THE WORLD HERITAGE SITES
of UNESCO
WITH THE PATRONAGE OF

ITALIAN NATIONAL COMMISSION

NATURE SANTUARIES

WHITE STAR
PUBLISHERS

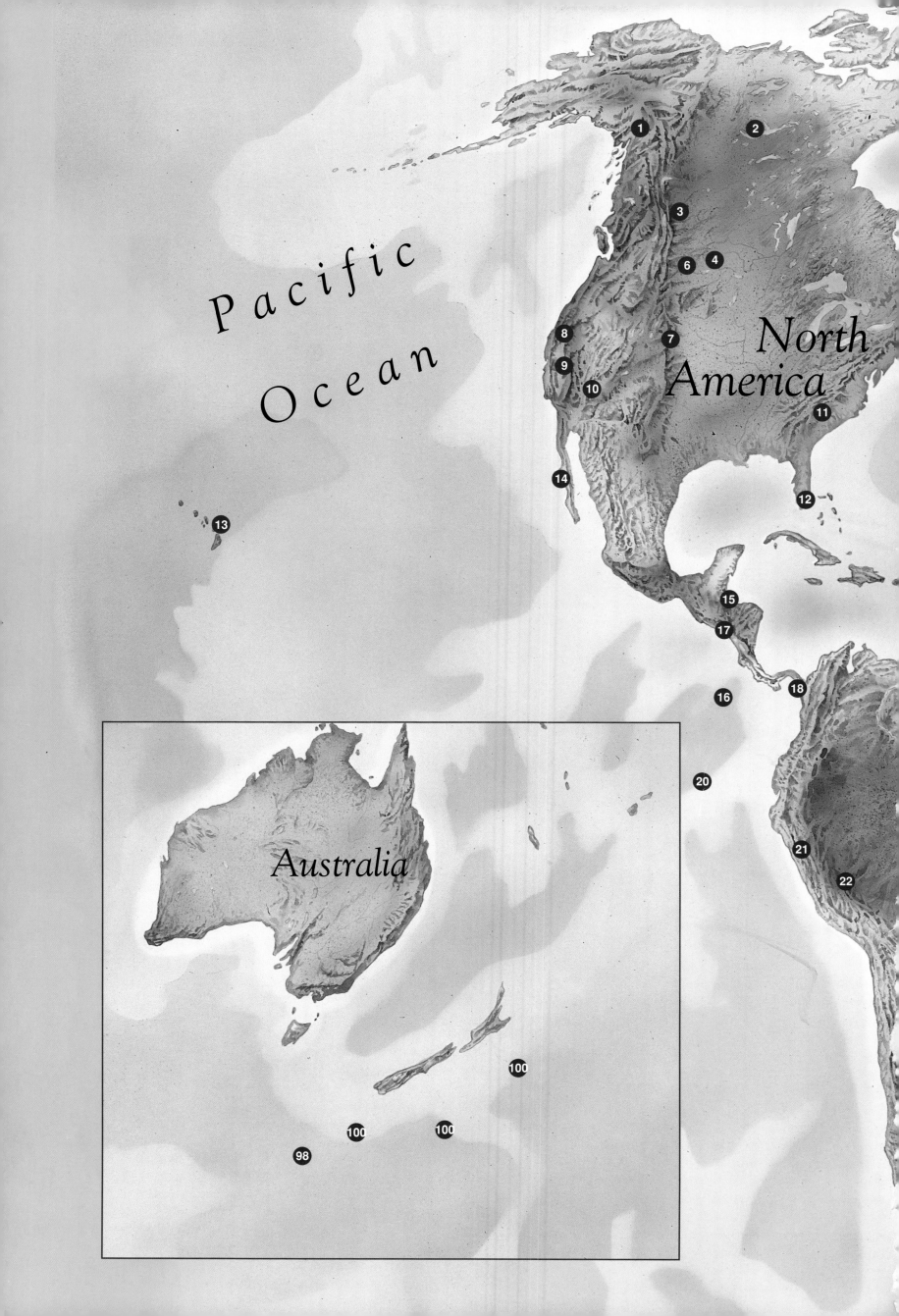

TEXTS BY
MARCO CATTANEO
JASMINA TRIFONI

GRAPHIC DESIGN
PATRIZIA BALOCCO LOVISETTI

GRAPHIC LAYOUT
PAOLA PIACCO

TRANSLATION
TIMOTHY STROUD

© 2003 White Star S.r.l.
Via Candido Sassone, 22/24
13100 Vercelli, Italy
www.whitestar.it

ISBN 88-8095-228-5

REPRINTS:
1 2 3 4 5 6   07 06 05 04 03

Printed in Italy by Arti Grafiche Amilcare Pizzi, Milan
Color separation: Grafotitoli, Milan

Contents

PREFACE
PAGE 8

INTRODUCTION
PAGE 10

2 Unconquered until 1953, at 29,029 feet Everest is the world's highest mountain. This rock and ice colossus is part of Sagarmatha National Park in Nepal, which was set up in 1976 and awarded the status of a UNESCO World Heritage site in 1979.

7 South Arlington Reef is one of the 3,400 stretches of coral reef that make up the Great Barrier Reef along the coasts of Australia and Papua New Guinea. Inscribed in the World Heritage list in 1981, with an area of 127,900 square miles, it is the largest protected area on the planet.

Nature Sanctuaries

THE AMERICAS

1   UNITED STATES/CANADA - KLUANE/WRANGELL-ST. ELIAS, GLACIER BAY AND TATSHENSHINI-ALSEK PARKS
2   CANADA - WOOD BUFFALO NATIONAL PARK
3   CANADA - CANADIAN ROCKY MOUNTAINS PARKS
4   CANADA - DINOSAUR PROVINCIAL PARK
5   CANADA - GROS MORNE NATIONAL PARK
6   CANADA/UNITED STATES - WATERTON GLACIER INTERNATIONAL PEACE PARK
7   UNITED STATES - YELLOWSTONE NATIONAL PARK
8   UNITED STATES - REDWOOD NATIONAL PARK
9   UNITED STATES - YOSEMITE NATIONAL PARK
10 UNITED STATES - GRAND CANYON NATIONAL PARK
11 UNITED STATES - GREAT SMOKY MOUNTAINS NATIONAL PARK
12 UNITED STATES - EVERGLADES NATIONAL PARK
13 UNITED STATES - HAWAII VOLCANOES NATIONAL PARK
14 MEXICO - WHALE SANCTUARY OF EL VIZCAÍNO
15 BELIZE - BELIZE BARRIER REEF
16 COSTA RICA - ISLA DE COCOS
17 COSTA RICA- GUANACASTE CONSERVATION AREA
18 PANAMA - PARQUE NACIONÁL DARIÉN
19 VENEZUELA - PARQUE NACIONÁL CANAIMA
20 ECUADOR - THE GALÁPAGOS ISLANDS
21 PERU - PARQUE NACIONÁL HUASCARÁN
22 PERU - PARQUE NACIONÁL MANU
23 BOLIVIA - PARQUE NACIONÁL NOEL KEMPFF MERCADO
24 BRAZIL - PANTANAL CONSERVATION AREA
25 BRAZIL - ATLANTIC FOREST SOUTH-EAST RESERVES
26 BRAZIL - FERNANDO DE NORONHA AND ATOL DAS ROCAS RESERVES
27 ARGENTINA/BRAZIL - IGUAZÚ FALLS
28 ARGENTINA - PARQUE NACIONÁL LOS GLACIARES
29 ARGENTINA - PENÍNSULA VALDÉS

EUROPE

30 SWEDEN - LAPLAND
31 BELARUS/POLAND - BIALOWIEZA FOREST
32 UNITED KINGDOM - THE GIANT'S CAUSEWAY
33 UNITED KINGDOM - THE COAST OF DORSET AND EAST DEVON
34 FRANCE (CORSICA) - CAP GIROLATA, CAP PORTO, SCANDOLA NATURE RESERVE AND PIANA CALANCHES
35 FRANCE/SPAIN - PYRÉNÉES - MONT PERDU
36 SPAIN - PARQUE NACIONAL DE COTO DOÑANA
37 PORTUGAL - THE LAURISILVA OF MADEIRA
38 SWITZERLAND - THE JUNGFRAU, ALETSCHHORN AND BIETSCHHORN
39 ITALY - THE AEOLIAN ISLANDS
40 SLOVENIA - THE CAVES OF SKOCJAN
41 CROATIA - THE LAKES OF PLITVICE
42 YUGOSLAVIA - DURMITOR NATIONAL PARK
43 SLOVAKIA/HUNGARY - THE CAVES OF AGGTELEK KARST AND SLOVAK KARST
44 RUMANIA - THE DELTA OF THE DANUBE
45 RUSSIAN FEDERATION - THE WESTERN CAUCASUS

AFRICA

46 MAURITANIA - BANC D'ARGUIN NATIONAL PARK
47 NIGER - AÏR AND TÉNÉRÉ NATURAL RESERVES
48 ETHIOPIA - SIMIEN NATIONAL PARK
49 UGANDA - RWENZORI MOUNTAINS NATIONAL PARK
50 UGANDA - BWINDI IMPENETRABLE NATIONAL PARK
51 KENYA - LAKE TURKANA NATIONAL PARKS
52 KENYA - MOUNT KENYA NATIONAL PARK/NATURAL FOREST
53 DEM. REP. OF CONGO - VIRUNGA NATIONAL PARK
54 TANZANIA - SERENGETI NATIONAL PARK
55 TANZANIA - KILIMANJARO NATIONAL PARK
56 TANZANIA - NGORONGORO CONSERVATION AREA
57 TANZANIA - SELOUS GAME RESERVE
58 ZAMBIA/ZIMBABWE - MOSI-OA-TUNYA, VICTORIA FALLS
59 ZIMBABWE - MANA POOLS NATIONAL PARK, SAPI AND CHEWORE RESERVES
60 SOUTH AFRICA - UKHAHLAMBA/DRAKENSBERG PARK
61 SOUTH AFRICA - GREATER ST. LUCIA WETLAND PARK
62 MADAGASCAR - TSINGY DE BEMARAHA STRICT NATURE RESERVE
63 SEYCHELLES - ALDABRA ATOLL

ASIA

64 TURKEY - THE VALLEY OF GÖREME
65 TURKEY - PAMUKKALE
66 RUSSIAN FEDERATION - THE KAMCHATKA VOLCANOES
67 RUSSIAN FEDERATION - LAKE BAIKAL
68 RUSSIAN FEDERATION - CENTRAL SIKHOTE-ALIN
69 RUSSIAN FEDERATION - THE GOLDEN MOUNTAINS OF ALTAI
70 CHINA - HUANGLONG AND JIUZHAIGOU
71 CHINA- HUANGSHAN
72 CHINA - WULINGYUAN
73 JAPAN - SHIRAKAMI-SANCHI
74 NEPAL - ROYAL CHITWAN NATIONAL PARK
75 NEPAL - SAGARMATHA NATIONAL PARK
76 INDIA - NANDA DEVI NATIONAL PARK
77 INDIA- KAZIRANGA NATIONAL PARK
78 INDIA - MANAS WILDLIFE SANCTUARY
79 INDIA - KEOLADEO NATIONAL PARK
80 SRI LANKA - SINHARAJA FOREST RESERVE
81 BANGLADESH - SUNDARBANS
82 THAILAND - THUNG YAI AND HUAI KHA KHAENG
83 VIETNAM - HA LONG BAY
84 PHILIPPINES - TUBBATAHA REEF MARINE PARK
85 MALAYSIA - KINABALU NATIONAL PARK
86 MALAYSIA - GUNUNG MULU NATIONAL PARK
87 INDONESIA - UJUNG KULON NATIONAL PARK
88 INDONESIA - KOMODO NATIONAL PARK

OCEANIA

89   AUSTRALIA - KAKADU NATIONAL PARK
90   AUSTRALIA - THE WET TROPICS IN QUEENSLAND
91   AUSTRALIA - THE GREAT BARRIER REEF
92   AUSTRALIA - FRASER ISLAND
93   AUSTRALIA - SHARK BAY
94   AUSTRALIA - ULURU-KATA TJUTA NATIONAL PARK
95   AUSTRALIA - CENTRAL EASTERN RAINFOREST RESERVES
96   AUSTRALIA - GREATER BLUE MOUNTAINS
97   AUSTRALIA - THE PARKS OF TASMANIA
98   AUSTRALIA - MACQUARIE ISLAND
99   NEW ZEALAND - TE WAHIPOUNAMU
100 NEW ZEALAND - THE SUB-ANTARCTIC ISLANDS OF NEW ZEALAND

Asia

Indian Ocean

Oceania

New Zealand

Preface

The first site inscribed in the Cultural and Natural World Heritage List in 1978 was the Galápagos Islands. These islands are of enormous naturalistic importance and, as is well known, provided the basis for the biological studies made by Charles Darwin, but some years back, they were seriously threatened by an oil spill in the Pacific Ocean. Volunteers flew in from all over the world to help while governments, institutes and individuals offered their skills and support. Although a disaster was mostly prevented, the consequences of the spill continue to create problems for the delicate environmental balance of the Galápagos. On the other hand, the situation demonstrated the extent of the awareness throughout the world of the World Heritage sites, particularly amongst the young. In the words of UNESCO's Director General, Koïchiro Matsuura, 'the Convention for the Conservation of the World Heritage is a vital and noble force that promotes peace in the world and honors our past and our future'.

At the time of writing, there are 730 World Heritage sites in 125 member states: of these 563 are cultural, 144 natural and 23 a combination of both. Much progress has therefore been made, but this does not in any way obfuscate how much remains to be done. First, it is clear from the statistics that the sites of naturalistic (or combined) interest total only about one quarter of the cultural sites, and therefore more emphasis needs to be placed on the planet's naturalistic heritage. Second, a glance at the list of states that have signed the Convention shows that not all of them have yet been represented with at least one site, and therefore that further effort needs to be made to right this situation. Those states that are weakest from the Organization's point of view (though this does not mean that they are without sites of universal importance) require support so that they can fully implement the conditions laid down by the UNESCO Convention and provide adequate resources and internal prescriptive mechanisms so that they too can nominate their sites for inclusion in the World Heritage List.

The celebrations held to mark the 30th anniversary of the Convention have recently ended, with Italy right up in the forefront making substantial organizational, scientific, cultural and economic contributions. The anniversary spawned a number of ventures, studies and artistic and media-based productions, including White Star's *The UNESCO World Heritage* of which this is the second volume in the series. The Commissione Nazionale Italiana per l'UNESCO, of which I have the honor to be President, has willingly supported White Star's publications as it is convinced that their intrinsic quality, superb photographs, wealth of information and clearness of text make them an important means for bringing people, in particular the young, closer to the environmental protection work that UNESCO carries out.

Tullia Carrettoni Romagnoli
President of the
UNESCO Italian National Commission

8 An immense gorge gouged out by the Colorado River, Arizona's Grand Canyon is 278 miles long and just over 1 mile wide. It was first placed under protection in 1893, became a national park in 1919 and has been a World Heritage site since 1979.

11 Kingdom of the African elephant, the Mana Pools National Park is home to one of southern Africa's densest concentrations of wildlife. Instituted in 1963, it was added to the UNESCO list in 1984.

12-13 Sunset enflames El Capitan, which rises almost 3,300 feet above Yosemite Valley in Yosemite National Park. In 1864 it became the world's first protected area and a World Heritage site in 1984.

Introduction

On 23 November 1972, the UNESCO General Conference in Paris approved the institutional Convention of the List of World Heritage sites that would come into force on 17 December 1975. The ambitious aim of the United Nations Educational, Scientific and Cultural Organization was to identify, study and protect monuments, groups of buildings and sites, created either by man or nature, that have an exceptional universal value from a historic, artistic, scientific, naturalistic, archeological or anthropological standpoint.

Thirty years on, the World Heritage List is an extraordinary inventory of places and works that embraces the twin histories of man and the Earth, and that enable us to understand nature, culture and, above all, the profound link that unites them. In short, the List represents human and planetary development.

The purpose of this work is to provide a cross-section of the priceless inheritance protected by UNESCO. In order to tackle such a vast and heterogeneous series of sites, the task has been divided into three volumes, dedicated respectively to artistic and archeological treasures, sites of naturalistic value and ancient civilizations. Although the distinction between cultural and natural properties was explicitly defined in the Convention, some sites have been inscribed on the World Heritage List as having both characteristics, owing to the importance they have to mankind both naturally and culturally. In total there are 23 such sites, some of which are included in this book owing to their peculiar geographical features, or because their ecosystems are of extreme importance and need to be conserved; in consequence, more emphasis is placed on their naturalistic aspects than their relevance to the development of human civilization.

To be registered on the World Heritage List as a natural site, a geographical area has to meet at least one of the following criteria:

I) be outstanding examples representing major stages of earth's history, including the record of life, significant on-going geological processes in the development of landforms or significant geomorphic or physiographic features; or

II) be outstanding examples representing significant on-going ecological and biological processes in the evolution and development of terrestrial, fresh water, coastal and marine ecosystems and communities of plants and animals; or

III) contain superlative natural phenomena or areas of exceptional natural beauty and aesthetic importance; or

IV) contain the most important and significant natural habitats for in-situ conservation of biological diversity, including those containing threatened species of outstanding universal value from the point of view of science or conservation.

Overall, the UNESCO Committee has so far recognized 167 sites, of which 100 have been selected for this book. The criteria that have guided our choice have taken account of geographic distribution, the size of the various sites and the uniqueness of the patrimony they represent.

For each park, reserve or protected area, we have considered it fitting to underline its geological and climatic phenomena and the richness of its ecosystem, whether regarding the wildlife or plantlife. Special attention has been given to species of exceptional zoological and botanical interest, especially endangered species. The causes of threats to survival have also been explained – which, in the majority of cases, can be traced back to man – as it is only through a thorough understanding of our responsibilities that we will be able to safeguard the extraordinary wealth of this planet.

List of the Sites

Europe

With more than 50 inhabitants per square mile, Europe is the continent with the highest density of population, six times greater than that of Africa. Europe is also the continent in which Neolithic man survived the Ice Age and began to alter his environment. And although agriculture came into existence in what we now call the Middle East, technology and urbanization – with the exception of the Nile Valley, Mesopotamia and Persia – underwent their first great development in Greece and Rome.

Many centuries later, the Industrial Revolution gave a new boost to human activities, generating a dizzying acceleration in production and bringing a radical change in the interactions between man and nature. Thus, what had been a sustainable exploitation of resources until the eighteenth century was transformed increasingly faster into man's impact on the environment that was destined in just two centuries to revolutionize the face of the Old Continent and to destroy much of its natural lavishness.

Only 20 of UNESCO's natural World Heritage sites lie in Europe, and these include the forests of Virgin Komi and the Western Caucasus that are geographically part of European Russia and the laurisilva of Madeira in the Atlantic Ocean off Portugal; they exclude the Henderson and Gough Islands, which are British possessions respectively in the eastern Pacific and southern Atlantic Oceans. Apart from the two Russian reserves, the Danube Delta, the forest of Bialowieza in Poland and Byelorussia and the reserve in Lapland, the sites in Europe are fairly small in size, being those remaining areas that have managed to escape the influence of man. Many of these are simply linked to geological phenomena – like the Giant's Causeway, the Aeolian Islands and the karstic complex of caves in Skocjan – or are the sites of important paleontological finds, like the Dorset and East Devon coast or the fossil bed in Messel, Germany.

That, however, does not mean that Europe is neglecting nature. Since the Second World War, the foundation and success of environmental movements, particularly in the large western European countries, have initiated the setting up of innumerable national parks and protected areas. In fact, seven out of the first 10 countries in the world, as ranked by the index of environmental sustainability, are European. Yet, in many cases, intervention has been dilatory and highly important species and vast tracts of residual forests have been lost. Despite the efforts being made, the naturalistic heritage of Europe is now mostly made up of tiny 'islands' set round by modern development.

Lapland

SWEDEN

COUNTY OF NORRBOTTEN
REGISTRATION: 1996
CRITERIA: N (I) (II) (III); C (III) (IV)

16 top An ancient forest of lodgepole pine lies in Stora-Sjofallet National Park. The park was set up in 1909 over 494 square miles to the southwest of Kiruna. This spectacular reserve contains more than 200 mountains higher than 5,900 feet.

The Folkhögskola has existed in the small Lap town of Jokkmokk since 1942. It is a school where young Sami, in addition to studying the normal Swedish syllabus, attend lessons in their own language and learn traditional handcrafts. Above all, they study the history of reindeer breeding, from its origins to the present, which lies at the base of their way of life. Protection of the Sami culture – and therefore reindeer breeding, which is practiced by 10% of the 20,000 Sami who live permanently in Swedish Lapland – was the reason that UNESCO decided to include an area of 3,630 square miles, which includes nine protected areas, in the list of World Heritage sites. This region is also the territory where the seasonal migration of reindeer takes place.

Sami have a traditional symbiotic relationship with reindeer. They obtain meat and milk from the animal, the tendons are used to sew their clothes and the hide and the tendons are used to make their *laitok* (traditional conical tents). Although many Sami today own a snowmobile, reindeer are still used for transport. During the long, dark months of winter inside the Arctic Circle, the Sami live on the flat, conifer-forested lands where the reindeer can survive on the lichens they find under the snow. In May, when the snow begins to melt, the young reindeer are born, and in June, after the new animals have been branded, the time arrives to migrate towards the mountains. There, they remain until August, when the arrival of the cold signals the return to the flatlands where the grass provides food for the herds.

Despite the fact that these herds number some 40,000 head, grazing does not have repercussions on the environmental balance. The combined territory of Lapland in Sweden, Finland and Norway is one of the last and largest areas of wilderness in Europe. It contains two wetlands – Sjaunja Nature Reserve and the Rapa Valley Delta in Sarek

16-17 Various species of birch dominate this beautiful autumnal panorama in the delta of the Rapa valley in Sarek National Park.

17 top Lying next to Stora-Sjofallet, Sarek National Park is one of the region's most difficult areas to reach. It is alpine in nature, with many glaciers and in great part devoid of vegetation.

National Park – and is considered of international importance by the Ramsar Convention.

Also of interest are the mountainous region in Stora-Sjöfallet National Park (more than 200 peaks over a height of 5,900 feet and a hundred or so glaciers) and Padjelanta National Park, which is a tundra of rare plant species and the location of Sweden's most beautiful lake, Lake Virihaure.

The conifer forest in Muddus National Park has trees over 700 years old, and, in summer, huge quantities of red myrtle (*Vaccinium vitis idaea*) and Arctic mulberry (*Rubus chamaemorus*).

17 center The osprey (Pandion haliaetus) was recorded by the Swedish naturalist Karl von Linné in 1758. It is one of many birds of prey that live in Lapland.

17 bottom The unstoppable increase in the number of lynx (Lynx lynx) – now estimated to number 700-1,000 – has begun to create serious problems for the Sami. The government has allowed the Sami to hunt them to protect their herds of reindeer.

STOCKHOLM

18 top The brown bear (Ursus arctos) disappeared from the southern regions of Sweden before the eighteenth century but there are still a thousand or so in Lapland.

18 center and bottom left The faint light of a Scandinavian winter girdles the open valleys and trees of Sarek National Park in an almost unreal light. Daytime in winter only lasts a few hours.

18 bottom right A herd of reindeer (Rangifer tarandus) runs through the conifer woods. In Scandinavia there are around 500,000 of these animals that are traditionally raised by the Sami.

18-19 Although the golden eagle (Aquila chrysaetos) is hunted for being a threat to reindeer fawns, its population in Lapland is stable.

19 top left Camouflaged by the paleness of the landscape, the most valuable of the fur animals, ermines (Mustela erminea), are hunted with often cruel methods.

19 top right The arctic fox (Alopex lagopus) lives in the circumpolar region in the northern hemisphere. Its coat turns white in winter and tawny in summer and offers superb camouflage.

The orange-colored mulberry is used throughout Scandinavia to make jam and a liqueur.

The fauna in Swedish Lapland has several species requiring protection, for example, the wolverine (*Gulo gulo*) and the white-tailed eagle (*Haliaeetus albicilla*), plus the brown bear, lynx, Arctic fox, otter and elk. There are roughly 200 species of birds, 100 of which reproduce in Sjaunja water meadows.

Though Sweden looks after Lapland stringently, prohibiting all entry to several of the protected areas, a law passed in 1971 gives special transit rights – even using motor vehicles – to Sami hunters and fishermen. This is in recognition of the fact that this people have always lived in harmony with nature.

Bialowieza Forest
BELARUS/POLAND

REGIONS OF BREST AND GRODNO POLAND
REGION OF BIALOSTOKIE
REGISTRATION: 1979, 1982
CRITERIA: N (III)

Though much less well known and visited, Bialowieza (or *Belovezhskaya Pushcha* in Russian) is the European equivalent of the Serengeti in Africa or Yellowstone in America. Situated in the hydrogeological basin between the Baltic and the Black Sea, and belonging to Belarus and Poland, it is a 'photograph' of how Europe was about 10,000 years ago, before man changed its natural balance forever.

The immense territory is protected as a Biosphere Reserve, with roughly 695 square miles lying in Belarus and 39 in Poland, small sections of which have been designated National Parks. The land is 88% covered by a virgin forest of conifers such as pines (*Pinus silvestris*) and fir (*Picea abies*) and broadleaf trees like lime (*Tilia cordata*), oak (*Quercus*

robur), birch (*Betula pubescens* and *Betula verrucosa*), sycamore (*Acer platanoides*) and ash (*Fraxinus excelsior*), some of which have achieved an exceptional age and size. In the Polish section of the forest, 864 trees are so large that they have been given the status of a National Monument.

Also in Poland – where Bialowieza was declared a National Park in 1932, making it one of Europe's first protected areas – the flora has been studied in great detail as a result of a tradition begun in 1929 by Jerzy Karpinski, the botanist who was made Director of the park on its creation. In total, 900 species of vascular plants have been recorded in the forest, of which there are 26 forest trees, 12 orchids, 254 lichens, 80 bryophytes and 3,000 fungi, as well as

aquatic plants near the Hwozna and Narewka rivers that bound Polish Bialowieza to the north and west.

The exceptional botanical wealth of the area is only part of the forest's treasures. Of equal interest is its fauna, which includes the moose (*Alces alces*), the grey wolf (*Canis lupus*), the boar (*Sus scrofa*), the lynx (*Felis lynx*), the beaver (*Castor fiber*), the otter (*Lutra lutra*), many species of deer, 232 species of birds and 8,500 types of insects. Unsurprisingly, the forest was used as a hunting reserve by the czars of Russia and the monarchs of Poland.

The symbol of Bialowieza is the European bison (*Bison bonastus*). Called *zubr* locally, the bison has had a tortured history in Europe. In prehistoric times this large herbivore extended from

20 bottom right The undergrowth in Bialoweza Forest is typified by widespread bryophytes and spermatophytes, like wild garlic (Allium roseum), which, as the photograph shows, covers huge areas.

20 top Boars are one of the most common wild mammals in the woods of central and southern Europe; they play an important role in the balance of faunal nature in areas as yet unaffected by man.

20 bottom left On the border between Poland and Byelorussia, Bialoweza is the last virgin forest in Europe. Overall, it covers 734 square miles. The Polish section was turned into a royal hunting park in the fourteenth century and is now a national park.

21 left Ferns and conifers looking onto a hidden pool are a typical sight in this forest where over 900 species of vascular plants grow.

21 right Grayish-brown and with a long tail, the wild cat (Felis silvestris) is slightly larger than a domestic cat and widespread in European forests.

MINSK

WARSAW

22 top left Studies made on mammals in Bialoweza forest by the Polish Research Institute have shown that roe deer (Capreolus capreolus) is a favorite prey of wolves and lynxes.

22 top right The European or gray wolf (Canis lupus) is the principal predator in this region. According to a study made in 1993, 66% of deer, 25% of roe deer and almost all elk fall prey to wolves.

Russia to Spain and from Scandinavia to Italy, as is proven by the many rock paintings that depict it. With deforestation, its habitat was progressively reduced, and during the First World War, followed by the Russian civil wars after the October Revolution, it was slaughtered by the rural poor suffering from hunger. In 1927 only 29 males and 25 females remained in the zoos around the world and the European bison seemed destined for extinction. However, a group of zoologists championed its cause and selected 13 of these bison, which were then encouraged to reproduce in captivity for 25 years. When the herd was large enough, the decisive moment had arrived: the first bison were freed in Poland in 1952 and others in Lithuania, Ukraine and Russia. Today their population, kept under close observation, numbers 3,200, of which 400 graze undisturbed in the habitat of their prehistoric progenitors: the forest of Bialowieza.

22-23 The deer population (Cervus elaphus) increased constantly in Bialoweza Forest in the nineteenth and twentieth centuries, thanks to protection programs adopted by the Polish government.

23 top A solitary animal, the lynx (Lynx lynx) is often hunted in Poland. There is a fair number of lynx in Bialoweza though the animal is more common in the Carpathians and in Russia.

23 bottom After coming close to extinction in the twentieth century, the European bison (Bison bonasus) was raised in captivity. The program was a success and now the population of these herbivores in Bialoweza is estimated at 400 – the largest population in Europe.

The Giant's Causeway
UNITED KINGDOM

In 1693 Sir Richard Bulkeley, an eminent scholar at Trinity College, Dublin, caused a stir among the members of the Royal Society when he presented a paper in which he described the discovery, made a year previous by the Count-Bishop of Derry, of a singular stretch of coast on the northeastern tip of Ireland. On the coastline of County Antrim stood some rocks that were too regular in shape to have been molded by nature. Four years later, the London institution sent an artist to the spot to illustrate the 'natural curiosity'.

For all of the eighteenth century the Giant's Causeway was visited by artists and scientists who wondered at the origin of the 40,000 basalt columns that are aligned so that they seem to form a paved road leading out to sea. For the ancient inhabitants of the area, the columns were the work of the giant Finn McCool, the commander for the king of Ireland's army. At this point versions of the legend differ. In the most common version, McCool built the stretch of rock to go to win his consort on Staffa in the Hebride Islands (where there is a similar formation); in another version, the giant made use of them so that he could fight his enemy in Scotland.

It was only at the end of the eighteenth century that one group of geologists offered the theory that the formation of rocks was of volcanic origin; while another, led by Richard Kirwan, believed that they were the result of the precipitation of minerals in the sea water. From 1830, when the first road alongside the Giant's Causeway was built, the cliffs began to become part of the Grand Tour made by the well-to-do of the period and was referred to in the works of Romantic poets.

At this time the official explanation of the origin of the Giant's Causeway was about to crumble. In the Tertiary period, between 60 and 50 million years ago, the area of Antrim was subject to intense volcanic activity. Masses of extremely fluid, molten rock were pushed upwards through cracks in the limestone surface to form a lava plateau. Rapid cooling caused the solidifying lava to contract and the different speeds at which the material cooled (which were the result of the different depths) created vertical cracks similar to those seen in mud when it dries.

With time the softest rock was eroded away by the action of the sea to leave the spectacular and perfectly adjacent columns that line the coast for 300 yards and that stretch 160 yards out to sea. Most of the columns are hexagonal (but there are also four-,

24 top The Atlantic puffin (Fratercula arctica) is a member of the charadriiform family that lives in large groups on the coasts of all northern seas. The species is characterized by unmistakable colored stripes on the beak.

24 bottom left First described in 1693, the Giant's Causeway was embroiled in legend and scientific disputes until the mid-nineteenth century, when knowledge of earth sciences became extensive enough to explain its formation.

24 bottom right The Auks razorbill (Alca torda) is one of about 80 species of birds, resident and migratory, that stop around the Giant's Causeway. For this reason the Royal Society for the Protection of Birds considers the area an important regional zone for birdlife.

BELFAST

DUBLIN

LONDON

25 With the passing of the
millennia, erosion caused
by tidal action where the
sea is most powerful has
slowly worn away the
geometrical shapes of the
basalt.

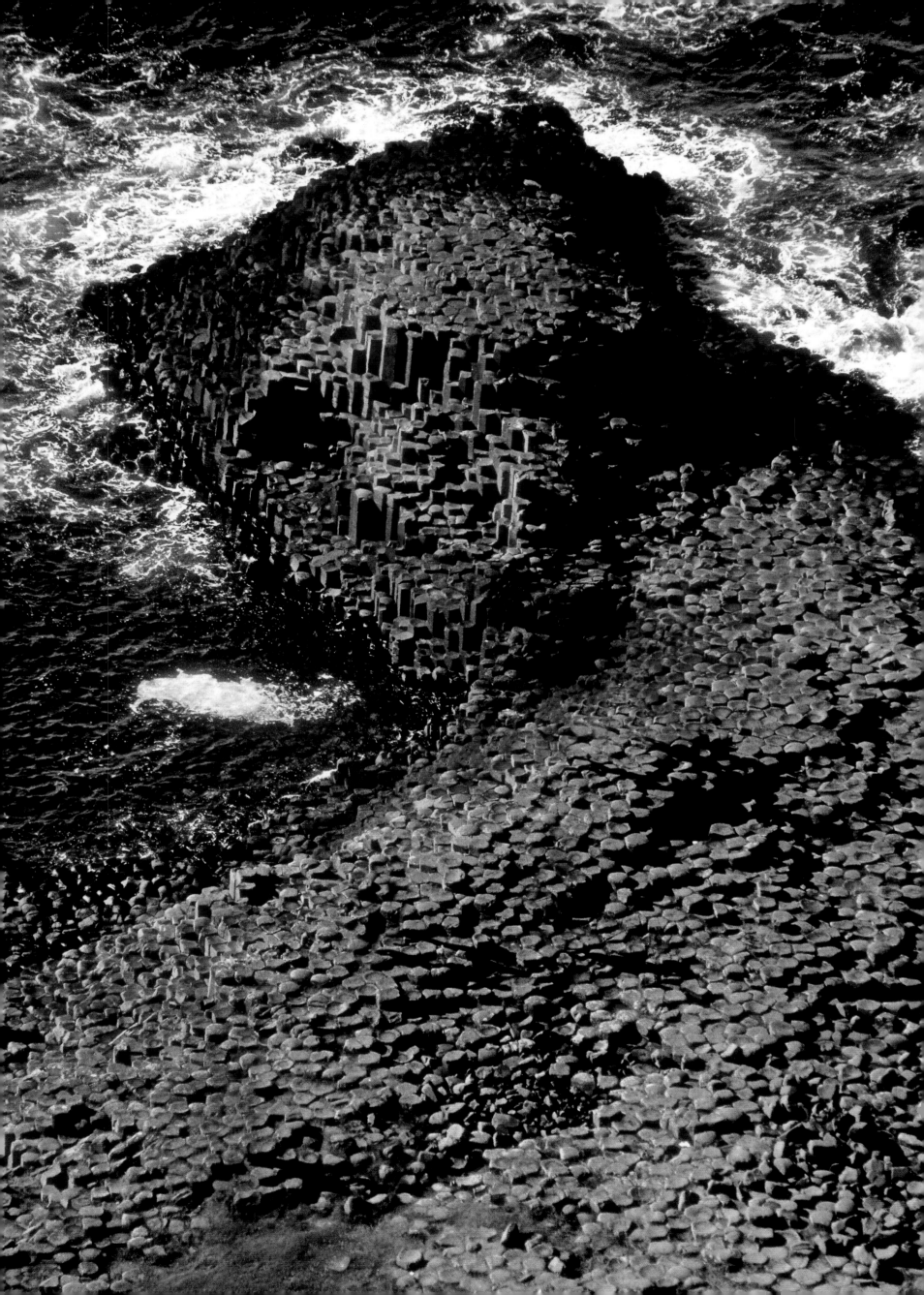

five-, eight- and ten-sided columns) and do not exceed 20 feet in height. Exceptions to these are those in the Giant's Organ, which reach a height of 40 feet. Erosion by atmospheric agents has also created circular formations around basalt cores known as the Giant's Eyes.

Although the geological aspects of the Giant's Causeway are its major attraction, the coastline is also a habitat for many species of sea birds, including the Arctic petrel, double-crested cormorant and razorbill. And The National Trust has drawn up an inventory of the many botanical species found on the top of the cliffs, which have survived three centuries of visitors.

26 Formed after intense volcanic activity 60-50 million years ago, the Giant's Causeway numbers roughly 40,000 basalt columns along a stretch of coast around 320 yards long and extending under the sea for about 160 yards.

27 top left The columns in the Giant's Organ – some of the tallest in the Causeway – reach 40 feet in height.

27 top right Normally the shape of the basalt columns is hexagonal, but there are some with four, five, eight and 10 sides.

27 center right Along with the Arctic ptarmigan, the Arctic petrel (Fulmarus glacialis) is one of the birds that nests in the far north, even in the Arctic Circle.

27 bottom The Causeway Coast is a striking set of basalt cliffs about 330 feet high formed by lava during the Tertiary period on the Antrim Plateau and covering about 1,500 square miles.

The coast of Dorset and East Devon
UNITED KINGDOM

DORSET AND EAST DEVON, ENGLAND
REGISTRATION: 2001
CRITERIA: N (I)

Mary Anning was just 12 years old when she discovered the first fossil of an ichthyosaur as she walked along the cliffs of the coastal town of Lyme Regis. At the time – the early nineteenth century – collecting fossils was a fashionable occupation in London, and that precious curiosity found its way to the house of the Duke of Buckingham before ending up in the main atrium of the Natural History Museum in London. In the years that followed, Mary Anning also provided science with the first fossil of a plesiosaur (a gigantic marine reptile) and a pterodactyl (the progenitor of the birds), which she donated to Oxford University. She made her living by selling fossils and, in a certain sense, revolutionized the history of paleontology.

The wealth of fossils on the coast of Dorset and East Devon had already been noted by John Ray in 1673 and, since then, that stretch of south England has been at the center of all the principal advances in the history of geology. The area was successively visited by scientists of the caliber of William Smith, the author of the first geological map of England, Gideon Mantell, discoverer of the iguanodont, Sir Henry De la Beche, founder of the British Geological Survey, John Stevens Henslow, Darwin's professor at Cambridge, and Louis Agassiz, the founder of

the science of glacial geomorphology. In short, Dorset and East Devon became the gymnasium in which the world's greatest minds of the natural sciences were exercised. This corner of south England stretches for 96 miles from Orcombe Rocks, near Exmouth in East Devon, to Studland Bay in Dorset and boasts an unusual geology. Due to the erosion of the cliffs that run the length of the coast, a practically continuous sequence of rocks from the Triassic, Jurassic and Cretaceous periods (i.e., the whole of the Mesozoic era) are laid bare, revealing an arc of almost 190 million years. The rock layers were deposited on an area known as the Wessex Basin that is subject to slight subsidence. The enormous volume of rock accumulated here slowly sank eastwards so that the oldest rocks are found in the western zone. As one heads east, the strata gradually become more recent.

The incredible variety of fossils in the protected area – which was instituted in 1957 and 1963, and covers 6,300 acres – spans the period represented by the two mass extinctions in the Permian and Cretaceous periods that include plants, insects, marine invertebrates, fish, terrestrial and marine reptiles and mammals.

But Dorset and East Devon are also interesting geomorphologically as they demonstrate a variety of movements of landmasses, including the formation of beaches and lagoons, cliffs produced by erosion, landslips and the motion of subduction. Three centuries of scientific study has produced the 5,000 documents that make up the *Bibliography and Index of Dorset Geology*, but the site continues to attract scholars, as a result of which, in 2000 and 2001, the British Geological Survey decided to publish a series of new maps of the coast, 180 years on from the original and memorable work by William Smith.

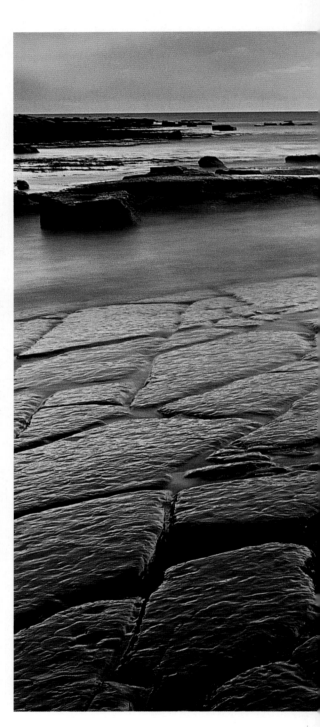

28 bottom Durdle Door is one of the most interesting geological landscapes on the Dorset coast. It has been known since the seventeenth century for its extraordinary variety of fossils.

28-29 The Kimmeridge coast, with its smoothed cliffs, dates to the early Jurassic period. Sea erosion has created a wide bay in the soft clay-like rock.

29 top The name Durdle Door first appeared on a map in 1811. The 'Door' refers to the dramatic opening in the rock, and 'Durdle' is derived from an ancient name whose meaning is unknown.

29 center right The white cliffs of Dorset and East Devon represent a remarkable series of rocks that cover the whole of the Mesozoic era (190 million years). The local sedimentation provides science with an invaluable treasure of knowledge about the era of the dinosaurs.

29 bottom A fossil forest dating to the Jurassic period can be seen near Lulworth Cove. It is evidence of the widespread diffusion of conifers in temperate regions during that epoch.

BELFAST

DUBLIN

LONDON

Cap Girolata, Cap Porto, Scandola Nature Reserve and Piana Calanches

FRANCE

CORSICA
REGISTRATION: 1983
CRITERIA: N (II) (III) (IV)

30

At the end of the Middle Ages, Corsica was a land ripe for conquest not just by France but also by the powerful sea republics of Pisa and Genoa on the Tyrrhenian coast of Italy. In 1559 Genoa finally triumphed and administered the island for almost two centuries. To protect their investment, the Genoese turned to the best military architects to build them splendid citadels like Calvi and Bonifacio, churches, palaces – for example the Governor's Palace in Bastia – and small forts such as those in Aleria, Tizzano and Porto Girolata.

It is from Porto Girolata fort on the rocky promontory that overlooks the Gulf of Girolata that one reaches the village of the same name. It is an isolated fishing village, only accessible by sea or along the difficult mule track that zigzags from the fort to the sea between reddish rock masses covered with Mediterranean scrub. Porto Girolata is a good starting point for long walks in Scandola Nature Reserve, which, with Cap Porto and Piana Calanches, was one of the first nature sites to be registered as a World Heritage site.

Covering an area of 7.5 square miles, Scandola Nature Reserve was set up in 1975 and was the first both marine and terrestrial park in France. The UNESCO site, however, is much larger as it covers 46 square miles, much of which falls in the Regional Natural Park of Corsica. Its confines lie at Punta Muchillina and the estuary of the Forno Torrent.

Geologically, Scandola Peninsula was the result of the intense volcanic activity that characterized the area during the Permian period, during which red igneous rhyolite and basalt were brought to the surface where they have since been modeled by the action of the sea and the weather. The result is a series of sharp peaks, caves, cliffs and rocky islets that make the landscape one of the most fascinating sights in the Mediterranean.

The flora numbers 600 species, of which 34 are endemic, and 450 algae that cover all the aquatic botanic biodiversity in this area of the Mediterranean. Some of them are not found elsewhere on the Corsican coast; there is also a carpet of posidonia that covers the seabed down to a depth of 150 feet and a species of algae called *lythophyllum* that forms limestone

30-31 Scandola Nature Reserve was set up in 1975 over 7.5 square miles of beautiful coastline. The vegetation among the rocks is mostly of myrtle, lentisks, heathers, holm-oaks and strawberry trees.

31 top left The red rhyolites of Cap Porto are the result of volcanic activity that modeled the west coast of Corsica during the Permian period (320-280 million years ago).

31 top right A solitary juniper (Juniperus communis) overlooks the Gulf of Porto and the calanches of Piana. The slopes that rise out of the water reach a maximum height of 8,904 feet on Mount Cinto to the northeast, which is the highest point on the island.

30 bottom The mouflon (Ovis musimon) has lived for thousands of years in Corsica and Sardinia and is the only species of wild sheep in Europe. Estimates put its numbers on the island at around 500.

AJACCIO

32 top left The osprey (Pandion haliaetus) is the conservation symbol of Scandola Nature Reserve. Its numbers are down to a few dozen pairs in the Mediterranean, many of which nest in this stretch of the Corsican coast.

32 top right Several dozens of pairs of the European shag (Phalacrocorax aristotelis) live in the reserve. Smaller than a cormorant and with a slimmer beak, it displays a tuft of feathers on its head during courtship.

32 center left About 12 inches in length, the bee-eater (Merops apiaster) is a migratory bird that winters in southern Africa but nests in Italy and Corsica.

cushions along the rocks. At Punta Palazzu, it has grown to form a sidewalk over 330 feet in length and 6 feet wide. The cliffs are covered by a mixed vegetation of myrtle, mastic, arborescent euphorbias, heather, ilex and arbutus.

Scandola also has an assortment of sea fauna that numbers 125 species of fish and many marine invertebrates, two of which are protected right across Europe. The birdlife totals 230 sedentary and migrating species, including the peregrine falcon (*Falco peregrinus*), the osprey (*Pandion haliaetus*), the sooty shearwater (*Puffinus griseus*) and the European shag (*Phalacrocorax aristotelis*). Until a few years ago, the peninsula was a refuge for one of the last colonies of monk seal (*Monachus monachus*), but now this creature is very rare in the Mediterranean. Since its disappearance from this site, the symbol of the conservation policy in Scandola has passed to the osprey.

32 bottom The cliffs of the Girolata Gulf make the area so difficult to reach that the village of Porto Girolata in the northwest of the bay can only be reached by sea or by following a steep muletrack.

33 The cliffs at Capo Rosso are the southernmost point of the Porto Gulf. The 463 square miles of the World Heritage site mostly lie inside the Regional Natural Park of Corsica.

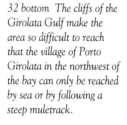

Pyrénées-Mont Perdu

FRANCE/SPAIN

DEPARTMENT OF HAUTES-PYRÉNÉES (FRANCE),
AUTONOMOUS COMMUNITY OF ARAGONA,
PROVINCE OF HUESCA (SPAIN)
REGISTRATION: 1997; EXTENSION: 1999
CRITERIA: N (I) (III); C (III) (IV) (V)

Although over the last century industrial development has profoundly changed the customs of mountain communities across Europe; in spring it is not unusual to encounter shepherds taking their flocks to graze at higher altitudes on the slopes of the Pyrénées. Summer grazing is a method of animal breeding begun by semi-nomadic shepherds in the Neolithic period that spread throughout southern Europe, though today it is restricted to small communities.

Ancient Europeans had adapted to the cold climate of Mont Perdu valley (*Monte Perdido* in Spanish) during the Paleolithic period, as is demonstrated by

the remains of human settlements dating from 40,000 years ago. Since then, the inhabitants of these zones have lived with nature that has been both hostile and unthreatening, adapting themselves to its demands over the millennia.

Constituted by the Parque Nacionál de Ordesa y Monte Perdído, in Spain, and the Parque National des Pyrénées Occidentales, in France, the site identified by UNESCO as Pyrénées-Mont Perdu lies in the central area of the Pyrénées, covering an area of 115 square miles that rises from the slopes at just 1,970 feet to the summit of Mont Perdu at 10,997 feet. This setting – a calcareous massif containing lakes, waterfalls, glacial rings, rock spurs, ravines and precipices – can be divided into three geomorphological regions. The first, to the north, is formed by three convergent valleys topped by mountain crests of schist and sandstone. The second is a steep limestone formation whose peaks are almost all above 9,840 feet. And the third, to the south, is constituted by plateaus of schist and sandstone.

The different heights correspond to five different types of vegetation: sub-Mediterranean, hill, mountain, subalpine and alpine. Low levels (in the valleys) are dominated by oaks of the species *Quercus ilex rotundifolia* and *Quercus faginea*. As the elevation rises, these give way to woods of *Quercus sessiliflora* and then beech (*Fagus sylvatica*), fir (*Abies alba*) and pine (*Pinus sylvestris*). The subalpine vegetation is dominated by hooked pine (*Pinus uncinata*), while the alpine zone is home to the endemic species (*Saxifraga iratiana*) and (*Androsace pyrenaica*).

With regard to fauna, the Pyrénées-Mont Perdu parks are inhabited by many species of reptiles and amphibians, plus birds typical of mountain habitats, including birds of prey. Important for reasons of conservation is the gypetus (*Gypetus barbatus*), whose numbers have fallen worryingly all over Europe. There are also many mammals typical of mountain habitats, such as marmots (*Marmota marmota*) and ermine (*Mustela erminea*) and hoofed animals like the roe deer (*Capreolus capreolus*) and the Pyrenean chamois (*Rupicapra pyrenaica pyrenaica*), of which only 800 remain.

Even worse was the fate of the Pyrenean ibex (*Capra pyrenaica pyrenaica*), a species of ibex of which only three remained, all female. On 5 January 2000, the Aragonese government officially confirmed that the last one – to which a radio-collar had been attached so that its movements could be followed – had been found dead near Faja de Pelay inside the Parque Nacionál de Ordesa y Monte Perdido.

34 top left Also known as the 'lamb vulture' the lammergeier had disappeared from the Alps in the early 1900s but survived in the Pyrenees. With a wingspan that can span over 9 feet, this large bird of prey is not a predator but eats mostly carcasses.

34 bottom left The griffon was thought to be endangered back in the nineteenth century. In the French Pyrenees only about

40 pairs were left in 1945 but conservation policies from the 1970s have helped to create a population of 1200-1500 individuals.

34 top right The Spanish ibex (Capra pyrenaica victoriae) is one of the four subspecies of goat endemic to the Pyrénées.

PARIS

MADRID

35 Ordesa canyon lies in
the Spanish section of the
park. It was cut out by
glaciation and, later, by the
flow of the Río Arazas.

This dramatic gorge is
nearly 3,000 feet deep and
cuts spectacularly into the
sandstone massif of Mount
Perdído.

Parque Nacional de Coto Doñana
SPAIN

GUADALQUIVÍR DELTA, ANDALUSIA
REGISTRATION: 1994
CRITERIA: N (II) (III) (IV)

It was, it is said, a disappointment in love that prompted Ana de Silva y Mendoza, the Duchess of Medina Sidonia, to isolate herself in the Spartan residence that stands in the Guadalquivír Delta where the monarchs of Castille had established a hunting reserve. From that time on, the inhabitants of the nearby fishing villages referred to the area as the forest of Doña Ana or, more simply, Doñana.

Many centuries later, in 1969, the Spanish government set up the Parque Nacional de Coto Doñana that extends over 135 square miles of the delta of what the Moors named the Wada-al-Kebir ('big river') and that is now known as the Guadalquivír. The delta is a very unusual one, to the extent that some prefer to call it an estuary, as only

one branch of the river enters the Atlantic, which it does to the north of Sanlúcar de Barramela. The other branches have been progressively blocked by the barrier of sandbar that stretches from the mouth of the Rio Tinto near Palos to the opposite bank to Sanlúcar. This barrier has gradually been modeled into a complex formation of tall dunes by the winds. On the other side of the dunes lie the *marismas*, or marshes, that make Doñana a unique area in Europe.

Currently the Arenas Gordas ('fat sands') that mark the edge of the Doñana marshes extend for roughly 45 miles north to south but are cut at the southernmost point by the mouth of the river. The *marismas* themselves cover an area of 444 square miles. The complex ecosystem of coastal dunes, marshes and freshwater pools forms an environment for typical Mediterranean vegetation such as heather, lentisc, rosemary and lavender, beyond which extend the remains of forests of cork oak.

For 12 months a year, the Parque Nacional de Coto Doñana is a refuge to over 300 species of birds, some of which are non-migratory. Some migrate from northern Europe during winter and others arrive from Africa to spend summer there. The winter rains

36 The marismas of the Parque Nacionál de Coto Doñana is the meeting place for over 300 species of birds, only a few of which are permanent residents. Some migrate from northern Europe during the winter and others arrive from Africa to spend the summer.

36-37 Established in 1969, the park covers an area of 135 square miles across, more or less, the Guadalquivír Delta, and includes a complex ecosystem of coastal dunes, marshes and freshwater pools with Mediterranean flora.

37 top A group of female fallow deer (Dama dama) explores the marsh called Madre de las Marismas del Rocio in search of food. Originally from Asia Minor, fallow deer were introduced to Europe by the Phoenicians.

MADRID

37 center The plumage of the purple heron (Ardea purpurea) has rich tones of brown and ocher. With a slender neck and long beak, the lower parts of its body are reddish and the upper part light to slate gray.

37 bottom Found right around the world, the cattle egret (Bubulcus ibis) frequents wetlands in colonies. It nests in trees, reed beds or bushes.

38 top The common tern
(Sterna hirundo) is a
migratory bird about 17
inches long. Those that nest
in Doñana leave Europe
between August and
October to pass the winter
in west Africa.

38-39 The coastal dunes
of the Cerro de los Ansares

('hill of the ducks') create a
constantly changing barrier
that stretches inland. It
changes the morphology
of the land each day.

39 top left Seen from
above, the coastal vegetation
in north Coto Doñana
stretches out of sight near
Matalascañas beach.

contribute to the formation of a vast marsh from 12-24 inches in depth in which *vetas* (islands) are used as nesting grounds by waders, terns and other aquatic birds. The presence too in winter of ducks and geese make Doñana a crossroads where at least a million birds find shelter.

In February the white spoonbills (*Platalea leucorodia*) arrive from North Africa to nest in the cork oaks. A month later the water level begins to drop and this is the period in which the Spanish imperial eagle (*Aquila heliaca*) lays its eggs. Researchers then have the opportunity to count this fearsome bird of prey, which is on the way to extinction.

The park is home to about fifteen pairs, which represent a third of all those in existence. For survival, each pair needs 1 square mile of hunting ground in the summer months and even more in winter, and this requirement makes its survival all the more difficult.

At the time of the duchess, Doñana was unmarked on maps but, over recent decades, the boundaries of the area have been built up. However, it is the proximity of agriculture that is the most serious threat as it washes quantities of pesticides into the water; in addition, the sulfur mines in Aznalcóliar, near Seville, contribute to the pollution of the waters with their waste products.

39 top right Doñana is home to large hoofed animals, like the deer (Cervo elaphus), of which about 90 live in the park.

39 bottom The huge expanse of Pinar de la Algaida – one of the few European forests still in good condition – is populated by communities of common pine (Pinus pinea) and lentisk.

The laurisilva of Madeira
PORGUTAL
PORTUGAL

THE ISLAND OF MADEIRA
REGISTRATION: 1999
CRITERIA: N (II) (IV)

40 top Noctules are disappearing from all Europe owing to the reduction of their habitat, the cutting down of trees in which they live and the elimination of their prey: insects. The Madeiran noctule (Nyctalus leisleri, in the verrucosus variety) is considered very vulnerable but the creation of the protected area of the Laurisilva has given this 'cousin' of the bat another chance.

40 bottom Although the laurisilva is a principal component of the vegetation on Madeira, the local flora includes many species of Euphorbiaceae, in particular Euphorbia canariensis and Euphorbia balsamifera, which are typical of the dry zones.

During the Tertiary period much of southern Europe and northwestern Africa were covered by thick forests of Lauraceae, the family of plants that includes the laurel and camphor. This luxuriant vegetation began to disappear from the Mediterranean basin around 10,000 years ago as a result of climatic change that caused the advance south of the arctic glaciers and a sudden decrease in the average temperature.

Laurel forests survived in regions spared from glaciations, including the archipelagos of Cape Verde, the Canary and Azores Islands and the Funchals (the islands of Madeira, Porto Santo, Desertas and Salvagens). Much later, in 1419, when the Portuguese João Goncalves Zarco sought shelter in Porto Santo from a storm, thereby discovering the archipelago, he found 90% of the uninhabited island of Madeira covered by a forest of Lauraceae.

Although it still remains the largest forest of its type in the world, the laurisilva (from the Latin silva = forest and laurus = laurel) has been reduced to 22% of the island's surface and now covers a total of 57.8 square miles, mostly on the north side of the island at a height of between 1,000 and 4,300 feet. It lies completely in the Parque Natural da Madeira, which was created in 1982 and is a wet subtropical zone with a rare ecosystem.

The forest is composed of species of tree that are endemic to the archipelago. There are two types: the dry laurisilva on the south-facing slopes, comprising Apollonias barbujana, Visnea mocarena, and Picconia excelsa, and the wet laurisilva on the northern slopes and in the gullies, in which Laurus azorica, Ocotea foetans and Persea indica predominate. The undergrowth is rich in species, many of which are endemic: bryophytes and lichens are particularly exemplary of the biodiversity. Overall, the flora of the laurisilva on Madeira numbers 1,226 species of vascular plants, with over 120 being endemic to the archipelago and 66 to the island.

The fauna is relatively poor and many species have been placed on the conservation list. Of primary importance are the birds, of which 295 species have been recorded and 42 of which nest on the island. Two are native to Madeira: the Zino's petrel (Pterodroma madeira) and the long-toed pigeon (Colomba trocaz). Together with the Fea's petrel (Pterodroma feae), these two are on the International Union for Conservation of Nature's Red List of species in danger.

The laurisilva is also home to 500 species of invertebrates, such as mollusks, insects and spiders, plus one lizard (Lacerta duguesii) and just two species of mammals, the noctule (Nyctalus leisleri verruscosus) and the Madeira bat (Pipistrellus maderensis).

This extraordinary forest has preserved the island from erosive phenomena. Its vegetal mosaic is in good health and has dynamism typical of balanced ecosystems. Nonetheless, the danger of further reduction in its surface area is always a threat. In particular, exogenous species like the acacias and pittosforum prevent the natural expansion of the laurisilva into abandoned rural areas as does poor management of grazing areas. Lastly, the recent increase in tourism has generated further pressure on Madeira's fragile habitat, to the extent that the authorities of the island have decided to regulate its flow.

40-41 The wet zone of the Laurisilva on the north-facing slopes and in the gorges is characterized by heavy growth of lichens (Usnea spp.) on the tree trunks.

41 bottom left The flora in the Laurisilva has a high biodiversity with 1,226 vascular plants, more than 120 of which are endemic to the archipelago and 66 to the island.

41 bottom right The Laurisilva enjoys a wet subtropical climate with a stable average temperature all year round and heavy rainfall. Primary forest represents 90% of Madeira's laurisilva.

FUNCHAL

The Jungfrau, Aletschhorn and Bietschhorn

SWITZERLAND

CANTONS OF BERNE AND VALLESE
REGISTRATION: 2001
CRITERIA: N (I) (II) (III)

BERNE

W̲hen it became popular as a destination for tourists two centuries ago, the pioneers of which were naturalists and 'gentlemen' climbers, Switzerland earned itself the sobriquet 'glacier country'. Its peaks and white expanses have been celebrated by poets and scientists like Goethe, von Haller, Scheutzer and de Saussure, and its romantic reputation was consolidated by legions of illustrators, first and foremost Caspar Wolf, who, between 1773 and 1778, paid tribute to the mountain country by producing hundreds of watercolors and oil paintings.

More recently, statisticians have calculated that if the enormous mass of glaciers were stretched out across the confederation of cantons, it would entirely cover the country to a depth of 4.5 feet. In fact, that was probably what Switzerland looked like during the many ice ages that occurred during the Quaternary period. The largest legacy of that time is the Aletschhorn, which, measuring 34 square miles and with a maximum thickness of 2,920 feet at Konkordiaplatz, is the largest glacier in western Eurasia.

The Aletschhorn also has other claims. The sight of this white sea fell within the reach of all when, more than a century ago, the rack railway was built on the Jungfrau, the highest of the Alps, whose topmost station – the Jungfraujoch – lies at a height of 11,332 feet. It was between the Aletschhorn and the Jungfrau that,

from 1841 to 1846, the scientist Louis Agassiz formulated his theory of glacial cycles that still lies at the base of all modern glaciology. Thanks to sophisticated instrumentation and satellite surveys, this science is now able to measure with precision the worrying shrinkage of the mass of glaciers around the world.

The area under the protection of UNESCO measures 208 square miles and lies at a height of between 2,950 and 14,022 feet. It is dominated by the jagged Aar massif formed by metamorphic rocks between 450-400 million years ago and by more recent granitic intrusions. Gneiss and schist characterize the Jungfrau, Mönch, Aletschhorn, Fiescherhorn, Grünhorn and Finsteraahorn, i.e., the peaks over 13,123 feet in height that are situated in the outer areas of the massif. Its central section, where the Bietschhorn stands, is formed by a mass of granite 62 miles long and 6 miles wide.

The Aar is marked by an exceptional

assortment of glacial phenomena: U-shaped valleys, morainic formations, proglacial edges and fissures, each of which has its own characteristics, making the massif an outstanding laboratory for studying future geomorphological changes resulting from climate change. The high level flora is also of great interest, with 529 species of phanerogams and pteridophytes. In addition to this is the huge wooded area up to a height of 6,500 feet that includes mountain pine (Pinus mugo) on the north-facing slopes and sycamore (Acer pseudoplatanus) and beech (Fagus sylvatica) on the south-facing slopes.

This zone has been protected for 70 years and is home to an abundant variety of fauna. Here live many species of ungulates, foxes, marmots and birds of prey, and the European lynx (Felis lynx), reintroduced several decades ago, is now common. From the train up the Jungfrau, it may even be seen running agilely on the snow.

The Aeolian Islands

ITALY

SICILY
REGISTRATION: 2000
CRITERIA: N (I)

44-45 *The village of Piano del Porto lies at the foot of Vulcano. It separates the crater of the main volcano from the other small volcanic system on the island, which ceased activity in the mid-sixteenth century.*

44 *Vulcano (seen here from Lipari) is the largest island in the Aeolians. People arrived from Sicily and settled on its highlands in the fifth millennium BC.*

Archeological research has shown that the peopling of the Aeolian Islands began at least in the fifth millennium BC when the archipelago became an important trading center between East and West. Their volcanic origins made the islands a valuable source of obsidian (a stone resembling black glass) that, when smoothed and sharpened, was used in ancient times to make weapons and tools. Trade in this resource made the first civilizations that lived on the highlands of Lipari prosperous.

Much later, in 580 BC, the seven islands – Lipari, Panarea, Vulcano, Stromboli, Alicudi, Filicudi and Salina – were conquered by the Greeks who consecrated them to Aeolus, the Greek god of the wind. Homer took his hero Odysseus to the islands, to whom Aeolus made a present of the winds to blow his ships back to Ithaca. Unfortunately, Odysseus' crew opened the goatskins in which the winds were enclosed, letting them escape, and the ship's odyssey continued.

The existence of the legend is an indication of the importance that this tiny archipelago north of the Sicilian coast had on the history of the Mediterranean. In geological terms, it was formed around 100,000 years ago following a series of violent volcanic eruptions, but despite the long time span, the islands are still interesting to students of vulcanology. Earth scientists began to visit the Aeolians at least two hundred years ago. In 1891, Giuseppe Mercalli, whose name is used on a scale that measures seismic activity, was the first to define a 'vulcanian' eruption, when he described the eruption of the island Vulcano in 1888-90. It is an explosive sort that throws fragments of lava into the air that do not take on a round form during their flight as they

are already partially solidified. 'Strombolian' activity, on the other hand, indicates a series of explosions and small spurts of basalt lava from the same crater.

So the names of two types of volcanic action are derived from islands in the Aeolians, the two that are still the most active. Though what Mercalli described was the last great eruption of Vulcano, Stromboli is in continuous, though

moderate, activity and its last two manifestations of violence occurred in 1919 and 1930, when several deaths were incurred. In fact, the volcano itself is the island's greatest attraction and lures tens of thousands of tourists every year.

Overall, the area of the entire archipelago is less than 5 square miles: Lipari, the largest, covers 1.5 while Panarea, the smallest, covers just 85

45 top Spectral concretions emerge from the fumes of Vulcano. The plateau (the largest in the Aeolians) on the island is composed of lava, tufa and Quaternary deposits, and is furrowed by deep valleys.

45 center Fossa di Vulcano in fact is composed of two craters: Fossa I and, 420 yards to the southwest, the current crater, Fossa II, which has a diameter of 1,640 feet and a depth of 650.

45 bottom Since its last eruptive season (1888-90), only the fumaroles of Fossa di Vulcano have been active, with emissions that have a maximum temperature of 1100-1300°F.

acres (slightly over one tenth of a square mile). The vegetation is typically Mediterranean with 900 species recorded, of which five are endemic: *Bassia saxicola, Dianthus rupicola, Silene hicesiae, Cytiscus aeolicus* and *Ophrys lunata*. The most famous species is undoubtedly *Capparis spinosa*, the caper plant, whose fruits are fundamental to the local cuisine.

The fauna has some 40 species of birds, most of which stop off on the islands on their migrations. Mammals worthy of note are the dormouse (*Elyomis quercinus liparensis*), an endemic wild rabbit and seven species of bats. There are also seven types of reptiles, including the Aeolian lizard (*Podarcis raffonei*), which lives on Vulcano.

Loved by Alexandre Dumas Père and Curzio Malaparte, the Aeolians began to become a tourist destination in the 1950s after Roberto Rossellini filmed *Stromboli* there starring Ingrid Bergman. Since then, the almost 10,000 inhabitants of the islands have turned their closed agricultural economy into one based on tourism, providing services to the volcanic islands' annual 200,000 visitors.

46 top Eruptive lava flows down the sides of the Sciara del Fuoco, which has been produced over the millennia on the northwest face of Stromboli by landslides.

46 center Stromboli's comparative youth is indicated by its many landslides, which have been facilitated by the fragility of the silicon- and rhyolite-rich lava.

46 bottom 'Strombolian' (i.e., explosive) eruptions are named after this island. It is the only volcano in Europe that is in a constant state of eruption.

46-47 Stromboli is a stratovolcano with a regular and steep-sided cone. It rises over 13,000 feet from the bottom of the sea, 3,030 of which are above sea level.

47 bottom left Strombolian eruptions occur when enough of the gas contained in the magma accumulates to blow out the 'plug'.

47 bottom right The threatening cone of Stromboli towers over the village of San Vincenzo. During the last two large eruptions (1919 and 1930), the volcano showed its unpredictability and killed a number of people.

48 The cave known as Saint Rudolf's Church takes its name from the 'natural Baroque style' of its limestone concretions. Since antiquity, the caves of Skocjan have combined an exceptional geological formation with a highly unusual faunal and floral ecosystem.

49 left The Cave of Silence – this is the entrance – has three sections, called Paradise, Calvary and Great Hall. It is the largest underground cavern in Europe and one of the most spectacular.

49 right Over hundreds of millennia, the Timavo River has cut a deep canyon to the Skocjan Caves where it disappears underground. The local karst extends underground for 3.6 miles.

LJUBLJANA

The caves of Skocjan
SLOVENIA

Kras, Municipality of Divača
Registration: 1986
Criteria: N (ii) (iii)

At the start of 1900, geologists received confirmation of what nineteenth-century 'water diviners' had always suspected: the mysterious Reka River that flowed underground in the area of Skocjan was the same one that reappeared in the form of three springs – under the new name Timavo – in San Giovanni di Duino, near Montefalcone in Italy, after a journey of 25 miles

Although Slovenia is particularly well endowed with caves (it has roughly 7,000), those in Skocjan are of notable geological importance. When the Reka passes from an area of *flysch* (ground formed of clay and marl) to one of calcareous rock, the water penetrates the subsoil and, over the geological eras, forms karst. In this zone of limestone, the dislocation of the points of entry of

and concretions in the world. This system proceeds along galleries to the sinkholes and arrives above the waters of the Reka that have cut a natural suspended bridge out of the rock. Visitors to Skocjan caves can descend to a depth of 690 feet.

The morphological characteristics of the caves have fostered particular climatic conditions that permit the

underground. The tracing elements used by the pioneers of karstism were colorants, radioactive substances and even eels; these were released in the Reka where the river went underground and seen on the surface when they emerged.

Separating the Roman world in the east from Illyria in antiquity, the Timavo (or Reka) rises on the slopes on Mount Sneznik in Slovenia before disappearing into the ground 31 miles later in the caves of Skocjan. Over the millennia, erosion caused by its waters has created those unusual geological formations referred to as karst, from Kras, the name of the Slovenian region through which the river runs.

the water has caused the formation of unique morphological features. One example is doline karst, in which the roofs of caves close to the surface have fallen in and left sinkholes. Doline karst is named after Velika Dolina and Malika Dolina in the Skocjan area; these are two sinkholes separated by a cave that plummet to a depth of 535 feet.

The imposing system of caves and galleries in Skocjan is over 3 miles in length and the longest example of true karst. It is entered through the Cave of Silence – the largest cave in Europe with a section measuring nearly 130,000 square feet – that contains some of the most fascinating stalactites, stalagmites

highly unusual coexistence, in the sinkholes and entrances to the caves, of botanical species belonging to alpine and Mediterranean environments. Similarly, living creatures have adapted to the peculiar habitat of the karst.

This unusual ecology makes Skocjan caves a unique laboratory of biodiversity and has earned it special attention from a conservation standpoint. With the contribution of the local populace, the management of the Regional Park of Skocjan (which covers nearly 2 square miles around the caves) is making a considerable effort to protect these fragile ecosystems, whose survival necessitates the cautious and compatible development of the surrounding territory.

The lakes of Plitvice
CROATIA

LIKA
REGISTRATION: 1979, 2000
CRITERIA: N (II) (III)

Even today, the elderly inhabitants of Lika like to recount a legend. One particular year in the distant past, the region was afflicted by a terrible drought. The crops shriveled up, the livestock died and the people prayed for rain in vain; until, moved to pity by their pleading, the Black Queen appeared in the sky and sent a thunderbolt into the valley whereupon it began to rain. It rained for so many days that streams flowed, meadows quickly turned green once more and lakes and waterfalls were formed: all of which now lie

within the National Park of Plitvice.

A mythological value has always been placed on water, particularly in karstic regions where an intricate network of underground streams flows, and the scenery in Plitvice is so beautiful that it is unsurprising that local tradition has attributed a supernatural origin to it. This extraordinary water system – created by waters from the Crna and Bijela Rivers – is formed by 16 main bodies of water with a joint surface area of nearly 500 acres. Grouped mainly in two sections, the Upper (Gornja Jezera) and Lower (Donja Jezera) Lakes, the pools are separated by a maximum difference in height of 443 feet and connected by a series of streams and waterfalls.

Lakes Kozjak and Prosce, both of which lie in the Upper Lake group, form three quarters of this area. Lake Kozjak receives the

waters of the Rjecica River and spills those of the Korana River downstream. From Novakovica Brod, the last of the Lower Lakes, the Korana makes a spectacular leap of 236 feet over Sastavci Waterfall ('encounter' in Croation), which collects all the waters that flow through Plitvice.

The distinction between the Upper and Lower Lakes may appear superfluous, given that all the lakes belong to a single system, however, there is a geological basis to this differentiation. The pools of the Upper Lakes lie in dolomitic rock,

whilst those of the Lower Lakes are in tufa. The point at which the two rock types meet occurs in the bed of the Lake Kozjak.

The landscape of the Plitvice Lakes is in constant evolution. Although scientists began studying the lakes at the start of the nineteenth century, it was only recently concluded that they are phytogenetic in character. In karst regions, and in a climate like that of Croatia, the tufa in contact with well-ventilated water becomes a form of living matter that favors the formation of mosses. Their roots capture calcium carbonate in solution, and, with the passing of time, the mosses grow on top of one another to form barriers; in doing so, they change the morphology of the pools. It is thought that in Plitvice, the bed of the lakes grows at a speed of up to an inch a year.

The protected area of Plitvice is not limited to the lakes. Since 1949, a territory of roughly 496 acres has been declared a national park. It lies at an altitude of between 1,300 and 4,200 feet, includes underground caves and is almost entirely covered by woods of beech (*Fagus sylvatica*), fir (*Abies alba*), pines (*Pinus sylvestris*), birch (*Carpinus betulus*) and sycamore (*Acer*

51

50 left Plitvicka Jereza National Park has 16 interconnecting lakes joined by streams and waterfalls.

50-51 Formed by four lakes, the pools in the Donja Jezera system are formed of tufa, the morphology of which is constantly altered by the calcium carbonate produced by mosses.

50 bottom Lake Kozjak is the largest in the park and covers 200 acres. The drainage area lies in the 'Upper Lakes' section, which is covered by a beech forest (Fagus sylvatica).

51 top A migratory bird of prey, the magnificent brown kite (Milvus milvus) is one of the 70 types of bird that nest in this zone. Altogether, 216 species have been recorded in the park.

51 bottom The lynx (Lynx lynx) was reintroduced to nearby Slovenia in the 1970s. It was first seen in Plitvice park in 1983 and now it is believed that 60 pairs live in Croatia.

pseudoplatanus). Conservation of the woods is of crucial importance to the survival of the lakes: the trees prevent erosion and encourage the distribution of the water throughout the year, withholding the water during the wet season and releasing it during the dry season: in addition to the 126 species of birds recorded, the park is the perfect habitat for the brown bear and the wolf, which are increasingly rare elsewhere.

Durmitor National Park

YUGOSLAVIA

Montenegro
Registration: 1980
Criteria: N (ii) (iii) (iv)

In these parts it is known as 'the Grand Canyon's only rival'. Perhaps this claim may seem exaggerated but the canyon created by the Tara River is the largest in Europe, though it is less famous and visited, partly owing to Yugoslavia's recent history.

The clean, clear water runs through a series of rapids for 52 miles between vertical sandstone walls up to 4,260 feet high before leaping over the spectacular waterfalls of Sige Jovicica. From here the Tara – which has a flow of 2,260 cubic feet per second – widens and runs another 40 or so miles to where it flows into the Piva and, shortly after, into the Drina, the river that symbolizes the tormented history of the Balkans.

Tara canyon is just one of the natural marvels of Durmitor, Montenegro's oldest national park (Montenegro is the smallest of the former Yugoslavia's republics and the only one not to have claimed independence). Founded in 1952, the Durmitor is named after a massif of 48 peaks over 6,560 feet high. Its 350 square miles and altitude that ranges from 1,480 to 8,275 feet enclose various ecosystems, from Mediterranean to alpine. Its other rivers are the Susica and the Draga, fed by 748 springs, both of which also created deep and impressive canyons during the Quaternary period.

Considered one of the last wild places in Europe, the park contains 13 glacial rings and 18 turquoise lakes that are locally known as 'the eyes of the mountain'. The largest, Crno Jezero (Black Lake), feeds the basins of the Tara and Komarica, an underground karstic river system that rises to the surface outside the park's boundaries. Karstic and glacial phenomena were responsible for the formation of the Ledena Pecina (Cold Cavern) that, at an altitude of 6,890 feet just below the summit of Mount Obla Glava, is filled with a host of permanently ice-covered stalactites and stalagmites.

Durmitor boasts a vegetation of 1,300 species of vascular plants, of which 37 are specific to the area, such as a rare species of verbena (*Verbascum durmitoreum*) and another of gentian (*Gentiana levicalis*). The aquatic plants that grow beside the lakes are of particular interest, as are the vast wooded areas, of which 100 acres represent the last virgin forest of black pine (*Pinus nigrus*) in Europe. Some of its trees are over 400 years old, stand 500 feet high and have a diameter of 4 feet.

Durmitor is also home to 130 species of birds, many brown bears (*Ursus arctos*), gray wolves (*Canis lupus*), chamois and boar; and the rivers contain various species of salmonids,

BELGRADE

including *Salmo trutem*, *Huchi hucho* and
Thimalus thimalus.

The wild, rocky area is inhabited by
1,500 people but another 8,000 live in
the village of Zabljak on the edge of
the park; at 4,780 feet, Zabljak is the
highest inhabited center in the
Balkans.

The traditional life of the villagers
may be considered economically
backward, but it is in perfect balance
with nature and this is a value that is
celebrated in the constitution of
the small republic that, in its
introduction, defines Montenegro
as an 'Ecological State'.

*52 top left The rare golden
eagle is one of the many
birds of prey that find
Durmitor an ideal habitat
and the location of
abundant prey.*

*52 center The gray wolf
was once widespread across
North America and
Eurasia. In Europe it has
now been reduced to small
populations in the Balkans,
Russia, Italy and Spain.*

*52 bottom Durmitor
massif culminates in the
peak of Bobotov Kuk
(8,275 feet) and is girded
by rocky pinnacles.*

*52-53 The Tara River
runs for 51 miles through a
vertiginous gorge. Here the
sides are lined by the last
virgin forest of black pine in
Europe.*

*53 bottom The Ledena
Pecina ('Cold Cave') is
permanently lined with ice
and was created below
Mount Obla Glava (6,890
feet) by karstic phenomena.*

The caves of Aggtelek Karst and Slovak Karst
SLOVAKIA AND HUNGARY

COUNTY OF BORSOD-ABAÚJ AEMPLÉN, HUNGARY
DISTRICTS OF ROZNAVA AND KOSICE, SLOVAKIA
REGISTRATION: 1995, 2000
CRITERIA: N (I)

In 1794 the speleologist Jószsef Sartory drew a map representing nearly a mile of Baradla Cave, a karstic formation in northeastern Hungary. This was the first map ever produced of a cave, but it took 30 years more before Sartory's work was completed to show over five miles of underground vaults and corridors. In the meantime, in 1806, after being fitted with steps and protective barriers, the curious natural phenomenon saw its first tourists.

It required more than another century before the obstinacy of another speleologist, Jan Majko, discovered that Baradla Cave connected with the nearby Certova Diera ('the Devil's abyss') and Licsia Diera ('the fox's den'). Yet more surprising was the fact that it formed a single complex over 13 miles long with

Domica Cave on the slopes of the Carpathian Mountains in what today is Slovakia.

In 1977, Slovakia established the Protected Area of Slovakian Karst and two years later Hungary established the National Park of Aggtelek, which covers 216 square miles along the southern edge of the Carpathians. This, the most fully explored karstic system in Europe, numbering 712 caves, many of which are distributed on different levels and contain extraordinary limestone formations, including the tallest stalagmite in the world at 107 feet. Almost all of them were formed during the Middle Triassic from sandstone modeled by the erosive action of underground rivers and the accumulation of sedimentary deposits.

The most attractive cave in the area – both to scientists and visitors – is Baradla-Domica, which attracts 200,000 tourists a year. It was formed 200 million years ago by the underground rivers, the Styx and the Domica. Its tunnels contain innumerable limestone formations, in the shapes of shields and drums, and also underground lakes – fed by water running down the smooth travertine walls – that are commonly known as the 'Roman Baths'.

The karstic system contains many more curiosities. Gombasecka Cave, near the village of Slavec in the district of Roznava, has a forest of white and pink stalactites up to 10 feet long but with a diameter of only a quarter of an inch. Jasovska Cave has pagoda-shaped formations of aragonite and travertine that reveal the composition of the carbonate rocks of which it is formed. There is also the frozen pool that covers the bed of sediments in Silicka Ladnika; in winter the ice reaches a volume of nearly 12,000 cubic feet, which makes it unique in continental Europe, particularly considering the relatively mild climate.

The fauna in the caves is of special interest. There are many species that have adapted to underground life, including coleopters, worms, mollusks, the endemic snail *Sadleriana pannonica*,

55 top Formations of aragonite and travertine form picturesque and evocative shapes in Gombasecka cave. The karst system of Aggtelek and Slovak Karst (which number 712 underground caves) draws 200,000 visitors a year.

and a primitive crab, *Niphargus aggtelekiensis*. The fauna that live at the entrance to the cave are abundant: 17 species of bats and numerous dipterans and butterflies.

During the Neolithic period, and occasionally in the Paleolithic, these grottoes offered shelter to man, as is clear from the graffiti and stone tools found in the area. Today, some of the caves have been fitted out with equipment to treat asthma and other pulmonary pathologies.

55 bottom Aggtelek's largest stalactite stands an amazing 122 feet high. This natural pillar is thought to be the world's tallest.

54 The limestone wall that stands near the main entrance to the Baradla Domica Cave well exemplifies the predominant geology in Aggtelek National Park.

54-55 Baradla Domica is the largest cave in Aggtelek. Its main chamber lies in Hungary and is large enough to hold 1,000 people.

BRATISLAVA

BUDAPEST

The delta of the Danube
RUMANIA

PROVINCE OF TULCEA
REGISTRATION: 1991
CRITERIA: N (III) (IV)

56 top In June the whiskered tern (Chlidonias hybridus) builds a nest from a raft of aquatic vegetation that it anchors to plants growing above the water surface. Sometimes it nests on a lily leaf.

The word 'delta' is used in several languages to mean the terminal section of a river – where arms branch off from the main course before the river flows into the sea – and was coined by the Greeks owing to the similarity in shape between the triangular letter 'delta' in the Greek alphabet and the river and its arms. The first river delta they saw, explored and described was that of the Danube, the great river that the historian Herodotus of Halicarnassus recognized in 450 BC as playing a fundamental role in European civilization.

With a length of 1,800 miles and navigable for almost its entire length, the basin of the Danube measures half a million square miles and contains roughly 80 million people in eight different countries. Its delta, of which 1,600 square miles lies in Rumania and the remaining 295 in Ukraine, is geologically the youngest zone in Europe. Declared a Biosphere Reserve in 1990 and inscribed as a UNESCO World Heritage site and on the Ramsar Convention a year later, the delta of the Danube is an area in continual evolution, being forged by the 180,000-325,000 cubic foot per second flow of the river itself and by the 55 million tons of alluvial detritus that are swept towards the sea each year.

There are four main branches in the Danube Delta, the Chilia, Tulcea, Sulina and Sfantu Gheorghe, to which can be added many freshwater lakes connected by canals. In the southern section there are vast brackish marshes separated from the Black Sea by sand banks, which are continually modeled by the combined action of the river and sea tides.

Only 10% of the delta territory is permanently above water level but, in recompense, the marshlands are the largest in Europe and home to what is probably the largest expanse of rushes on the planet. The rushes are mostly from the species *Phragmites australis* and form numerous small islands (called *plaur*) that stand above the water ferns and yellow and white lilies that cover the marshes.

Where the Danube meets the sea is where the scenery is most surprising: here, there are islands that exist by day but are submerged by night tides, grass-covered sand dunes that enclose wet

56 center The huge marshes of the Danube are often covered by white and yellow water lilies.

56 bottom Near the mouth of the Danube, oak trees have adapted to live with the trunk exposed to the action of the tides.

BUCHAREST

56-57 The terrain of the
Danube Delta is constantly
altered by the large river,
which has a flow of
180,000-325,000 cubic
feet per second and carries
50 million tons of alluvial
detritus downstream every
year.

57 top An example of a
glossy ibis (Plegadis
falcinellus) in its speckled
winter plumage. In
summer its colors are
brighter: the body and neck
are rust colored, while the
wings and head are
metallic green.

57 bottom A skilful diver,
swimmer and fisher, the
common pelican
(Pelecanus onocrotalus)
has no rivals for elegance
in flight. They fly in flocks
and exploit thermals to give
them height.

valleys and long barriers of alluvial land on which tall trees grow. The most interesting example of the land barriers is called Letea and lies at the mouth of the Sulina. It is about 13 miles long and no more than 10 miles wide and is characterized by oaks (*Quercus robur* and *Quercus pedunculiflora*) up to 115 feet tall and by pines and ash trees, which in turn are besieged by various climbing plants – *Periploca graeca, Clematis vitalba, Vitis sylvestris* and *Humulus lupulus* – giving the scene a curiously 'tropical' appearance.

The water meadows, lakes, dunes and other 'high' zones in the Danube Delta provide the largest ornithological reserve in Europe in terms of both quantity and

do not nest in the delta, in the winter months there are roughly 45,000 red-breasted geese (*Branta ruficollis*).

It has not yet been quantified precisely but the number of small mammals like the otter, coypu, hare, wild cat, viper and muskrat is important on a European level. And Letea Barrier is home to a moth, the *Rhyparioides metelkana*, which is unique in Europe.

Of the 70 or so species of freshwater fish (30 of which are typical of the delta), mention should be made of the Danube herring, the carp and, above all, the sturgeon, a favorite catch of fishermen for its caviar.

The inhabitants in the delta number about 15,000, are distributed in small

58 top Islets of rushes, which are mostly from the species Phragmites australis, are known as plaur. Overall, they cover an area of 368 square miles.

58 bottom left Unlike other herons, the shy purple heron (Ardea purpurea) spends its life among the rush beds in the huge marshes where it is best camouflaged.

58 bottom right Included in the IUCN's Red List, the pygmy cormorant (Phalacrocorax pygmaeus) is the smallest and rarest cormorant. Over half the world's population lives in the protected area.

variety of bird species. Of the over 300 species that visit the reserve from around the Mediterranean, continental Europe and even remote areas of Asia, 176 nest here. These include the pygmy cormorant (*Phalacrocorax pygmaeus*), whose population of 2,500 pairs represents 61% of the world total, and the largest European colony of the two pelicans, *Pelecanus onocrotalus* and *Pelecanus crispus*. There are also many ibis, purple herons, storks, egrets and white swans, of which there are at least 1,000 in each species. And, though they

villages and are mainly Orthodox Ukrainians. However, the delta is being depopulated as a result of the increasingly strict restrictions imposed by the Rumanian government following pressure from international organizations. Checks are being placed on activities related to systematic fishing and agriculture, both of which are considered unsustainable. This goes in complete contrast to the 1980s when, under the Ceausescu regime and aegis of the Soviet Union, a massive plan was introduced to exploit the zone. Numerous low-lying areas were dug for

experimentation with crops such as rice and maize, while vast areas were deforested to make space for poppy plantations in sight of paper mills. Meanwhile, heavy industries dumped tons of poisons into the Danube upstream.

Though the collapse of the Soviet Union and its satellite countries brought dramatic political, economic and social consequences, it was a cure-all for the delta's delicate ecosystem. According to experts, it is in good health, at least for the moment.

58-59 A group of common
pelicans gather in a marshy
area. It has been estimated
that the delta is home to
2,500 pairs, i.e., half of
the Palearctic population.

59 bottom With its
unmistakable green and
blue plumage and hooked
beak, the long common
roller (Coracias garrulus)
lives in pairs or small
groups.

Western Caucasus

RUSSIAN FEDERATION

REPUBLICS OF ADIGEA
AND KARACEVO-CIRCASSIA
REGISTRATION: 1999
CRITERIA: N (II) (IV)

60

MOSCOW

60-61 Lying in a mountainous region, the 130 glacial lakes in the western Caucasus all lie at high altitudes, between 6,500-9,900 feet, in the strip where glaciers once existed.

The plan to build ski resorts in what is, in all probability, the area in Europe least contaminated by man was the unusual accusation leveled by Russian environmentalists against the Moscow government on the occasion of the Johannesburg summit on sustainable development. The westernmost areas of the Caucasus Mountains, just a few dozen miles from the coast of the Black Sea, have not seen a human being for centuries.

In 1882 the Kuban Hunting Reserve was established there, named after one of the largest rivers in the area, for use by the Muscovite nobility, but by 1906 the czar had decided to return the land to its inhabitants. This act of generosity, however, aroused the indignation of the Academy of Sciences, which began pushing for the setting up of a nature park for scientific research. Consequently, in 1924, the Soviets instituted the Kavkazkyi Nature Reserve, which was followed many years later by the Sochi National Park and other small areas used for conservation.

Covering an area of over 1,150 square miles, the western Caucasus is occupied fully by the final offshoots of one of Europe's most impressive mountain chains. Its peaks range in height between 820 and the 13,274 feet of Mount Dunbai Ulgen. The geology of the region has formations of igneous, metamorphic and sedimentary rocks, and, in the northern section, is dominated by limestone massifs in which enormous fissures were eroded during the Ice Age. One includes Russia's largest cave, 5,250 feet in depth and 10 miles in length. The many rivers on the south sides of the mountains flow into the Black Sea after a short rough journey through lakes, waterfalls and deep ravines.

The vegetation inhabits different zones depending on altitude. Between 3,300-3,940 feet, a deciduous forest is predominated by oak (*Quercus petraea*), pear trees (*Pyrus communis*), chestnuts (*Castanea sativa*), hornbeam (*Carpinus caucasica*) and eastern beech (*Fagus orientalis*). At higher levels, these give way to various species of pine and Caucasian fir (*Abies nordmanniana*). Above 6,500 feet it is the turn of the birch (*Betula pendula* and *Betula litwinowii*) and maple (*Acer laetum*). At higher altitudes grows the endemic Caucasian rhododendron (*Rhododendron caucasicum*). Overall, the vegetation

60 bottom Pink clouds create a fairytale backdrop to the rocky heights of the western Caucasus. The area includes igneous, metamorphic and sedimentary rocks and, in the northern part, limestone massifs.

61 top left A magnificent but extinct volcano, Mount Elbrus (18,481 feet) is the highest point in the Caucasus region.

61 top right Deep cracks in one of the 60 glaciers in the mountain range. Overall the glaciers cover nearly 7 square miles.

61 center The males in the Kuban tar (Capra caucasica) have large horns and can weigh up to 220 pounds. The females reach a maximum of 130 pounds.

61 bottom Thought to be in danger of extinction, the Kuban tar only lives in the western Caucasus, in an inaccessible grazing area of 1,500 square miles.

numbers 160 species of vascular plants and 700 types of fungi.

The 60 mammals in Kavkazkyi Nature Reserve and Sochi National Park include wolves, brown bears, lynxes, boars, the Caucasian red deer (*Cervus elaphus moral*), roe deer, chamois and the Kuban tur (*Capra caucasica*), a high altitude goat. The recently reintroduced European bison is considered endangered and is joined in this status by two species of bats (*Miniopterus Schreibersi* and *Nyctalus lasioterus*), the Caucasian otter (*Lutra lutra meridionalis*) and a subspecies of the leopard (*Panthera pardus ciscaucasica*). The list of vertebrates includes 160 species of birds and 17 reptiles.

Though remains of ancient human settlements have been found, nobody lives inside the protected areas. There are few, very twisting roads and most of the region can only be reached via helicopter. There are only a few thousand tourists each year, and these nearly all come during the summer when international canoe races are held on the foaming Belaya River.

62 top Solitary and non-migratory, the eagle owl (Bubo bubo) is the largest nocturnal bird of prey in Europe. It has a wingspan of over 6 feet and weighs up to 6.5 pounds.

62 center The knotty branch of this eastern beech (Fagus orientalis) belongs to a dominant species in the deciduous forest at 3,300-3,900 feet, along with oaks, hornbeams and chestnuts.

62 bottom left Apart from magnificent trees, the forests in the western Caucasus contain mosses and fungi. The fungi number 700 species, of which 12 are very rare.

62 bottom right At 13,275 feet, the severe looking Mount Donbai-Ulgen is the highest point in the western Caucasus. It dominates the entire northern section of the area protected by UNESCO.

63 The region has several large rivers that form waterfalls as they flow into the Black Sea. The highest fall has a drop of 820 feet.

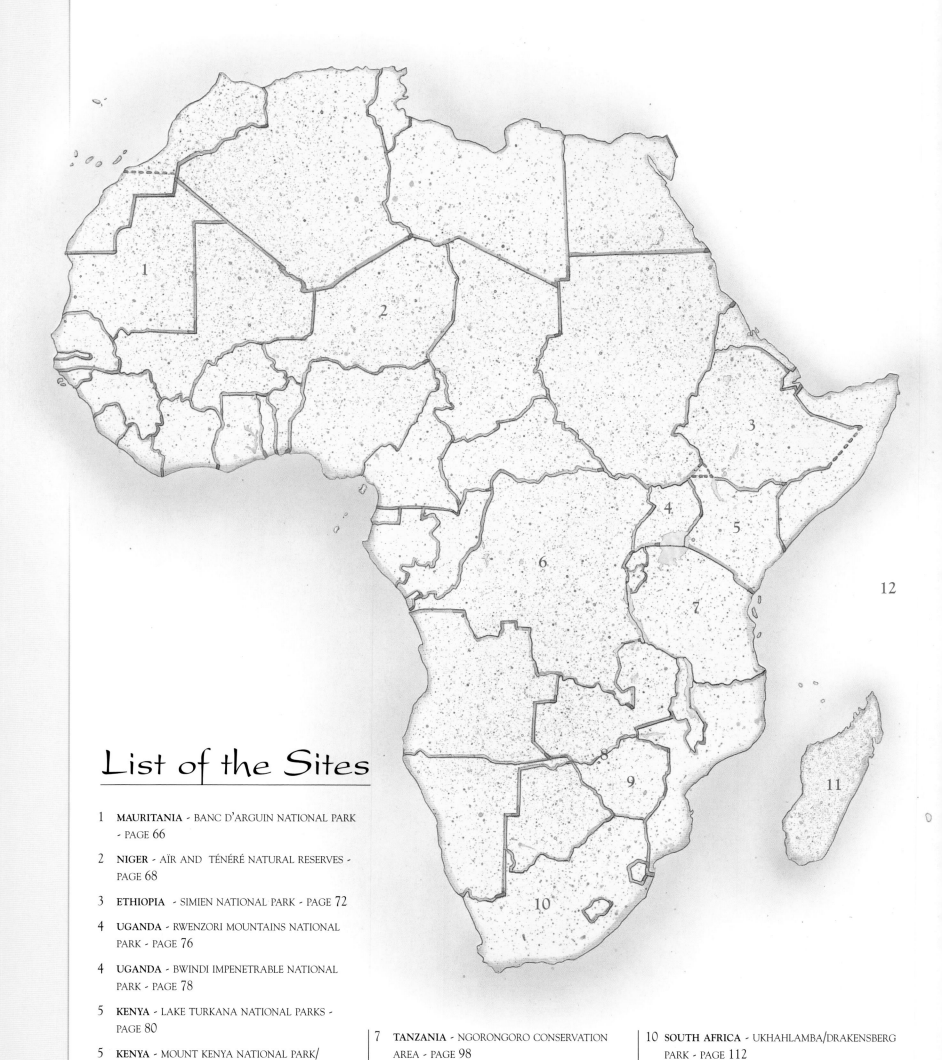

List of the Sites

Africa

When speaking of Africa and nature, one's imagination immediately jumps to the continent's parks and extraordinary wildlife, first and foremost the large mammals that have fascinated Westerners, from nineteenth-century explorers to modern tourists. The huge savannahs are the kingdom of magnificent predators like lions, leopards and cheetahs, but also of giant herbivores such as elephant, hippopotamus, buffalo, antelope, zebra and giraffe.

A continent of immense natural resources, Africa has some of the most abundant ecosystems in the world, for example, the immense alluvial plains of Manu National Park in Zimbabwe and Selous Game Reserve in Tanzania; the arid grasslands of Kenya and Ethiopia; the desolate expanses of the Sahara and Kalahari deserts; and the forests of Uganda, Rwanda and the Congo, where the greatly endangered species of mountain gorilla lives that was made famous by the zoologist Dian Fossey.

Africa has 32 of UNESCO's natural World Heritage sites, almost all of which were created to safeguard the continent's spectacular wildlife. Many of these areas are still unspoilt and their environmental balances remain unaltered thanks to the sustainable interaction of the local peoples. These are often small ethnic groups like the Maasai whose livelihood is based on livestock grazing.

Africa's natural heritage is probably the one most threatened by irrational development. Many animal species are considered to be at risk by the International Union for the Conservation of Nature. Although hunting – which was ruthlessly practiced until the mid-twentieth century – and ivory trading have been banned, local and international protective measures are often ineffective against poaching. Africa, of course, is the world's poorest continent so that, on the one hand, the means are lacking to protect the reserves, and, on the other hand, the poverty of the people means the poachers often find them complicit in their activity.

Furthermore, the modern era is arriving in Africa with a worrying demographic explosion that renders the situation even more critical. Many parks are already besieged by the external presence of humans. In some cases, like Mount Kenya and Mount Kilimanjaro, agriculture and grazing have already entered the parks' area, removing precious space from the animals' natural habitat. Elsewhere, for instance in the Congo, the tribal wars that periodically shake the continent constitute an increasing threat to the environment. And the African population, which depends on the land more than any other, is paying the price for shortsighted colonial and imperialist policies and damage caused by global climate change.

Banc d'Arguin National Park
MAURITANIA

NOUADHIBOU AND AZEFAL
REGISTRATION: 1989
CRITERIA: N (II) (IV)

During the period 4,000-7,000 years ago, the Sahara offered a reasonably hospitable environment, and the climate favored human settlement and large communities of wildlife. At that time, the landscape of the Banc d'Arguin would have resembled the present estuary of the Senegal River, with the Wadis Téguédé, Chibka and Chrack that carried their waters to the bay of St. Jean; however, desertification was about to begin. The large mammals moved south and the villages of Neolithic fishermen and livestock raisers were abandoned. The only vestige of that period is the 11 square miles of mangroves (*Avicennia africana*) on the coastal mudbanks and inland water meadows.

The coastline that separates the Sahara from the Atlantic includes a system of 15 or so islands – the largest of which, Tidra, measures 21 miles in length by 5 miles in width – that are mainly composed of sand carried from the Sahara by the wind. The islands have been created because the ocean here, 38 miles from the coast, at low tide is no more than 16 feet deep. The 4,633 square-mile Banc d'Arguin National Park was created in 1976 by the government of Mauritania to protect the migrating birds that spend winter in this extraordinary habitat where the desert environment and biodiversity of the Atlantic Ocean coexist.

The park lies in a region where the paleoarctic and afrotropical vegetation meet. The sandy coast is home to salt-tolerant plants such as *Salsola baryosma*, *Salicornia senegalensis* and *Suaeda fructicosa*, while the dunes are covered by *Stipagrostis pungens*, *Cornulaca monacantha* and *Euphorbia balsamifera*. Inland, the desert-like climate is suitable for acacias like *Acacia raddiana* and plants such as *Balanites aegyptiaca*, *Maerva crassifolia* and *Capparis deciduas*, a plant in the caper family.

Of the 7 million or so migratory birds that follow the Atlantic routes, more than 2 million spend winter on the Banc d'Arguin, finding food in the fish-filled gulf waters. The 108 recorded species include the black tern (*Chlidonias nigra*) and pink flamingo (*Phoenocopterus ruber*), of which there are hundreds of thousands. In addition, during the mating season, there are 45,000 pairs of white pelicans (*Pelecanus onocrotalus*), European spoonbills (*Platalea leucorodia*), herons (*Ardea cinerea and Egretta gularis*), black-footed terns (*Gelochelidon nilotica*), Caspian terns (*Hydroprogne caspia*), sandpipers (*Calidris acuminata*) and African

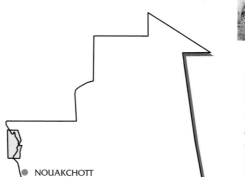

66 top right The windborne sand of the Sahara and mangrove swamps push into the Banc d'Arguin park. Covering 4,633 square miles, this extraordinary habitat is home to roughly 2 million birds during the winter months.

66 center left Cap Blanc is a nature reserve annexed to Banc d'Arguin where cliffs fall sheer into the waters of the Atlantic. A population of 150 monk seals (Monachus monachus) live in its shadow.

NOUAKCHOTT

66 bottom left Pterioftalmi, known as 'land fish', are able to live in water and to behave like amphibians. The park's mangrove swamps are therefore an ideal habitat for them.

66-67 Included in the IUCN's Red List of endangered species, the Caspian tern (Hydroprogne caspia) spends the winter months on the sandy expanses of the Banc d'Arguin safe from predators.

cormorants (Phalacrocorax africanus). The presence of mammals is also remarkable, with Dorcas gazelles, jackals, hyenas and various cats, and marine mammals like the (Sousa teuszii), rough-toothed dolphin (Steno bredanensis), bottle-nosed dolphins (Tursiops truncates and Delphinus delphis), finwhales (Balaenoptera physalus) and 150 monk seals (Monachus monachus).

The secret of this environment is the extraordinary richness of its aquatic fauna, as the shallow waters of the Banc d'Arguin are an important mating area for many species of fish and crustaceans. These are the principal source of food, not just to the wildlife, but also to the 500 inhabitants of the Imraguen ethnic group that populate the seven villages inside the park.

And finally, they provide a source of income to the economy of the whole of Mauritania, of which fishing is one of the pillars.

67 top Accustomed to living in crowded populations, the Caspian tern can be recognized by its black head and bright red beak. It eats almost only fish and for this is a skilful swimmer.

67 center Roughly 6,000 pairs of white (or common) pelicans (Pelecanus onocrotalus) come to the Banc d'Arguin for the mating season.

67 bottom The European spoonbill (Platalea leucorodia) gets its name from the shape of its bill. It uses this as a tool to sieve the sand in search of shrimps, its favorite food.

Aïr and Ténéré Natural Reserves

NIGER

Department of Agadès
Registration: 1991
Inscription on the World Heritage in
Danger list: 1992
Criteria: N (II) (III) (IV)

After becoming famous for being the decisive stretch of the exhausting Paris-Dakar car and motorcycle race, during the 1990s the Ténéré Desert hit the headlines for political reasons.

The revolt by the Tuareg, who were at one time the unchallenged masters of the Sahara, was putting the stability of Niger and Mali at risk and interrupting the already few north-south routes across the huge African desert.

The kidnapping in February 1992 of six members of the staff of the Aïr and Ténéré Natural Reserves produced the request by the government of Niger to include the area in the World Heritage in Danger list.

The kidnapping ended without victims and on 20 April 1995 the parties signed an agreement that opened the way for the World Wildlife Fund to examine the area. Fortunately, the delicate local environment had suffered less damage than expected, even though some species, like the ostrich, continue to be at grave risk owing to poaching.

With an area of just under 30,000 square miles, the Aïr and Ténéré Natural Reserves form the largest protected area in Africa. Approximately rectangular in shape, approximately 35-40% of its surface is occupied by the Aïr Mountains. These are nine granite massifs with igneous elements that rise out of the desert sands.

The rest of the area is the Ténéré Desert, one of the largest sand seas in the Sahara, whose platform is composed of Cambrian metamorphic rocks subjected to continual and intense erosion. Out of this emerge the ergs – huge fields of sand dunes whose height can reach 1,000 feet where they have a rocky base to rest on.

Amply described in the scientific literature, the vegetation runs to more than 350 species that are particularly widespread in the Sahelian environment of Aïr. The main communities are of Balanites

68 top The paleolithic paintings of Anakom are one of the most important examples of early human existence in the Sahara. 0

68 bottom Much of Ténéré is covered by ergs, the immense sand dunes that are created by the constant erosion of the Cambrian substrate.

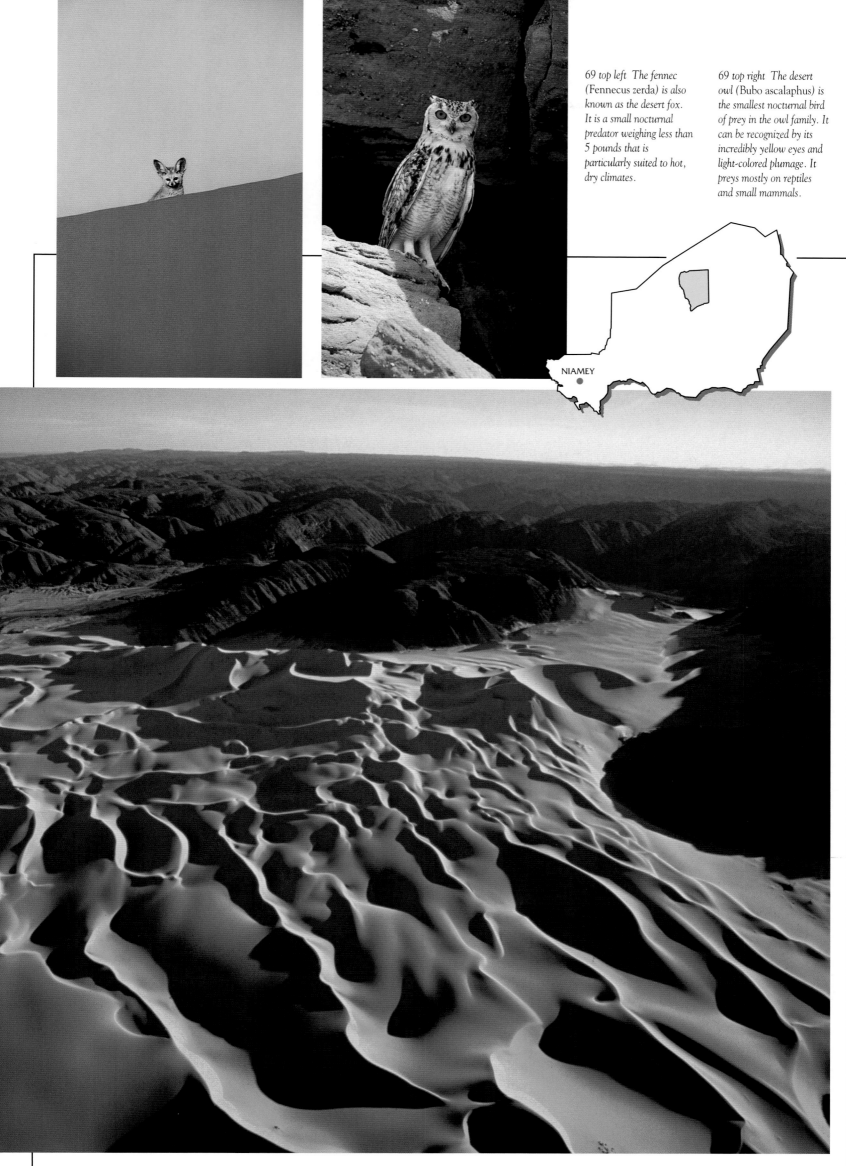

69 top left The fennec (Fennecus zerda) is also known as the desert fox. It is a small nocturnal predator weighing less than 5 pounds that is particularly suited to hot, dry climates.

69 top right The desert owl (Bubo ascalaphus) is the smallest nocturnal bird of prey in the owl family. It can be recognized by its incredibly yellow eyes and light-colored plumage. It preys mostly on reptiles and small mammals.

NIAMEY

68-69 Measuring 30,000 odd square miles, the Aïr and Ténéré reserves together form the largest protected area in Africa.

This aerial view shows the outreaches of the mountains of Aïr rising beyond the enormous expanse of sand sea.

70 top right A sand cat (Felis margarita) struggles with a deadly prey, the horned viper (Cerastes cerastes), which is one of the 18 endemic reptiles in the Ténéré.

70 center left Three fennec cubs peep out of a crack. Only 2 inches long at birth, the cubs reach the size of their parents in just 4 months.

70 bottom left A desert jerboa (Jaculus jaculus) digs its shelter in the sands of the Ténéré.

aegyptiaca, which contains a steroid that cures schistosomiasis, Salvadora persica, which is the green shrub used in the Sahel to clean teeth, Ziziphus mauritiana and Acacia laeta.

In the Ténéré, the acacias are Acacia tortilis raddiana and Acacia ehrenbergiana.

The wild varieties of some food plants such as olives, millet and sorghum are particularly important and have recently been subjected to genetic study by the International Board for Plant Genetic Resources.

Despite the harshness of the climate, with recorded temperatures at an annual average of 28 degrees and rainfall scarce or non-existent, there are 165 species of birds, 18 reptiles and 40 mammals, many of which are in danger of extinction, for example, the 12,000 dorcade gazelles (Gazella dorcas), the 170 Dama gazelles (Gazella dama), and the 3,500 Barbary sheep or aoudad (Ammotragus lervia).

Even the Addax antelope (Addax nasomaculatus), which to the Tuareg is the 'queen of the desert', is in continual decline from indiscriminate hunting. It is estimated there are only 15 left.

The climatic conditions make Aïr and Ténéré difficult for man to inhabit and the villages of Iférouane and Tin Telloust have only 2,500 fixed inhabitants plus 1,500-4,500 Tuareg nomads. Yet this region has traces of settlements dating to 30,000 years ago when the glacial age had made the Sahara a land able to support the livestock-grazing lifestyle of its inhabitants. Their passing is documented in many rock paintings.

70-71 With about 12,000 remaining, the dorcas gazelle (Gazella dorcas) is one of the ungulates in danger of extinction that finds refuge in the protected area. Others are the Dama gazelle, barbary sheep and Addaz antelope.

71 top Ruthlessly hunted during the Tuareg rebellion, the ostrich (Struthio camelus) has become quite rare in the Aïr and Ténéré reserves.

71 right Bee-eater is the common name for various species of birds belonging to the Meropidae family (Merops spp.), whose diet is almost exclusively composed of bees and wasps.

Simien National Park

ETHIOPIA

REGION OF GONDAR
REGISTRATION: 1978
INSCRIPTION IN THE LIST OF WORLD
HERITAGE IN DANGER: 1996
CRITERIA: N (III) (IV)

ADDIS ABEBA

72-73 Endemic to the highlands, the Abyssinian wolf (Canis simensis) is the rarest dog in the world. In Simien National Park there are only a few hundred left and not one exists in captivity.

72 bottom An Egyptian vulture (Neophron percnopterus) is followed by a lappet-faced vulture (Torgos tracheliotus). The presence of carcass-eating birds of prey is typical of the birdlife in the Simien National Park.

Its horns are more than 3 feet long and are the most sought after trophy of Ethiopian warriors. Its coat is hazel in color; it is strong and can weigh up to 290 pounds. It is the Abyssinian ibex (*Walia ibex*), a species that has survived from the early incursion of paleoarctic fauna in the tropics.

Often featuring in Ethiopian myths and legends, this ibex – haughty in appearance and stubborn by nature – is also the symbol of the country. But despite this consecration, today there are only 150 remaining. The threat to it from man has forced the creatures to take refuge in the most inaccessible ravines in the Simien Highlands in Gondar.

Back in 1963 the Abyssinian ibex was added to the International Union for the Conservation of Nature's Red List of species under threat of extinction and, in order to preserve its habitat, Ethiopia instituted the first national park in the country in 1969. Sadly, however, the protection offered by the 85 square miles of Simien National Park is theoretical rather than practical.

The area has often been the theater of war in the long conflict between Ethiopia and Eritrea and, as a result, many refugees have fled there; indeed, the Ethiopian Highland Plateau is one of the most densely populated agricultural areas in eastern Africa. And if that were not enough, in recent years the zone has been hit by a dreadful drought.

The landscape in Simien National Park is of unusual beauty. In addition to Ras Dashan Terara – the highest peak in Ethiopia at 15,190 feet – the plateau is a

series of dizzying ravines and cliffs, formed by erosion of the volcanic lava, with walls up to 5,000 feet high and 22 miles long.

The vegetation is of great botanical interest, being prevalently herbaceous or typical of mountain savannah, with giant lobelias (*Lobelia rhynchopetalum*), but it is also threatened by demographic pressure. Agriculture and grazing have caused a reduction in the grass cover, which has led to the crossbreeding of the Abyssinian ibex.

Another species endemic to the plateau is the Abyssinian wolf (*Canis Simiensis*). It is the most rare member of

73 top The majestic lamergeyer (Gypeatus barbatus) has a wingspan of 9 feet and nests for the most part on the inaccessible walls of ravines.

73 center Stretches of giant lobelias animate the landscape of Simien National Park. These plants have developed strategies for adaptation to the harsh highland climate that experiences large fluctuations in temperature.

73 bottom During the day the leaves of the giant lobelia stand almost vertical so as not to expose their surface to the strong sunlight.

74 *Like other giant lobelias, this Kniphofia foliosa only flowers once in its lifespan.*

74-75 *Once widespread in Africa, the gelada (Theropithecus gelada) is a large baboon of which only 400 remain, all on Simien's plateau.*

the dog family in the world with only a few hundred left and not a single one in captivity.

The other species that survives on the Simien Plateau, which was once common to the entire continent but of which only 400 remain, is the Gelada baboon (*Theropithecus gelada*). This creature with a mane similar to that of a lion is less aggressive and curious than its closest relatives and is special in two other ways: it is the only ape to feed exclusively on grass and it is the most dexterous.

The park is home to other mammals considered to be under threat of extinction even though they also live in other areas of Africa: they are the serval (*Felix serval*), the caracal (*Felis caracal*)

and the spotted hyena (*Crocuta crocuta*). It was the threat to the animal species that led UNESCO to include Simien National Park on the List of World Heritage in Danger in 1996. Although the Ethiopian government in Addis Ababa has voiced support and reassurances, international interest in the area has brought it little benefit as local authorities have scarce interest in the park and its fauna.

The overriding concern of the local chiefs is to alleviate the suffering of the human population, which is stricken by famine and sickness.

75 top Despite its threatening leonine mane, the gelada is less aggressive than other baboons; however, this characteristic is one reason for its continual decline.

75 center A small honeyeater of the genus Nectarinia flies among the lichens on the leaves of an arboreal heather.

75 bottom Incapable of climbing trees, the gelada is a ground-based primate that feeds only on grasses. Despite being extremely dexterous, its skills (remarkable compared to other monkeys) adapted for living on the ground made it an easy prey for early examples of Homo spp.

Rwenzori Mountains National Park

UGANDA

DISTRICTS OF KABAROLE, KASESE AND BUNDIBUGYO
REGISTRATION: 1994
REGISTRATION ON THE LIST OF WORLD HERITAGE
SITES IN DANGER: 1999
CRITERIA: N (III) (IV)

Although it was way back in the second century AD that the Roman geographer Ptolemy claimed that the source of the Nile was to be found in the heart of Africa, at the top of the 'mountains of the Moon', Europeans only discovered the Rwenzori chain in 1889. It must have been a wonderful surprise to Arthur Jephson and Thomas Parke, members of Henry Morton Stanley's expedition, to find themselves gazing at snowy peaks right on the equator.

However, the Englishmen had other aims at the time and the chain of mountains remained unexplored until 1906 when prince Luigi of Savoy organized an expedition. And thus it was that though the most important mountain in the Rwenzori range was named after the British Lord Stanley, its highest peak (at 16,761 feet the third highest in Africa) was named Mount Margherita after the then queen of Italy.

Running 80 miles north to south and 30 miles wide, the Rwenzori Mountains are an unusual formation of non-volcanic Precambrian rocks. They were formed from a block that was thrust up during the creation of the western arm of the Great East African Rift Valley. The area of the Rwenzori Mountains National Park, created in 1991, covers almost 386 square miles in western Uganda on its borders with the Congo. The park encloses 25 mountains over 14,750 feet high, roughly 30 glaciers and permanent snow cover.

As it lies between altitudes of 5,500 and 16,761 feet, the park has several vegetative zones. In addition, its geographic position has fostered the

development of an Afro-alpine flora with many endemic examples: of the 278 species of forest tree catalogued, 81% are endemic to East Africa. Bamboo forests dominate at heights over 10,000 feet, but these are replaced at higher levels by vegetation featuring giant heathers, such as *Erika kingaensis* and *Philippia trimera*, which can reach 30 feet in height, and certain species of lobelia, like *Lobelia rhynchopetalum* that weigh up to 130 pounds.

In terms of fauna, the inventory of the species in the Rwenzori is far from complete. We know, however, that there are at least 89 species of forest birds, four diurnal primates and 15 butterflies. Some of them are actually subspecies restricted to the region of Lake Albert, for example, the Rwenzori colobus monkey, the hyrax (a small primitive plantigrade) and the leopard. A recent study identified 60 species of invertebrates of which 25 were completely new discoveries, which is a clear illustration of the biodiversity of the region.

Rwenzori forests are of crucial importance as they feed Lakes Albert and Edward, and the water that these lakes collect is used by at least half a million Ugandan farmers in the region. This is another reason why UNESCO, with the World Conservation Union and the Rwenzori Mountains Service, is committed to protecting the park. Since 1997, the Rwenzori area has been the theater of clashes between the army and rebel groups. In addition to reducing tourist income used to develop the territory, continued tension may seriously endanger the mountain habitats.

76 top left Mounts Margherita (16,762 feet) and Alexandra (16,713 feet) are the highest peaks in the Rwenzori range.

76 bottom left Bujuku Valley, at roughly 13,150 feet, is dominated by Mount Baker in the background.

77

76 bottom right Below a height of 7,900 feet, the forest is typified by endemic species of tree from East Africa, such as Prunus Africana and Symphonia globulifera.

77 top The flora in the Rwenzori has many endemic species. Of particular interest are the many large species, like

the giant lobelias that can weigh 130 pounds and the giant heathers that can reach 32 feet in height.

77 bottom An expanse of Senecio johnstonii, which is an arboreal species of cineraria, grows above 9,800 feet on slopes less exposed to the wind.

KAMPALA

Bwindi Impenetrable National Park

UGANDA

Districts of Kabale, Kisoro and Rukungiri
Registration: 1994
Criteria: N (III) (IV)

KAMPALA

N oisy crowds of chimpanzees (*Pan troglodytes*) search for fruits and edible plants, the black-and-white-coated colobus monkeys (*Colobus polykomos*) leap from tree to tree screeching warnings to their companions and Hoest's monkeys (*Cercopithecus l'hoesti*) drowse in the tallest branches, occasionally descending to search among the roots for food.

There are a dozen or so species of primates that live in the forests of Bwindi Impenetrable National Park, which, as its name suggests, is one of the most inaccessible areas in East Africa, but one of these species attracts more attention than the others. Tourists arrive here in tiny groups, no more than 10 per day, in line with the strict Ugandan laws, and paying a hefty price for the privilege. They are here to see the mountain gorilla (*Gorilla gorilla beringei*), the most rare of the three subspecies belonging to the largest and most 'human' of the anthropomorphic primates, and which were made famous by the studies of Dian Fossey.

Of the 650 remaining in the world,

these creatures can be seen in the wild. Created in 1932 as a forest reserve, the area was turned into Bwindi Impenetrable National Park in 1991. It covers 116 square miles that lie between the altitudes of 3,900 and 8,550 feet. It is one of the largest forested watersheds in the region with several tributaries of Lake Albert and Lake Mutanda running through it. Its conservation is also of fundamental importance to agriculture in the surrounding rural areas.

Due to the range of altitudes over which it spreads, Bwindi is the meeting point for the valley and mountain communities of plant life and together create the most profuse biodiversity in east Africa. It numbers over 200 species of forest tree and more than 100 ferns, but Bwindi is also famous for the extraordinary richness of the undergrowth in which the density of climbing plants, herbaceous plants and shrubs on the valley floors makes them impenetrable. In addition to plants requiring protection, such as *Prunus africana*, *Newtonia buchananii* and *Symphonia globulifera*, at least 10 endemic species have been recorded.

The park is home to 340 species of birds, 120 mammals and more than 200 butterflies. At risk are the elephants, which are now down to 30 or so in number. The buffalo suffered a worse fate, hunted to extinction in the 1960s, and the leopard too has recently disappeared. Another factor is that Bwindi lies in one of Uganda's most densely populated rural areas and a recent investigation revealed that much of the park showed signs of human presence, including hunting, tree cutting, animal breeding and even gold hunting in the river beds.

78-79 The community of 300 or so mountain gorillas (Gorilla gorilla beringei) in Bwindi Impenetrable National Park is the largest in existence. The world population has now dwindled to circa 650.

78 bottom left The suffocating undergrowth of Bwindi Impenetrable Forest has over 100 species of ferns. The vegetation is so thick that it is almost impossible to fight one's way through to the valley bottoms that lie between the mountain ridges.

78 bottom right With over 200 species of forest trees girdled by lichens, lianas and climbing plants, Bwindi Impenetrable Forest has perhaps the richest biodiversity in East Africa.

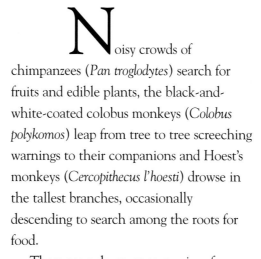

79 top Mountain gorillas are the mot rare of the three subspecies of gorilla. Those in Bwindi live in about 10 families which, despite the serious commitment of the Ugandan government, see their fragile habitat progressively reduced.

79 bottom The dominant male mountain gorillas can be recognized by their 'silver backs', the name by which they are sometimes known.

roughly 300 live in this forest on the western edge of the Rift Valley, on the border with Zaire. The large silverback males grow nearly 6 feet tall and can weigh 350 pounds; they lead 30 or so families and see their ecosystem progressively diminished despite the efforts of the Ugandan government to protect what represents a significant entry in the state coffers, for tourists to the game park spend close on 1 million dollars a year.

Given the political chaos in western Zaire and Rwanda, where the other communities of mountain gorilla live, Bwindi is currently the only place where

Lake Turkana National Parks

KENYA

Marsabit District, Eastern Province

Registration: 1997, 2001

Criteria: N (i) (iv)

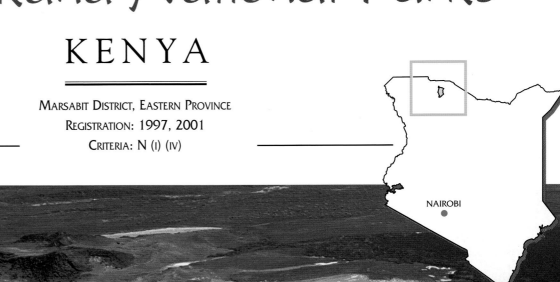

NAIROBI

When Richard Leakey first flew over the east shore of Lake Turkana in 1967, he noticed a tangle of blackened sandstone that looked like the waste from a coal mine and began to wonder about the past of the place. Months later, when he had been appointed director of the Kenya National Museum, the young scholar (the son of the world's most famous pair of 'hominid hunters') began exploring Koobi Fora, where he discovered the richest fossil beds on the African continent. They are especially valuable for the period from 3 to 1 million years ago.

First, he found a fragment of a skull 2 million years old, which was classified as *Homo habilis*, but over the course of a decade, Leakey uncovered more than 160 remains of hominid fossils and their stone tools. In addition there are more than 4,000 parts of mammals and fish, including giant tortoises (*Petusios broadleyi*), crocodiles up to 50 feet in length (*Euthecodon brumpti*), prehistoric elephants (*Elephas recki*), giant baboons, pigs the size of rhinoceroses and the ancestors of the modern horse, cat and antelope families.

Called Lake Rudolf by the first Europeans to reach it in 1888, Lake Turkana is not just important for the extraordinary collection of fossils found in Koobi Fora. Lying in a position with a semi-desert climate, Lake Turkana is the most saline of the great African lakes and the northernmost of those in the Great Rift Valley. The area was classified a World Heritage site in 1997 and includes Sibiloi National Park (there is a petrified forest 7 million years old on the slopes of Mount Sibiloi) and Central Island National Park, a small volcanic island. To these was added South Island National Park in 2001, creating an overall site of more than 620 square miles.

The aridity of the region restricts the growth of vegetation, with what little there is being dominated by acacias and savannah. Nonetheless, Lake Turkana is an exceptional location for studying the wildlife on its banks.

The mammals to be observed there are Burchell's and Grevy's zebras (*Equus burchelli and Equus grevyi*), Grant's gazelles (*Gazella granti*), oryx (*Oryx gazella beisa*), antelopes like the red hartebeest (*Alcelaphus buselaphus*), the sassaby (*Damaliscus korrigum*) and the lesser kudu (*Tragelaphus imberbis*) and predators like lions (*Panthera leo*) and cheetahs (*Acinonyx jubatus*).

The lake is also an important stopping-off point for migrating birds, of which 350 species have been recorded, including a population of African skimmers (*Rynchops flavirostris*), which nests on Central Island, flamingos, nightingales, yellow wagtails and sandpipers (*Calidris minuta*). Above all, it is home to the largest community in existence of Nile crocodiles (*Crocodylus niloticus*), of which 12,000 inhabit these waters.

The future of what used to be one of the largest tributaries to the White Nile,

and which today is a lake without an emissary, is under threat. Not so much from man – who has restricted his activities to a subsistence economy practiced by small groups of nomadic herders from the Turkana, Gabbra and Rendille peoples – as from global warming. And the state of the lake has been further jeopardized by the disastrous drought that has affected East Africa in recent years.

80-81 Nyabuyatom Volcano lies on the south shore of Lake Turkana. Its name means 'elephant stomach' in the Turkana language.

80 bottom left Lake Turkana is the most saline lake in Africa. It covers an area of 2,606 square miles.

80 bottom right Called the 'Jade Sea' for its greenish blue water, Lake Turkana is surrounded by spectacular desert scenery.

81 top Similar to rocks, the petrified forest trees on Mount Sibiloi date to roughly 7 million years ago and suggest the area used to be rainy and densely populated.

81 center A colony of flamingos (Phoenicopterus ruber) crowds the water in Lake Turkana. It is an important refuge for over 350 species of birds, most of which are migratory.

81 bottom Grant's gazelle (Gazella granti) is the most common of the 13 species of this genus and one of the most tolerant of drought.

Mount Kenya
National Park/Natural Forest

KENYA

EMBU, CENTRAL HIGHLANDS
REGISTRATION: 1997
CRITERIA: N (II) (III)

In search of fertile soil in the sixteenth and seventeenth centuries, the Kikuyu people reached this region from the flatlands east of Lake Turkana and just south of the equator. They found grazing land but also a gigantic mountain that they considered to be the home of the god Ngai (or Mwene Nyaga, 'the master of light') and his wife Mumbi. The mountain came to be called Kere Nyaga, 'mountain of light', and from there, having been distorted by Swahili, it became Mount Kenya after which the whole country is named.

The second highest mountain in Africa at 17,057 feet, Mount Kenya was formed by intermittent volcanic eruptions between 3.1 and 2.6 million years ago. In antiquity it is estimated that it was once 21,300 feet high but since then it has been eroded by atmospheric agents. Today the cone measures 60 miles across and at its peak, marked by deep furrows and moraines, there are 12 glaciers and 20 or so glacial lakes. During the wet season, the glaciers are covered by thick snow and the forests on the mountainsides turn Mount Kenya into the most important

hydrological reserve in eastern Africa from which the rural economy of 7 million people depends.

The protected area includes Mount Kenya National Park, instituted in 1949 and covering an area of 276 square miles, and Mount Kenya Natural Forest, which covers a further 272 square miles. The strength of the winds blowing off the Indian Ocean cause highly differentiated precipitation, which ranges from 35 inches a year in the north to 90 inches in the southeast. Combined with a variety of altitudes of between 5,250 and 17,060 feet, the result is a huge biodiversity of vegetation. In the lower, drier areas species of *podocarpaceae* and junipers (*Juniperus procera*) dominate, whereas in the wet zones it is *Cassipourea malosana* that prevails. Between 8,200 and 9,850 feet, in particular in the wet strip to the southeast, the slopes are covered by 110 square miles of bamboo forest. A further 10,000 feet up, the forest opens, making space for indigenous species of vegetation such as camphor (*Ocotea usambarensis*), wild olives (*Olea europeae*) and Hagenia abyssinica.

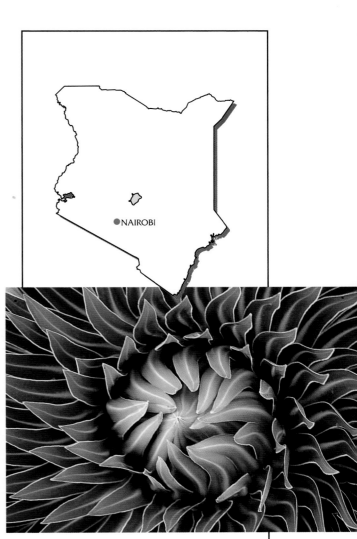

82 A small honeyeater (Nectarinia johnstoni) feeds on the nectar of a giant lobelia. In return it pollinates the plant.

83 left Present in the alpine strip of Mount Kenya between the altitudes of 12,500 and 14,750 feet, Senecio keniodendron is a composite plant with rosette leaves that can reach a height of almost 20 feet.

83 right Giant lobelias like those on the slopes of Mount Kenya (Lobelia keniensis in the picture, Lobelia telekii and the less common Lobelia aberdarica) can reach 30 feet in height. The rosette of leaves at the top of the plant is adapted to catch the largest possible quantity of rainwater and has a diameter of almost 18 inches.

84 left The local undergrowth has many species of orchid, which grow in altitudes up to 11,150 feet.

84 right The bamboo forest is mainly of the species Arundinaria alpina *and covers 310 square miles on the southwest flank of Mount Kenya.*

The fauna is prevalently diffused in the lower areas and the bamboo forests. There are many species of mammal, for example, the tree hyrax (*Dendrohyrax arboreus*), the whitetailed mongoose (*Ichneumia albicauda*), elephant, black rhino (*Diceros bicornis*) and the leopard, which climbs higher to avoid the increasing pressure on its habitat.

A recent study by Christian Lambrechts of the United Nations Environment Programme has revealed evidence of wide-ranging human activity in the protected area. The forests up to a height of 8,200 feet are severely threatened by agriculture and animal breeding, and at higher altitudes commercial logging, charcoal production and even the cultivation of marijuana have been recorded.

Following these discoveries, the government in Nairobi passed the Forest Act in 1999, in which the Kenya Wildlife Service is entrusted with the protection of the entire area of Mount Kenya; the protected area has been extended to 820 square miles, and only non-indigenous species can be cut on the lower slopes of the mountain.

84-85 The summit of Mount Kenya, Africa's second highest mountain at 17,057 feet, is nearly always covered by stratiform cloud. Surrounded by a dozen glaciers and many glacial lakes, it is a highly valuable water resource for East Africa.

85 top With two wet seasons, Mount Kenya's climate has relatively modest rainfall on the north slopes (35 inches) but much more abundant precipitation on the south flank (90 inches).

85 bottom left The species Senecio brassica *is one of the low trees that dominate the alpine and subalpine strips between 11,150 and 14,700 feet.*

85 bottom right A waterfall slips down the sides of Mount Kenya. The livelihoods of 7 million people depend on the environmental health of this ancient volcano.

Virunga National Park
DEM. REP. OF CONGO

DEMOCRATIC REPUBLIC OF THE CONGO REGIONS OF KIVU AND UPPER ZAIRE
REGISTRATION: 1979
INSCRIPTION IN THE WORLD HERITAGE IN DANGER LIST: 1994
CRITERIA: N (II) (III) (IV)

The cover of the January 1970 *National Geographic* had a photograph of a young veterinary doctor from Louisville who, for three years, with the help of the National Geographic Society and the Wilkie Foundation, had settled in Zaire and, later, the Karisoke Research Center in Rwanda to study the most fascinating of the large primates: the mountain gorilla.

After poachers had shot Digit, the silverback male to which she had come to care about, Dian Fossey launched a campaign to raise awareness of the future of a community that was being thinned down year after year.

It was in the Karisoke Research Center that her strenuous defense of the gorilla came to a sudden end when, on 27 December 1985, Dian Fossey became the victim of a raid on her camp.

Her cry for help, however, was heard by Hollywood and the autobiography she had published just two years previous – *Gorillas in the Mist* – was turned into a highly successful film.

More than 30 years after the magazine cover appeared, the future of

KINSHASA

the mountain gorillas in Virunga National Park, where Dian Fossey did her research, is still uncertain.

In memory of Dian Fossey, the foundation continues to look after the gorillas, and its work is less troubled. Since 1994, the 3,050 square mile park, which borders the Ugandan Rwenzori Mountains National Park, has been inscribed in the World Heritage in Danger list as a result of the massive influx of refugees caused by the civil war in Rwanda.

According to the UN High Committee for Refugees, there are roughly 2 million people camping mainly in the province of Kivu, thereby increasing the population in the area of Virunga out of all proportion.

The war between Rwanda and the Democratic Republic of the Congo – which came to an end when peace was signed on 30 July 2002 – resulted in the occupation of the eastern Congo by the Rwandan army with disastrous consequences for the park. It is estimated that at least 1,900 square miles were transformed into agricultural land or their trees were cut down for firewood, with an average consumption of 600 tons per day. But poaching is just as insidious a risk. The population of the hippopotamus has collapsed from 30,000 to 3,000 and of the elephant from 3,000 to less than 500. And although they live in the most remote areas of the mountains, not even the gorillas escaped the destruction. Poachers shot 12, not

86 bottom The dense rainforest on the slopes of the Rwenzori mountain range is mainly constituted of bamboo and Hagenia abyssinica.

87 top Standing over 5 feet tall and weighing as much as 350 pounds, male silverbacks are the dominant individuals in the extended families of gorillas that number up to 30 members.

87 bottom Mountain gorillas in Virunga were made famous in the 1970s by the awareness campaign carried out by Dian Fossey whose autobiography, Gorillas in the Mist, became a very successful film.

86 left Sabinyo Volcano is one of the numerous cones in the Virunga volcanic region. Two others are Nyiragongo and Nyamuragira, both of which have recently recorded violent activity.

86-87 Estimated to have a population of 280 in 1986, the mountain gorillas of Virunga have suffered from the recent crisis in the Great Lakes region and have been reduced in number by at least a dozen from poaching and killing.

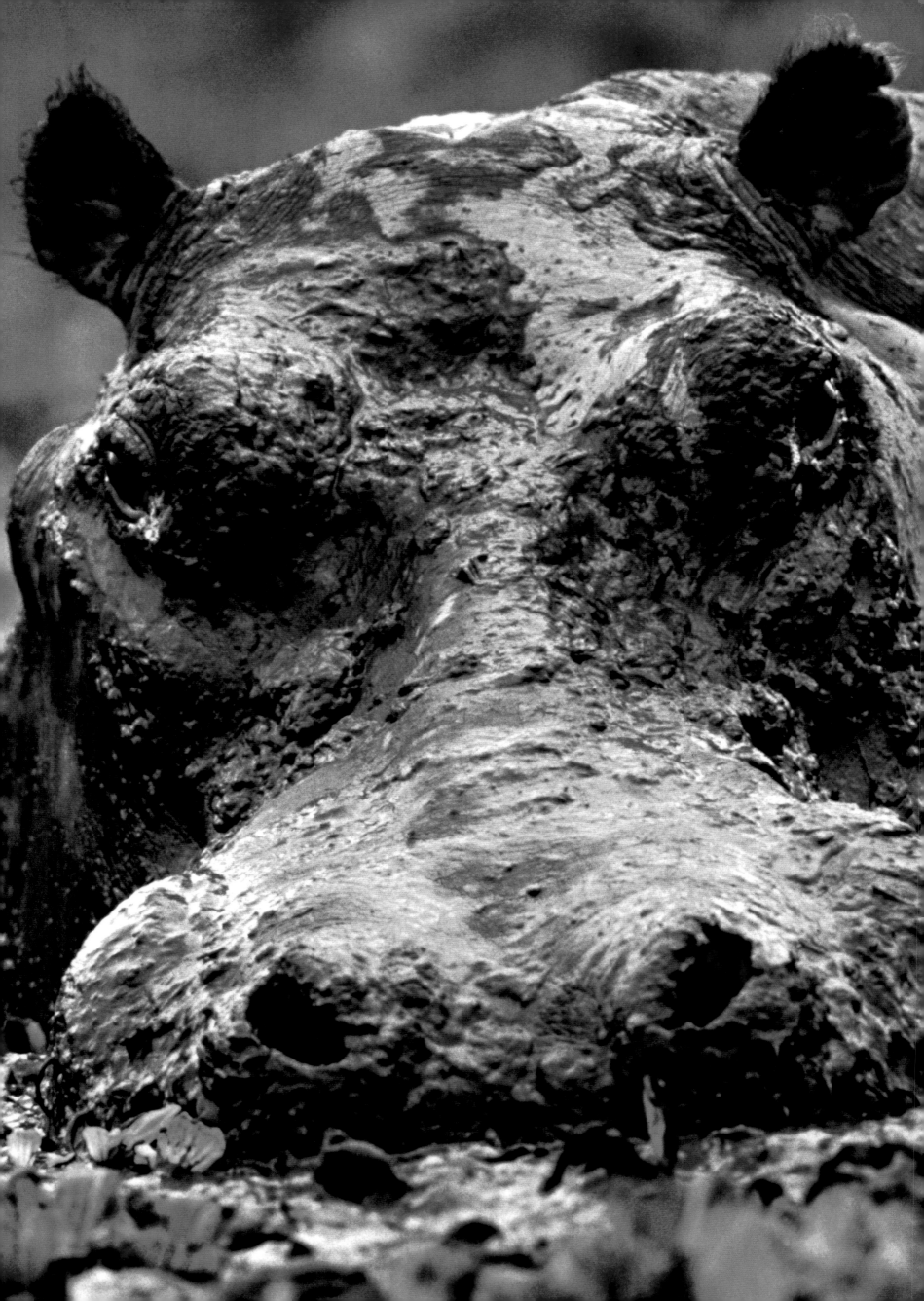

to mention several of the park's guards.

Despite these setbacks, Virunga remains one of the world's most extraordinary protected areas, above all for the diversity of its habitats.

There are spectacular environments between the lowest valleys at 2,600 feet above sea level and the 16,795 feet of the summits of the Rwenzori Mountains.

The territory covers a part of Lake Edward (part of the Nile Basin), the Semliki River Valley and Lake Kivu, from which a branch of the Congo River departs. There are inland deltas, savannahs, lavic plateaus, glaciers, snowfields and low-level equatorial forests.

Owing to its position at the boundaries of several different biogeographic zones, the park includes both tropical rainforests and steppes.

The mountain slopes are dominated by forests of bamboo and *Hagenia abyssinica*, whilst along the Semliki

Valley there are species typical of equatorial forests. Trees and grasslands predominate in the Rwindi Plains, and there are steppes featuring the genera *Carissa*, *Capparis*, *Maerua* and *Euphorbia*.

The lavic plateaus are suitable terrain for species like Neobutonia *macrocalyx*, while the marshes feature various types of reeds. At higher altitudes, the alpine forest includes giant lobelias.

Up until 10 or more years ago, there used to be one of the greatest concentrations of wild animals in Africa along the rivers of Virunga National Park. In addition to those already mentioned, the most important populations were of buffalo (*Syncerus caffer*), waterhog (*Phacochoerus aethiopicus*), lion (*Panthera leo*) and antelopes like the kob (*Kobus kob*), waterbuck (*Kobus ellipsiprymnus*) and topi (*Damaliscus lunatus*).

Unlike that of other animals, the

number of lions seems to be on the increase.

A census carried out in 1986 estimated that there were roughly 280 mountain gorillas (*Gorilla gorilla berengei*), but no one has any idea of the current situation.

The danger imposed by man is added to by various volcanoes, which were formed during the Pleistocene epoch along the Rift Valley.

The highest, at 14,786 feet, is Karisimbi, in Ruandan territory.

The most active is Nyiragongo, which, in January 2002, erupted spectacularly and devastatingly, forcing half a million people to flee and destroying various villages near Goma. The explosion was the worst volcanic eruption in the last decade.

Less damaging but still violent was the successive eruption of Nyamuragira, whose rivers of lava destroyed dozens of square miles of cultivated land and polluted many water sources in July 2002.

88 *An amphibian mammal more active at night, the hippo (*Hippopotamus amphibius*) weighs up to 3 tons. This bulk requires a diet of 90 to 130 pounds of grass a day.*

89 top *The flatter parts of Virunga are threaded by many watercourses that make the region one of the most important hydrological basins in central Africa.*

89 center left *The lion (*Panthera leo*) is one of the few species in Virunga National Park that does not seem to have been affected by the many years of war. Its population appears to be on the increase.*

89 center right *A jackal (*Canis aureus*) has just caught a Thomson's gazelle (*Gazella thomsonii*) in the grasslands of Rwanda.*

89 bottom *The largest community of hippos in all Africa lives in the rivers of Virunga National Park. With the war in Rwanda, their number dropped from 30,000 to just 3,000 in ten years.*

Serengeti National Park
TANZANIA

REGIONS OF MARA, ARUSHA AND SHINYANGA
REGISTRATION: 1981
CRITERIA: N (III) (IV)

90 top The largest terrestrial mammal, the African elephant, is also one with the most complex social behavior. The females live in small groups with their young, while the males are mainly solitary.

90 bottom The giraffe is taller than the elephant. The males can measure 18 feet in height and the females 15 feet. With the loss of their habitat and only giving birth to a single calf, the number of these magnificent animals is being reduced.

An African legend tells that the last animal that God created was the gnu, which he fashioned by putting together those few animal parts he had left over.

It is true that the gnu (*Connochaetes taurinus*) is not a gracious animal – with its overlarge head and the front part of its body that is higher and larger than its rear – especially when compared to the elegant antelopes that populate the savannah, yet this animal is the most important link in the chain that forms the Serengeti's ecosystem.

The seasonal migration of almost 2 million gnus–to which can be added those of 300,000 zebras and other antelopes – is a phenomenon that fascinates both naturalists and non-scientists. During the rainy season (between December and June), gnus gather in Ngorongoro crater where they reproduce.

Then, when the grass begins to dry out, they cross the large Serengeti Plain northwards where permanent watercourses provide them with the nourishment necessary to their survival. At the end of November comes the time to make the return journey.

The migration lasts four or five days during which time they cover a distance of roughly 120 miles.

This is an exhausting effort that many youngsters and old gnu do not complete, being pulled down by either the many feline predators on the march or by the crocodiles that wait for them in the rivers.

Despite the contrary opinion of the park rangers, at the start of the 1960s, the Tanzanian government decided to build a wood and metal fence to prevent the gnus from entering Ngorongoro National Park, but it only took a few hours before the fence was trampled to the ground. Man has neither the power nor the right to alter the behavior that animals have had as part of their genetic inheritance for thousands of years.

The biological and geographic region that contains the Serengeti and Ngorongoro National Parks in Tanzania and the Maasai-Mara National Park in Kenya is considered one of the oldest

90-91 The migration of the gnu takes place around the end of November when almost 2 million of them are joined by roughly 300,000 zebras and antelopes. The gnu can cover a distance of 130 miles in just 4-5 days.

healthy ecosystems in the world, given that the composition of its wildlife has remained more or less unchanged since the Pleistocene epoch (1 million years ago). Moreover, that was the period from which the first human finds date, which were found in Onduvai Gorge in the north section of Serengeti National Park, just below Ngorongoro Crater.

Covering slightly less than 5,800 square miles and declared a national park in 1951, the Serengeti (its Maasai name means 'the place of the land that runs forever') is a crystalline rock plateau covered with volcanic terrain. On this, at an average altitude of 3,020 feet, stand granite hills known as *kopjes* to the north and east, the highest of which reaches 5,900 feet.

There are two watercourses that only dry up completely during years of drought, but the plateau as a whole is marked by a number of pools and water meadows.

Besides the gnu, the habitat is also home to Burchell's zebra, eland, impala, Thompson's gazelle and many other species of antelope.

91 bottom left A male lion finishes its prey. This scene is not very common: usually it is the lionesses that hunt and by night.

91 bottom right The Serengeti Plain is formed of crystalline rocks covered over the millennia by layers of volcanic ashes.

DAR-ES-SALAAM

These are all possible prey to the leopards, cheetahs or the 3,000 lions in the region, and, when these have finished their meal, spotted hyenas and jackals scavenge the remains.

There are approximately 1,500 elephants as well as black rhinos, buffaloes, hippos, giraffes and crocodiles. Of the smaller animals, there are seven species each of mongoose and primates and two each of otters and warthogs.

The African wild dog was present here until a dozen years ago but was wiped out by rabies. There are 350 species of birds, including the world's largest, the ostrich.

With such a vast and varied population, the Serengeti is one of the most popular destinations for wildlife safaris. In a single day, the tourist might easily see all of the big five: elephant, rhino, buffalo, lion and leopard. Contrary to what has been thought, these animals did not earn themselves this nickname for their size, but because they were the most sought after trophies when big game hunting was permitted owing to the danger they posed to man.

During the rainy season, the Serengeti is like a grass meadow.

In the central and western sections, there are many species of acacias, wild date palms and what are commonly known as 'sausage trees' (*Kigelia africana*) named for the shape of their fruit. The extract of this fruit is used in the cosmetics industry.

During the dry season, the scenery changes drastically and resembles a desert.

Though not suitable for agriculture, pressure exerted by man's activities on the edges of the protected area is always strong. The Maasai communities are habitual poachers and it is calculated that on average 4,000 antelope are shot each year for food.

93 bottom The world's fastest animal is the cheetah (Acinonyx jubatus). It is an endangered species but attempts are being made to increase its numbers with animals born in captivity.

94-95 The number of gnu (Connochaetes taurinus) in the Serengeti has increased over the last 50 years from about 190,000 to almost 2 million.

The huge campaign undertaken by the government recently to make the local inhabitants more aware of the situation has brought scarce results. Although tourism is Tanzania's second largest earner, only the crumbs remain to the Maasai, who were made even poorer by the drought of 2000.

Kilimanjaro National Park
TANZANIA

REGION OF MOSHI
REGISTRATION: 1987
CRITERIA: N (III)

It must certainly have been a surprise to Johannes Rebmann when, in 1848, he reached the foot of a gigantic mountain covered with snow that stood just 186 miles south of the equator in the African highlands. The Chagga, the people who lived on its slopes, called it Kilimanjaro and worshipped it as a sacred mountain, but the geologist Hans Meyer, the first to climb it, in October 1889, renamed it Kaiser Wilhelm Spitze in honor of the German emperor.

Many years later, the independent Tanzanian government imposed the name Uhuru Peak after the Swahili word meaning 'freedom', but nonetheless, to everyone else, the solitary mountain has returned to being Kilimanjaro though the origins of this name remain uncertain. Rebmann believed it meant 'mountain of greatness' but others interpret it as 'shining mountain', 'white mountain' or 'mountain of water'.

Whatever it may be, Kilimanjaro remains as fascinating today as it was when seen by the first European visitors. Often its summit is covered by thick cloud that prevents the sight of its permanent snowcap. Kilimanjaro is 19,317 feet high, of volcanic origin and has three craters: Shira (12,999 feet), Mawenzi (16,893 feet) and Kibo, the highest. In all it is spread over an area measuring 1,500 square miles, making it one of the largest volcanoes in the world, and, though its last eruptions were 1 million years ago, it still shows traces of activity in a fumarole at the center of Kibo crater.

96 top Kilimanjaro is Africa's highest mountain. Although its last eruptions date to the Pleistocene, the center of the main crater still shows signs of modest activity.

96-97 Kilimanjaro covers an area of 1,500 square miles and has three craters: Shira, 12,999 feet, Mawenzi, 16,893 feet and Kibo, the highest at 19,317 feet.

Declared a nature reserve by the colonial German government in 1921, the current Kilimanjaro National Park covers an area of 291 square miles and is surrounded by a further forestry reserve of 358 square miles. Between the 6,000-foot high Marangu Gate, where the protected area begins, and the summit, there are four different botanical ecosystems that might be termed mountain forest, high-altitude heath, alpine marshes and alpine desert.

From 15,100 feet upwards only moss and lichen grow, whereas down at the level of the high-altitude heath the vegetation is mainly heather and shrubs. Apart from the two species of genus Senecio and an endemic giant lobelia (*Lobelia deckenii*), which are common at this height, the most interesting species grow in the forest band that lies between 6,000 and 8,900 feet, for example, camphor (*Ocotea usambarensis*) and various species of *Podocarpus*. Plants that are absent are bamboo and hagenia, which are common in other regions of central Africa.

Kilimanjaro provides shelter to many mammals, including eland, bushbuck, two types of duiker, buffalo (*Syncerus caffer*), leopards, an estimated population of 220 elephants and various primates (cercopithecids, galagos and colobus monkeys). There are no black rhinos, however.

Although the protection inside the park is absolute and the government has blocked all concessions for tree cutting, the resources available to the park personnel are insufficient.

A recent aerial reconnaissance of the entire area, promoted by the United Nations Environment Programme and local authorities, has shown that intense anthropic activities are continuing, for example, the cutting down of valuable species like camphor and cedar, agriculture, animal breeding and wood burning to make charcoal.

There are no longer any stretches of untouched mountain below the height of 8,200 feet.

97 top Kibo Crater is surrounded by perennial snow and glaciers at up to 14,760 feet but near Mawenzi, the snows are semi-permanent. Remains of past glaciations can be seen on all three peaks, with morainic detritus visible at up to 11,800 feet.

97 bottom A herd of elephants heads towards a waterhole at the foot of Kilimanjaro. Covering 291 square miles, Kilimanjaro National Park has five different botanical ecozones that support a rich and diverse fauna.

DAR-ES-SALAAM

Ngorongoro Conservation Area

TANZANIA

REGION OF ARUSHA
REGISTRATION: 1979
CRITERIA: N (II) (III) (IV)

Ngorongoro is almost a perfect circle just under 12 miles in diameter and, as such, is one of the largest craters in the world, though it has not turned into a lake over the millennia. Its rim now has walls that vary in height between 1,300 and 2,000 feet but it has not always been like that. When it formed at the end of the Mesozoic and start of the Cenozoic eras, Ngorongoro was a powerful volcano larger, according to scientists, than its neighbors (Loolmalasin, 11,768 feet; Oldeani, 10,394 feet; and even Kilimanjaro, Africa's highest mountain at 19,317 feet), however, it erupted with such force that it fell in on itself.

With the passage of time, its concave shape meant that it became a safe haven, unmatched in Africa, for wildlife, a sort of 'circus' that contains an extraordinary spectacle of nature at its wildest.

Considered a protected area since 1959, the crater is the culmination of the enormous ecosystem represented by the Serengeti Plain.

Besides being the point of arrival of large migrations of gnu, Burchell's zebra and many species of gazelle, it is also home to elephants, hippopotami, giraffes and buffaloes, a large number of baboons and birds (including 30 or so birds of prey) and all the large predators. In addition, it is one of the last refuges of the black rhinoceros.

The animal, however, that deserves a separate mention is the cheetah (Acinoryx jubatus), which here, unlike the rest of the continent where it is diminishing in numbers, still flourishes.

The cheetah has been identified as the forefather of all the large cats and is the fastest animal in the world, being able to accelerate to 68 mph in just 3 seconds, but scientists so fear for its survival that they are considering an extreme measure: cloning.

The reason for the abundant wildlife in the crater lies in the variety of vegetal habitats it contains, which provide excellent sources of food and shelter. The bottom of the crater has many pools of water that, during the rainy season, are turned into lakes, and the presence of water has produced a thick carpet of grass.

As one moves towards the edges of the crater, there are two springs that nourish the forests of Lerai (mostly *Acacia xanthopholea* and *Rauwfolia*

98-99 Ngorongoro Crater is almost a perfect circle enclosing 102 square miles of land and has walls varying in height between 1,300 and 2,000 feet.

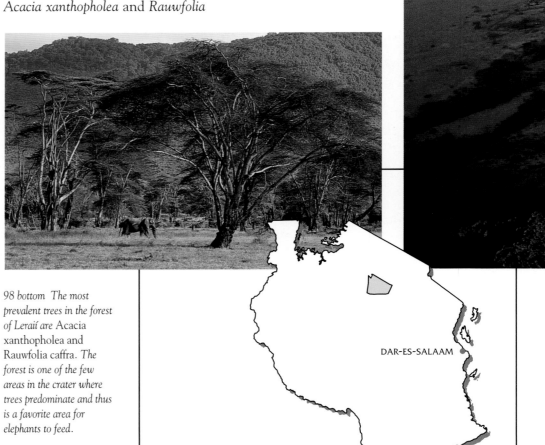

98 bottom The most prevalent trees in the forest of Lerai are Acacia xanthopholea and Rauwfolia caffra. The forest is one of the few areas in the crater where trees predominate and thus is a favorite area for elephants to feed.

DAR-ES-SALAAM

99 *top and bottom* During long droughts, the crater is turned into a desert but during normal conditions of rainfall it is covered by nutritious herbaceous plants that support the large populations of gnu, zebra and antelope.

caffra) and Laiyani (*Acacia lahai,
Albizzia gummifera* and *Cassipourea
malosana*).

The crater's highly fertile soil
provides excellent support to the flora.
The volcano Ol Doniyo Lengai lies at
the edge of Ngorongoro and, as it is still
active, periodically covers the crater
with ashes that are rich with nutritious
substances.

The crater has been important to
man too. Around the edge, fossils have
been found of *Homo erectus,
Australopitecus boisei* and *Homo habilis*,
which have contributed to the theory
that Africa was where our species
originated. And, more recently, for the
Maasai people, who have been the
dominant ethnic group in this region for
centuries, Ngorongoro has been crucial
to their subsistence based on livestock
grazing and, to a lesser extent,
agriculture. For this reason, notable

*100-101 Close-up of a
buffalo (Syncerus caffer)
covered with mud from a
pool. Recent estimates
suggest that there are about
4,000 buffaloe in
Ngorongoro.*

*100 bottom left Gazelles
do not need to drink much
as they absorb the liquid in
grass, leaves and succulent
fruit.*

*100 bottom right A group
of hippos passes a river
bank packed with egrets
(Ardeola ibis).*

*101 top The crater is the
destination of the gnus'
migration. Both males and
females have horns but the
male is taller (on average
4.5 feet at the withers) and
weighs 550 pounds against
the female's 350.*

*101 center Ostriches are
the largest birds on the
planet. Though they cannot
fly, they run extremely fast.
If threatened by predators
they can maintain a speed
of 31 mph for 30 minutes,
a demonstration of
endurance that is very rare
in the animal world.*

*101 bottom Thousands of
flamingos (Phoeiconaias
minor) crowd a pool. Few
species of large birds are as
gregarious as these.
Flamingos gather in large
numbers in pools and lakes
that are too saline or
alkaline for fish, with which
they would otherwise have
to compete for food.*

efforts have been made by the
government of Tanzania and
international organizations to create
an experimental project for multiple use
of the territory that will allow the needs
of the Maasai to be met as well as those
of the wildlife, and that will also
conserve the environment.

102 top The black rhino (Diceros bicornis) is increasingly rare. The population in the crater has declined over the last 40 years from several hundred to just 15 or so.

102 center left During daytime, lions generally laze in the shade. They hunt at night, usually led by the lionesses.

102 center right The behavior of the spotted hyena (Crocuta crocuta) is unusual. The female is dominant: she weighs at least 22 pounds more than the male and is much more aggressive.

102 bottom Thompson's gazelle is the most common antelope in central-eastern Africa. There are about 3,000 in Ngorongoro.

103 A lioness has between one and five cubs at a time and is very protective towards them. However, females in a group live in a sort of gynaecium and wean each others' cubs.

Selous Game Reserve

TANZANIA

Regions of Mogororo, Lindi,
Mtwara and Ruvuma
Registration: 1982
Criteria: N (ii) (iv)

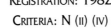

DAR-ES-SALAAM

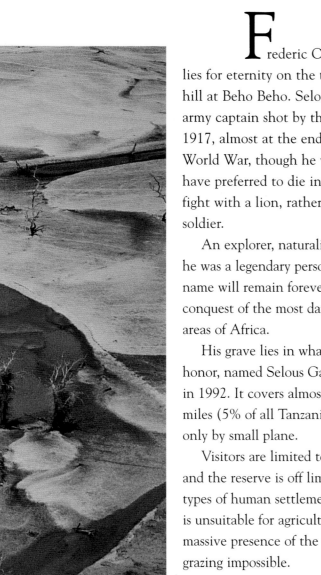

Frederic Courtney Selous lies for eternity on the top of a rocky hill at Beho Beho. Selous was a British army captain shot by the Germans in 1917, almost at the end of the First World War, though he would probably have preferred to die in a hand-to-hand fight with a lion, rather than as a soldier.

An explorer, naturalist and hunter, he was a legendary personality whose name will remain forever linked to the conquest of the most dangerous and wild areas of Africa.

His grave lies in what was, in his honor, named Selous Game Reserve in 1992. It covers almost 20,000 square miles (5% of all Tanzania) and is reached only by small plane.

Visitors are limited to 3,000 per year and the reserve is off limits also to all types of human settlement as the soil is unsuitable for agriculture and the massive presence of the tsetse fly makes grazing impossible.

In recompense, the park accommodates 800,000 large mammals. This is the largest community in the world and includes the highest concentration of elephants (50,000), buffaloes (110,000), African hunting dogs (1,300), lions (3,000-4,000) and huge herds of hippos and crocodiles.

In addition there are 100 or so black rhinos, predators like the leopard and cheetah, large communities of baboons, antelopes of several species, Burchell's zebras and giraffes. The latter are concentrated in the area to the north of the Rufiji, the largest river in Selous. Birds are represented by 440 species,

several of which require conservation measures, such as the *Bucorvus leadbeateri* from the hornbill family, and the bateleur (*Terathopius ecaudatus*), a sort of eagle.

In addition to the Rufiji River, this immense area is irrigated by its tributaries, the Luwegu, Kilombero, Great Ruaha, Luhombero and Mbarangardu, plus other watercourses formed during the rainy season between December and March. During the dry season, these run dry but leave pools known as *mbugas* in Swahili. The vast plain is only broken by the Beho Beho Hills and Steiger Gorge, which is a

104-105 The alluvial plain of Selous is practically inaccessible and thus the uncontested kingdom of wildlife. Agriculture is made impossible by the infertility of the soil and grazing by the widespread presence of the tsetse fly.

104 bottom left Resting on a muddy bank, a crocodile (Crocodylus niloticus) opens its mouth to regulate its body temperature. As an adult, Africa's largest reptile can reach 20 feet in length and weigh a ton.

104 bottom right The enormous mouth of a hippopotamus emerges from the calm surface of a river. Seemingly harmless in appearance, it is in fact an extremely aggressive animal that heads the list of African mankillers.

105 top A group of hippos (Hippopotamus amphibius) idles in the Rufiji River. Selous Game Reserve has the largest community of this species in the world.

105 bottom This young male elephant is from the reserve. Elephants, too, have their largest single community in the world (about 50,000) in this protected area.

granitic formation through which the Rufiji Riverruns.

It was named after a German hunter who, in 1907, was killed here by an elephant.

The flora is also of exceptional interest, with the 2,000 or so estimated species being mostly suited to the deciduous savannah and second only to the rainforest in biodiversity.

Called *miombo* in Bantu languages, this vegetative zone covers 75% of Selous Game Reserve and is dominated by acacias – mostly *Acacia zanzibarica* and *Acacia nigrescens* – and by other trees of genera *Brachystegia*, *Jubernadia* and *Pterocarpus*. Also to be found are baobabs (*Adansonia digitata*) up to 1,000 years old, which represent an important water resource to the fauna during the dry season as the trunk and branches of a large baobab can contain as close to 160 tons of water. Near the rivers there is an incredible variety of plants; the most interesting are palms like *Borassus aethiopium*, which reaches heights of 82 feet, and *Phoenix reclinata*. Both produce fruits similar to dates that are enjoyed by elephants and baboons.

The flora of the *miombo* has not yet been widely studied owing to the lack of roads, the size of the area and the shortage of funding; the same aspects that make the work of the anti-poaching teams difficult.

107 top The vegetation along the rivers is very thick and varied, including more than 2,000 species of plants, most of which is typical of a deciduous savannah and second in biodiversity only to a rainforest.

107 center A male leopard (Pantherus pardus) rests on an acacia after eating. The leopard's vastly varied diet (90 species from large insects to small elephants) is the basis for the excellent state of the species.

107 bottom Two Burchell's zebras fight for a female. Usually zebras live in communities of one male and a dozen or so females, which the male strenuously defends.

Mosi-oa-Tunya/ Victoria Falls

ZAMBIA/ZIMBABWE

LIVINGSTONE (ZAMBIA),
VICTORIA FALLS (ZIMBABWE)
REGISTRATION: 1989
CRITERIA: N (II) (III)

In early November 1855 a group of Kololo indigenes led Dr. Livingstone to the place they called Mosi-oa-Tunya, 'the smoke that thunders'. After a short trip along the Zambezi River, the British explorer saw for the first time what 'at a distance of 6 miles or so seemed the smoke that rises, in Africa, when vast tracts of savannah are burned'. Instead, he was looking at the vaporized water produced by the river as it leaps from Makgadikgadi Pan into the basalt gorges below.

Livingstone dedicated this spectacle of nature to Queen Victoria but he only made the discovery known in Europe when he returned to London four years later. On 3 August 1860 William Baldwin was the second traveler to reach Victoria Falls, which, from that time, became one of Africa's most popular tourist destinations. Visitors arrived on foot, horseback or ox-drawn carts following the route that ran from the Transvaal into the 'hunters' way' along the modern Botswana-Zimbabwe border. Later, it all became much easier thanks to Cecil Rhodes who, in 1900, organized a railway line to the falls, despite never having visited the place himself, and also the construction of a bridge near enough to the bottom of the waterfall for the carts to be reached by the spray.

The Victoria Falls Reserve was created by the colonial government in 1934 but was substituted in 1972 by two national parks (Mosi-oa-Tunya and Victoria Falls), which cover 34 square miles and protect the falls on both the Zambian and Zimbabwean sides of the river.

Formed roughly 2 million years ago

following the rise of the left bank of the river, Victoria Falls is the widest fluvial waterfall in the world: it stretches more than 5,500 feet across and has a maximum drop of 355 feet. During the flood season of the Zambezi (February and March) the river has a flow rate of over 140 million gallons per minute and the sound of the impact can be heard 13 miles away. Placid until that point, at the bottom of the falls the river becomes turbulent and runs violently between the basalt walls of seven successive gorges that correspond to the positions of the falls in remote epochs.

Although the area has no particular wildlife attractions of its own, its contiguity to the Zambezi National Park means that it is frequented by elephants, giraffes, zebras, warthogs and lions, whilst in the calm bends of the river colonies of hippos and crocodiles idle. In contrast, the fluvial fauna is noteworthy as the falls form an evolutional barrier between different sets of species. Equally interesting is the narrow strip of rainforest that grows on the Zimbabwean bank where the land is bathed by the water vapor. The forest is home to many species typical of latitudes closer to the equator

108 top Below the Victoria Falls, the Zambesi River threads its way through a series of basalt gorges creating violent rapids. These clefts mark the position of the falls in ancient times.

108 bottom Indifferent to the majesty of the falls, a Thomson's gazelle (Gazella thomsonii) stands on the Zimbabwean bank of the Zambesi River.

such as ebony (*Diospyros mespiliformis*), date palms (*Phoenix reclinata*) and various species of *Ficus*.

A century and a half after its discovery, Victoria Falls continues to exert an irresistible fascination on its thousands of visitors. And the ancient legend of Yami-Yami, the god of the waterfalls that a chosen few are lucky enough to espy in the churning waters, has developed into a business: the symbol of the pagan god is carved on fragments of basalt and sold as a souvenir, aiding the local economy that has become the most prosperous in all Zimbabwe.

108-109 Marking the border between Zimbabwe and Zambia, the Victoria Falls form the longest curtain of water in the world in February and March (during the flood season of the Zambesi River) with a flow of 140 million gallons per minute.

109 right Mosi-oa-Tunya ('the smoke that roars') is the Kololo name for the Victoria Falls. The nebulized water is similar to a curtain of smoke and the crash can be heard 13 miles away.

109 bottom The extraordinary morphology of the territory that has created the Victoria Falls has encouraged the differentiation of fluvial fauna to which the enormous drop represents an uncrossable evolutional boundary.

ZAMBIA

LUSAKA

HARARE

ZIMBABWE

Mana Pools National Park, Sapi and Chewore Reserves

ZIMBABWE

NORTHEAST OF LAKE KARIBA,
SOUTH BANK OF THE ZAMBEZI RIVER
REGISTRATION: 1984
CRITERIA: N (II) (III) (IV)

About 60 hippopotami laze together in a pool of water. They remain submerged all day long where they are protected from the sun, as their hide – despite its tough appearance – is delicate and easily burned. The group of Nile crocodiles (*Crocodylus niloticus*) seems equally relaxed as they idle almost immobile on a bend of the Zambezi River. A little further downstream, indifferent to the presence of the fearsome predators that can reach 23 feet in length, an enormous herd of antelope grazes.

This is just one of the innumerable sights to be seen in Mana Pools National Park – instituted in 1963 – and the adjacent Sapi and Chewore Reserves, which together cover a total of 2,600 square miles. During the dry season from May to October, this large alluvial plain and the pools, islands, ravines and the Zambezi River that marks the southern boundary of the area together provide sanctuary to one of the highest concentrations of wildlife in southern Africa.

In addition to the thousands of hippos and crocodiles, there are black rhinos, elephants, lions, leopards, cheetahs, spotted hyenas, warthogs, African hunting dogs and ratels (*Mellivora capensis*), which are a sort of badger that eat honey-producing hymenoptera. There are also large herds of zebra (*Equus burcelli*) and various species of antelope, for example, kudu (*Tragelaphus oryx*), shy common waterbuck (*Kobus ellipsiprymnus*), huge eland (*Taurotragus oryx*) and elegant nyala (*Tragelaphus angasi*). Then there are numerous

amphibians and fish and more than 380 species of birds of which 40 or so are birds of prey.

Such a rich and varied animal community owes its subsistence to dense

and highly nutritious vegetation. The hills in Chewore Reserve are predominantly covered with tall grasses,

while the alluvial plain is home to deciduous thorn bushes, called *jesse* locally, and mopane woodland (*Colophospermum mopane*). This leathery barked tree has butterfly-shaped leaves that, in the hottest hours of the day, fold up to limit their transpiration.

The fronds of the mopane are rich with protein and phosphorus and retain their nutritious qualities even when dry, which is why they are so important to the herbivores. The worms that live on the mopane – a sort of millipede that infests the branches during the rainy season – are a favorite food of the local birds. Equally important in Mana's food chain is a species of acacia (*Trichilia emetica*), whose leaves provide sustenance

110 top Communities of hippopotami can number 60 individuals. They spend their days in the water to protect their delicate skin from strong sunshine.

110-111 The vegetation in the alluvial plains of Mana is characterized by deciduous thorn bushes (jesse) and Trichilia emetica acacias. The leaves of the acacia are nutritious and enjoyed by antelopes and elephants.

110 bottom Female elephants and their young rest by a pool in Mana after their customary mudbath.

111 top left Similar in size to the impala, the puku (Aepyceros melamphus petersi) is an antelope that always lives near water and comes out at twilight. Antelopes are some of the most numerous animals in Mana Pools National Park.

111 top right The lower Zambesi River slowly winds along the border between Zimbabwe and Zambia before flowing into the enormous Lake Kariba. The rich flora on its banks supports a large variety of animals all year round.

HARARE

to antelopes and elephants.

In the local language, *Mana* means 'four'. This is the number of large pools that lie just to the south of the Zambezi in the northern section of the park. Centuries ago the river ran through that area and the pools are what have been left. Today the work of nature is threatened by the hand of man. In 1958 the government of what was then Rhodesia decided to build the Kariba Dam to produce electricity. However, this has reduced the flow of the river and consequently the flooded area during the rainy season has shrunk. The effect of this has impoverished the quality of the soil and reduced the vegetation that is so important to the ecosystem.

111 bottom Though numerous in southern Africa, leopards are solitary, shy animals, difficult to sight. A large population in Mana lives near the Ruckomechi River, the tributary of the Zambezi that marks the eastern boundary of the park.

SWAZILAND

PRETORIA

LESOTHO

112 top left With about 300 species of birds, the ecoregion of the Drakensberg is the last refuge of the lammergeier (Gypaetus barbatus) in southern Africa. About 85% of this bird's diet is formed by the bones of dead animals.

112 top right The Drakensberg massif is one of the richest hydrological basins in South Africa, mostly as a result of the abundant rainfall it receives, especially in the summer months from November to March.

Ukhahlamba/Drakensberg Park

SOUTH AFRICA

KwaZulu-Natal
REGISTRATION: 2000
CRITERIA: N (III) (IV); C (I) (III)

Around 8,000 years ago, when Europe and the Middle East were living through the early phases of the Neolithic period, southern Africa was still inhabited by groups of semi-nomadic hunter-gatherers who lived in caves or beneath rock spurs in the bare valleys of the Drakensberg Mountains. One of these peoples, the San, began to decorate the walls and roofs of their caves with paintings of idols, hunting scenes and life in an inhospitable environment where the struggle for survival was daily. Although the vestiges of human settlements suggest that the region has been inhabited for a million years, the rock 'chronicles' of the San are the most concrete evidence of the Paleolithic period in South Africa, and they cover a span of time that reaches right up to the nineteenth century. This was when the country's European colonists, coming up from the Cape, and African peoples like the Zulu and Zhosa, pushed the San out of the mountains towards the stony edges of the Kalahari.

The beauty of the Drakensberg Mountains and their wildness inspired the colonial government of Natal to set up a faunal park in 1903, which developed into the Natal National Park in 1916. In 1947 its boundaries were expanded and the park was renamed the Royal Natal National Park. And, in 1998, officially reverting to African idioms, the government of South Africa again renamed the park, this time the uKhahlamba-Drakensberg Park. Lying between altitudes of 4,200 and 11,480 feet, the 937 square miles of the Drakensberg park are characterized by an extraordinary variety of topography, including plateaus, mountain peaks, rock faces of basalt and sandstone, deep wide valleys and harsh rock formations. A rich hydrological basin favored by a subtropical climate, the park has a lush vegetation that differs strongly between the valleys, mountainsides and plateaus. Overall, there are 2,153 vegetal species, almost 2,000 of which belong to the angiosperm family. More than 200 are endemic to the park and region and 109 of these are considered to be in danger.

The fauna has 48 species of mammals, almost 300 birds, 48 reptiles, 26 amphibians and eight fish, but the invertebrates too – of which no precise census has been taken – contribute fundamentally to the ecological balance. They include 74 species of butterfly (equal to 7% of all those in South Africa), 32 millipedes and 44 dragonflies. The amphibians include three species of especially interesting frogs (*Rana vertebralis*, *R. dracomontana* and *Strongylopus hymenopus*) as they only live at high altitudes and in low temperatures, while the birds include many endemics. The mammals number 16 species of rodents, the largest population of otter in South Africa, 15 carnivores and 11 artiodactyls, of which there are 1,500 antelope (*Pelea capriolus*) and 2,000 eland (*Taurotragus oryx*), the world's largest antelope. The park is not home to mammals threatened by extinction and, surprisingly, has none of Africa's large predators. These can now only be seen in the hunting scenes painted by the San.

112-113 The natural amphitheater in the Drakensberg is a hemicircle of volcanic rock over 3 miles in diameter. The 937 square miles of the park enclose an extraordinary topographical variety.

113 bottom An expanse of red-hot poker plants (Kniphofia uvaria) covers the valley bottom overlooked by the massive Drakensberg amphitheater. The protected area lies at an altitude between 4,200 and 11,500 feet.

Greater St. Lucia Wetland Park

SOUTH AFRICA

KwaZulu-Natal
Registration: 1999
Criteria: N (II) (III) (IV)

114 top A community of lesser flamingos (Phoeniconaias minor) fills the banks and placid waters of Lake Kosi. The Great St. Lucia Wetland Park is home to over 50,000 of this species.

114 bottom Known as the 'voice of Africa' because of its unmistakable cry, the African fish eagle (Haliaeetus vocifer) is an extremely territorial bird of prey that eats fish and small aquatic birds.

In September 2002, the Italian cargo ship Jolly Rubino ran aground off the coast of KwaZulu-Natal, spilling part of its 1,000 tons of fuel from its holds. What was worse, however, was that about 70 containers of highly pollutant toxic substances also finished in the sea.

Fortunately, the prompt intervention of safety teams and clement weather and sea conditions prevented what could have turned into a colossal environmental disaster.

The boat was blocked a short distance from the protected areas of the Greater St. Lucia Wetland Park, a delicate ecosystem of river estuaries unique for its physical biodiversity, complex hydrological structure and the associated adaptation of the species that inhabit the zone.

Running for 140 miles along the east coast of South Africa to the south of Mozambique and Swaziland, the park comprises 13 protected areas that cover a surface area of 926 square miles, within which lie two geomorphic areas: the coastal plain and the continental platform that rises up to 1,640 feet above sea level.

Instituted in 1997, the park encloses the final section of the course of several rivers, the most important being the Mkuze and the Umfolozi.

There are also several coastal lakes such as Lake St. Lucia and Lake Kosi, whose waters are of average salinity, and the freshwater lakes Sibayi, Bhangazi and Ngoboreleni.

Vegetation-covered dunes are the most noteworthy feature of the external edge of the coastal plain, which lead down to huge beaches dotted with rocky outcrops.

St. Lucia lies in southern Africa's most fertile area of vegetal biodiversity and boasts species belonging to 152 families and 734 genera.

These represent 30% of the flora of all South Africa. At least 44 species are endemic to the park, including *Brachychloa, Ephippiocarpa, Helichrysopsis, Inhambanella,* South Africa's recently discovered smallest flowering plant, *Wolffiella welwitschii,* and the only marine flowering plant in the country, *Thallasodendron cilliata.*

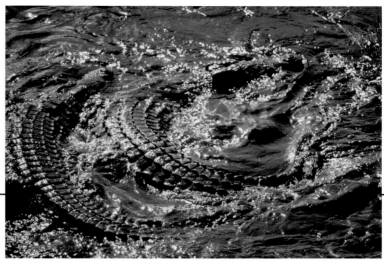

SWAZILAND

PRETORIA

LESOTHO

114-115 A Nile crocodile (Crocodylus niloticus) catches a frog in the reeds (Hyperolius mariae). The park has five amphibians endemic to KwaZulu-Natal and six reptiles on the IUCN's Red List.

115 top left Roughly 27 square miles of the park are formed by marshes of reeds and papyrus, making this the largest protected wetland in South Africa.

115 top right There are many scientific research stations in the park. These Nile crocodiles are monitored by the Pooley Crocodile Research Station.

The aquatic vegetation contributes largely to the richness of the area with roughly 27 square miles of marshland covered by rushes and papyrus, 325 species of algae and many other species typical of wetlands.

This being Africa, it may seem strange but the fauna is not particularly linked to large predators, though there are 129 species of mammals, including 150 white rhinos and 100 or so black rhinos. More interesting are those that are generally unobserved by tourists, like the butterflies (of which there are about 200 species), the dragonflies (52) and the stercorariidea (139).

Then there are marine invertebrates, including 53 genera of corals and 812 mollusks. A particularly impressive statistic is the 991 species of fish in St. Lucia of which only 55 inhabit fresh water. In total there are 109 species of reptiles and 521 of birds, including a population of flamingos that sometimes reaches 50,000.

Finally, the amphibians, in decline around the world, are a sensitive indicator of the environment's state of

health: in St. Lucia there are 50 species whose populations seem stable.

This is owing to the fact that there are no human settlements in the habitat and therefore the environment has remained relatively unspoilt – cargo ships permitting.

116

116 top The small antelope Cephalophus natalensis *has the ability to camouflage itself in the vegetation.*

116 bottom Covered with vegetation right up to the tide line, the coastal dunes average 525 feet in height, with the tallest reaching 597 feet.

116-117 There are about 150 examples of the white rhinoceros but only 80 or so black rhinos.

117 bottom left Large groups of hippos can be seen in the two main rivers in Greater St. Lucia Wetland Park, the Mkuze and Mfolozi.

117 bottom right A herd of Burchell's zebras slakes its thirst. There are no large predators in the park, but there are 129 species of sea and land mammals and 521 species of birds, which represent 60% of South Africa's bird population.

Tsingy de Bemaraha Strict Nature Reserve

MADAGASCAR

NORTHERN PART OF THE REGION
OF ANTSINGY
REGISTRATION: 1990
CRITERIA: N (III) (IV)

The sifaka (*Propithecus verraux deckeni*) is the largest and mainly a daytime creature, whereas the tilitilivaha (*Microcebus murinus*) is no larger than a rat and only comes out at night, but there are nine other species of lemur in the Tsingy de Bemaraha reserve that range between these two extremes.

There are golden-crowned Sifaka *Propithecus tattersalli* and the mongoose lemur (*Eulemur mongoz*), Perrier's sifaka (*Propithecus diadema perrieri*) and the Milne-Edwards lemur (*Lepilemur edwardsi*). And recently observed is one of the most rare species of lemur, the aye-aye (*Daubentonia madagascariensis*), which loves the depths of the forest.

The 587 square miles of the Tsingy de Bemaraha Nature Reserve, in the west of Madagascar, were placed under protection for the first time in 1927 to safeguard an environment of extraordinary beauty that was once almost inaccessible to man. Bounded to the east by a 1,000-1,300-foot precipice that drops down to the Manabolo River, the Bemaraha Plateau is formed by a karstic limestone mass that the erosive action of the river and rain waters has sculpted into a network of ravines and fissures separated by sharp pinnacles and spires: the Tsingy.

The climate is tropical with a dry season that lasts six to eight months and a wet one from November to March. The relatively high rainfall has fostered the proliferation of a dense deciduous forest that alternates, in the less hostile areas, with anthropogenic savannah. The few studies made on the vegetation have recorded roughly 430 species of which 85% are endemic, owing to the different evolution of island species. For example, the east coast ebony (*Diospyros perrieri*), the only wild banana tree in Madagascar (*Musa perrieri*) and various species of *Delonix* are unique. There are also baobabs, Orchidaceae, Euphorbiaceae,

Bombaceae and leguminous plants and many xerophytic plants like the aloe.

Equally scarce have been studies on the park's fauna, for which the number of species is very uncertain and the sources are in disagreement. Besides the lemurs, the more interesting species are a small endemic rodent (*Nesomys rufus lambertoni*) and the chameleon (*Brookesia perarmata*) of which only a few have been seen. In total, there are 13 species of amphibians and some dozens of reptiles, including the Nile crocodile (*Crocodylus niloticus*) and species of the *Uroplatus* and *Brookesia* genera. The zone is also frequented by numerous birds, both terrestrial and aquatic: 30 of the 100 pairs of ospreys in Madagascar – one of the rarest birds of prey in the world – nest at the entrances to the ravines or by the Tsingy Lakes.

A curious fact is that though Tsingy de Bemaraha is the largest protected area in west Madagascar in size and biodiversity, it suffers from lack of maintenance. In fact the World Wildlife Fund emphasized the need for greater attention to be paid to its conservation. Whereas the park was impenetrable by man until a few years ago, now several families have settled inside it where they graze animals and cultivate crops, as do the inhabitants of nearby villages. This means fires in the open areas and on the edges of the forests; and the primary deciduous forests that used to cover Madagascar before human settlement have already been reduced by 3%.

118-119 The chaotic deciduous forest in Tsingy grows in ravines, fissures and gorges and has a very high percentage of endemic species.

119 top Extraordinary canyons exist in Tsingy. The difficulty of moving around in this zone has prevented accurate classification of the flora and fauna, which still remain largely unknown.

119 bottom Having remained impenetrable to man until the mid-twentieth century, today Tsingy de Bemaraha Natural Reserve has been invaded by local peoples, with the consequent risk of compromising the exceptional biodiversity with their agriculture and livestock grazing.

118 Bemaraha highland is an immense mass of limestone with karstic phenomena. Erosion by rainwater and surface water has created the pinnacles ('tsingi') that has given the park its name.

ANTANANARIVO

Aldabra Atoll

SEYCHELLES

REGISTRATION: 1982
CRITERIA: N (II) (III) (IV)

120 top Aldabra is the only place in the Indian Ocean where the red-footed booby nests.

120 bottom The atoll is home to 150,000 giant tortoises, the last on the planet.

Aldabra is the largest atoll in the world and lies to the south of the main island in the Seychelles, Mahé, towards Madagascar. The first documentation of the atoll was made in 1511 by the Portuguese when one of their maps mentioned Ilha Dara (Aldabra), a name with an Arab origin: *al Khadra* ('the Green One'). It seems that the Portuguese navigators were facing in such a direction that they saw the green reflection of the waters inside the atoll.

The first to place a flag on one of the 13 islands that compose the atoll were the French in 1742 when the expedition led by Lazare Picault and Jean Grossin discovered the Seychelles Archipelago. At the start of the nineteenth century the islands were conquered by the British navy and, later, began to be appreciated by British naturalists, first and foremost Charles Darwin.

The first to make extensive studies of the atoll's ecosystem was Jacques-Yves Cousteau when he sailed there in 1954 on the Calypso. The distance of the atoll from the other islands in the archipelago and its lack of fresh water have prevented permanent human settlement but that did not stop the British navy from proposing it as a naval base at the start of the 1960s.

The intervention of the Royal Society and the Smithsonian Institution brought an end to the project and so Aldabra Atoll has remained one of the most remote and unspoiled environments in the world.

Like all formations of this type, the atoll is volcanic in origin, created roughly 125,000 years ago.

The islands that surround it are set on two separate tables, at 13 and 26 feet above sea level. The lagoon is nearly 22 miles across and covers a surface area of roughly 40 square miles. It communicates with the ocean through four main outlets. The maximum depth of the lagoon is little more than 10 feet at high tide and 80% of the bed is exposed at low tide.

The flora on the atoll consists of 198 vegetal species, 19 of which are endemic, but what makes Aldabra so special is the variety of its fauna.

Its most outstanding inhabitant is the giant tortoise (*Geochelone gigantea*), which was one of the first species to be protected in the world thanks to the efforts of Darwin who made entreaties on its behalf to the Governor of Mauritius. Once common throughout the Indian Ocean, this animal now remains only on Aldabra, where there are approximately 150,000, three times the population of the famous tortoises in the Galápagos Islands. As a male adult can reach a length of nearly 4 feet, weigh 550 pounds and live for 100 years, the impact of the species on the atoll's fragile environment is comparable to that of the elephants in the African savannah. Aldabra is also an egg-laying area for the green turtle (*Chelonia mydas*).

There are many species of birds, some of which are very rare, like the white-throated rail (*Dryolimnas cuvieri aldabranus, the last flightless bird in the Indian Ocean*), a species of egret

121 top Seen from above, Aldabra Atoll is a patchwork of crystalline colors, with all shades of turquoise, aquamarine, lapis lazuli and cobalt. The lagoon has a diameter of 21 miles and has a surface area of 37 square miles.

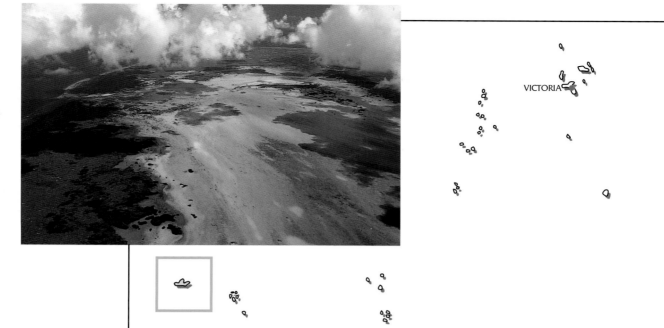

120-121 Aldabra has four outlets to the ocean, one of which can be seen like a branched river in the upper right of the picture. The maximum depth is roughly 10 feet at high tide, but 80% of the bed remains exposed at low tide.

121 bottom In the western channel of Aldabra atoll there are spectacular rock 'mushrooms' shaped by the erosion of the sea. The local currents are considered by some to be one of the strongest natural forces on the planet.

122 top A tangle of mangrove roots in the shallow waters of the atoll. Aldabra has 198 species of vegetation, 19 of which are endemic.

122 center A nurse shark (Nebrus ferrugineus) moves cautiously over the lagoon bed. About 10 feet long, like other sharks of this type it is generally harmless to man.

122 bottom Aldabra is the kingdom of turtles and tortoises. Besides the Geochelone gigantica, here there are green turtles (Chelonia mydas), the loggerhead turtle (Caretta caretta), and the hawksbill turtle (Eretmochelys imbricate). These long-living reptiles rival the sharks for being the most ancient creatures on the planet.

(Egretta gularis dimorpha) and the sacred ibis of Aldabra (Threskiornis aethiopica abbottii).

Particular mention should be made of the marine fauna that lives along the coral reef. The many varieties of coral and sponges favor the proliferation of microorganisms that provide

nourishment to approximately 200 species of highly colored tropical fish. These include angel fish, butterfly fish, scorpion fish, needlefish and puffer fish; then there are many species of crab, large bivalves, anemones and mollusks, which make Aldabra a paradise for the few and fortunate divers allowed here.

122-123 A shoal of snappers (Lutjanus monostigma and Lutjanus eherembergi) explore the submerged mangrove roots. Snappers get their name from their aggressive behavior towards other members of the same species.

123 bottom Of Aldabra's 13 land birds, there are the Aldabran drongo (Dicrurus aldabranus), which nests in the mangroves, and the white-throated rail (Dryolimnas cuvieri aldabranus), which is the only flightless bird in the Indian Ocean.

124 top right Gorgonias (sea fans) are so called for their similarity to the hair of the ancient Greek gorgon. They form colonies with an appearance like trees. They belong to the Class Anthozoa and have a horny skeleton but, unlike calcareous corals, they are flexible.

124 center A long-nose hawkfish (Oxycirrhites typus) rests on a soft coral or alcyonaria.

124 bottom The sea cucumber is a member of the echinoderm family. It has a soft, flexible and warty skin and it moves slowly, contracting its longitudinal and circular muscles.

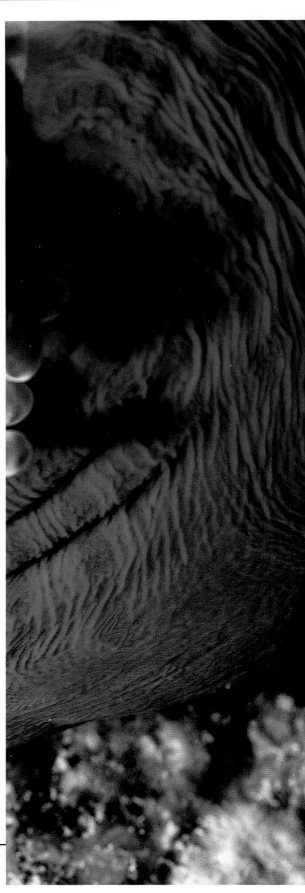

124-125 The porcelain crab is found throughout the Indian Ocean. It lives in association with large anemones (seen here with a Hetaractis magnifica), and it camouflages itself in their tentacles.

125 top A school of snubnose pompano (Trachinotus blochii) dazzles the reef waters with silvery glints. These fish are generally mid-sea dwellers but towards sundown they move close to rocks or coral where they feed mainly on bivalve mollusks.

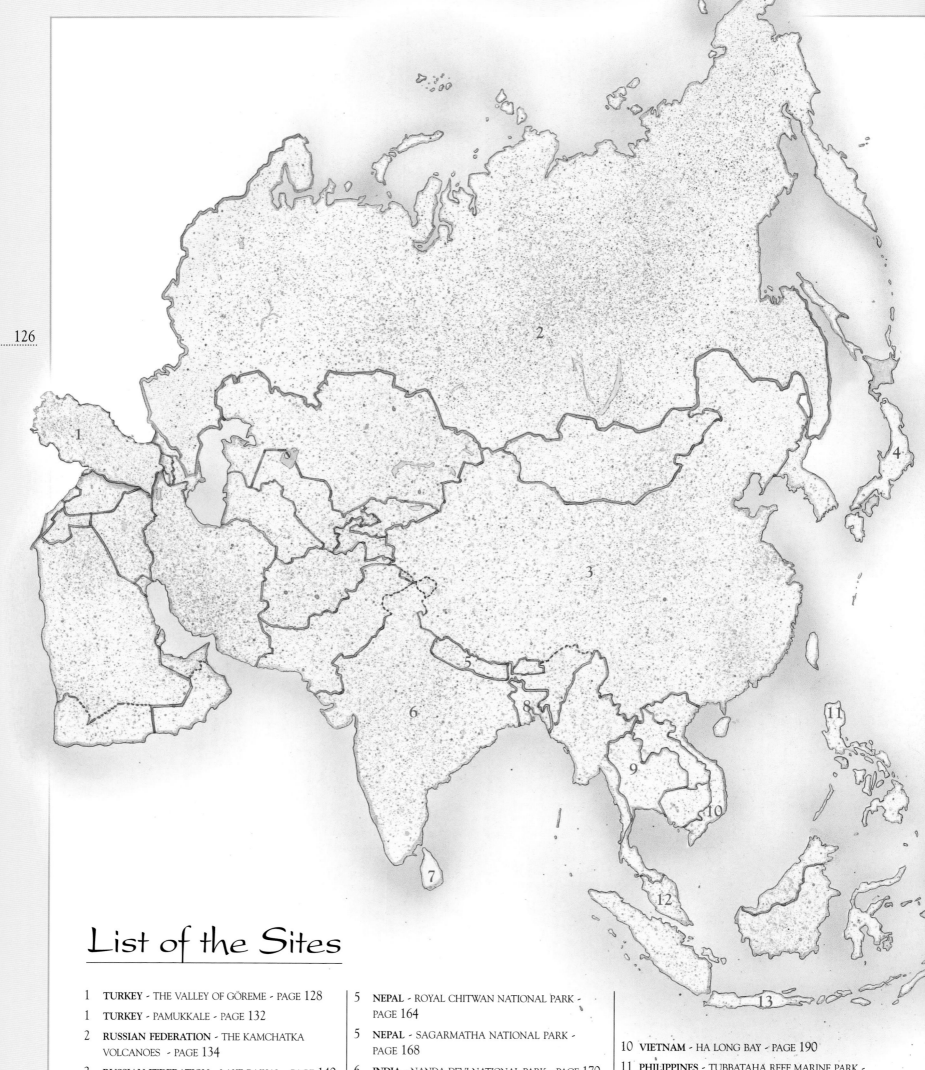

List of the Sites

Asia

This is the continent of a thousand peoples and the great religions and cultures thousands of years old. China and India alone hold almost half of the world population, and Java, in Indonesia, is the planet's most densely populated island. Consequently, it is unusual to associate Asia with a heritage of nature, yet the immensity of this continent contains some of the most extraordinarily beautiful areas in the world. It has the highest mountains on Earth in the chains of the Himalayas, Karakorum and Hindukush; huge rivers, with the Yangtze, Yellow River, Mekong, Amu Darya, Ob and Indus; and almost inaccessible sites of beauty in the delta of the Ganges and Brahmaputra, where the intricate mangrove forest on the border between India and Bangladesh offers the last stronghold for the formidable Bengal tiger. Then there are places of exceptional geological interest, like the Kamchatka Peninsula in Russia, which is a land of volcanoes in continual eruption, and the enchanting landscape of the Vietnamese bay of Ha Long.

From the Arabian Peninsula to Japan, from Siberia to the Sonda Archipelago, the vastness of Asia offers innumerable climates and environments, fauna and flora. Given these extraordinary possibilities, it is perhaps surprising that Asia contains just 27 of the UNESCO

World Heritage nature sites, even though overall they represent an unequalled range of habitats, for example, China's last bamboo forests are the refuge of the symbol of nature conservation, the giant panda, central Asia is the land of the snow leopard and Indonesia provides a limited habitat for the fearsome Komodo dragons and the Javan rhinoceros. Even if one only considers mammals, the list of unique species in remote Asian regions is almost endless.

Up until a few decades ago nature was able to withstand the demographic growth in Asia without detriment, but today the continent's growth is becoming worrisome for the fragile environments of some regions. In the last 20 years, China, India and the countries of Southeast Asia have experienced a huge economic boom that has brought better conditions of life to the lowest levels of society but has also entailed the development of heavy industry and progressive urbanization that together threaten the health of the environment.

It also does not seem that the rapid decline in the population of the Asian tiger will slow, and unless drastic measures are taken to defend the protected areas, the danger that the last wild regions in the continent will be overwhelmed could suddenly become a reality.

The valley of Göreme

TURKEY

CAPPADOCIA, CENTRAL ANATOLIA
REGISTRATION: 1985
CRITERIA: C (I) (III) (V) N (III)

In the villages of Cappadocia mothers like to tell their children the story of the evil giants who wanted to take possession of their country but who were turned to stone by Allah. This is how the devout Moslem mothers explain the origin of the highly unusual rock formations found in the lunar landscape of the valley of Göreme. Over the 16 centuries of human habitation in the region, both inhabitants and travelers have turned to legend to account for these 'fairy chimneys', up to 130 feet high, whose shapes resemble mushrooms, chimneys and pyramids.

The geological explanation of the pillars' existence, being neither romantic nor imaginative in its approach, is that the original morphology of the valley was created by a volcano, Erciyas Dag, that lies in the plain of Kayseri (the Roman city of Caesarea).

Erciyas Dag stands 12,847 feet high and is now extinct, even if every so often seismic activity is recorded in the zone, but during the Pliocene and early Pleistocene epochs it produced violent eruptions. The flow of volcanic material covered 3,860 square miles of surrounding countryside in horizontal layers of lava and ash, then the lava cooled to form a solid layer of black basalt and the ash fused into crumbly white rock known as andesite.

Later, the area experienced a climate of heavy precipitation that created a great number of waterways, and it was these that forged the extraordinary landscape in the valley of Göreme.

Stretching 40 square miles and protected as a national park since 1986, a year after being inscribed as a UNESCO World Heritage site, the valley is unique in the world thanks to the surprising combination of the actions of nature and man.

It contains evidence of the ancient Hittite civilization and that Cappadocia was later under the dominion of

128 left Standing 130 feet high, the rock formations of Göreme have provided the stuff of innumerable legends and are known popularly as 'fairy chimneys'.

128 right Göreme's dramatic landscape was caused by ancient eruptions of the volcano Erciyas Dag, which, over the millennia, deposited thick layers of lava and

ash on the plain. The deposits solidified into hard basalt and crumbly andesite, which were then shaped by atmospheric agents.

129 To fly over the Göreme Valley in a balloon is a stirring experience: the intricate maze of columns, created by thousands of years of fluvial erosion, can only be appreciated from above.

ANKARA

130 top and 130-131
The structure of the white
sedimentary rock in
Göreme Valley clearly
shows how it was shaped:
for the most part it has
been rain that has cut
through the layers of ash to
create bizarre towers and
rocks shaped like whipped
cream.

Phrygia, Rome, Byzantium and finally under the aegis of Islam. In the single village of Göreme, 365 churches were built in the 'fairy chimneys' so that mass could be celebrated every day on a different altar.

Over the centuries, man adapted the natural andesite formations into housing. Even today about 10,000 people live in the valley, to whom are added another 20,000 in the areas bordering the national park.

The bareness of the valley may be deceptive as the site has fertile soil and the vegetal species number 110 endemics, like *Acanthus irsutus, Alkanna orientalis* and *Dinathus zederbauriana.*

The major livelihood of the local population is agriculture, which is still practiced using traditional methods that are considered sustainable.

As for wildlife, the valley is also home to gray wolves, foxes, badgers, stone martins and a multitude of birds, especially pigeons (*Alectoris graeca*). Another positive interaction between man and the environment can be seen in the rock formations that have been turned into pigeon lofts, some of which make use of abandoned rock churches. Pigeons have long been an important source of food and fertilizer to the people of the valley and, even though elsewhere farmers make use of chemical products, here the fields are spread with pigeon guano.

It is said that this is the secret of the goodness of the fruit in Cappadocia, the best to be found in Turkey.

131 top Baglidere Valley is another surprising spectacle in Cappadocia. Abandoned a short while ago due to government orders, the local 'chimneys' were inhabited since ancient times, as is revealed by archaeological finds from Hittite people.

131 bottom Though the landscape in Göreme is bare, the soil of Cappadocia is fairly fertile, allowing agriculture and spontaneous vegetation to grow, and the region has 110 endemic species.

Pamukkale

TURKEY

DENIZLE PLAINS
REGISTRATION: 1988
CRITERIA: C (III) (IV) N (III)

The long colonnaded avenue, the Plateia, was a wide road paved with enormous blocks of travertine by the Romans in the second century AD and was the hub around which the daily life of Hierapolis revolved. Hierapolis was an important spa city, situated 14 or so miles north of Denizle in southwest Turkey, that was founded in the second century BC by Eumenes II, the king of Pergamum, on a site where a community had flourished many centuries earlier.

Hierapolis ('Sacred City') owed this

132 top Pamukkale ('cotton castle') is the modern Turkish name of the ancient spa town of Hierapolis. The name emphasizes the site's unusual limestone formations.

132 bottom The spring water that flows down the Cal Dag'i Plateau halts in large pools where it cools, freeing calcium carbonate that it has collected from the subsoil. The carbonate then flows over the edges of the pools to create columns of travertine.

attention to an unusual property found in its subsoil: water rich with the mineral salt calcium bicarbonate. The water collects the salt as it passes through a limestone stratum on its passage to the surface. This water provides the thermal baths that, according to the ancients, are of exceptional curative powers as well as

being of dramatic appearance. Their white rocky formations have given rise to their modern Turkish name, *Pamukkale*, which means 'cotton castle'. And this is their principal aspect of interest.

Descending the gentle slope of Cal Dag'i Plateau, the mineral rich spring water, which has a temperature of 95°F, collects in pools and ravines where it cools, thus liberating the dissolved calcium carbonate. As the water cools first on the edges of the pools, the travertine precipitates more quickly there and columns of increasingly thicker layers are formed. On average, Pamukkale's springs deposit over 140,000 cubic feet of travertine each year. Over their estimated life of 14,000 years, the accumulation of deposits has created an unreal landscape of mineral forests, petrified cascades, spires and terraces that has always attracted the curiosity of the local people.

The therapeutic powers of Pamukkale's waters have been legendary since before the Roman era. The geographer Strabo reported that Hierapolis was famous for its thermal waters and the Plutonium, a paved room that collected fumes that are poisonous to both men and animals. For the local population, the spring waters have the necessary chemical properties to clean the cotton produced in the area (another reason for Pamukkale's name) and to fix the colors of the materials when they are dyed. The therapeutic value of the thermal springs is derived from their mineral content, in particular, calcium carbonate and sulfate, and iron, sulfur and magnesium salts.

Pamukkale springs and the ruins of the cultural site of Roman Hierapolis continue to be a very popular tourist attraction. It is to preserve the naturalistic and archeological value of this site that the Turkish authorities have launched a series of conservation projects since 1976 as part of an agreement between the countries that ring the Mediterranean.

132-133 It is thought that 14,000 years were required for the water rich in mineral salts to form the 330-foot tall forest of petrified waterfalls, spires and terraces seen today.

133 bottom Spread across a mile and a half, the spring-water waterfalls of Pamukkale deposit a volume of 140,000 cubic feet of travertine each year. The mineral salt content is prevalently calcium carbonate and calcium sulphate and is responsible for the legendary curative properties of the water.

ANKARA

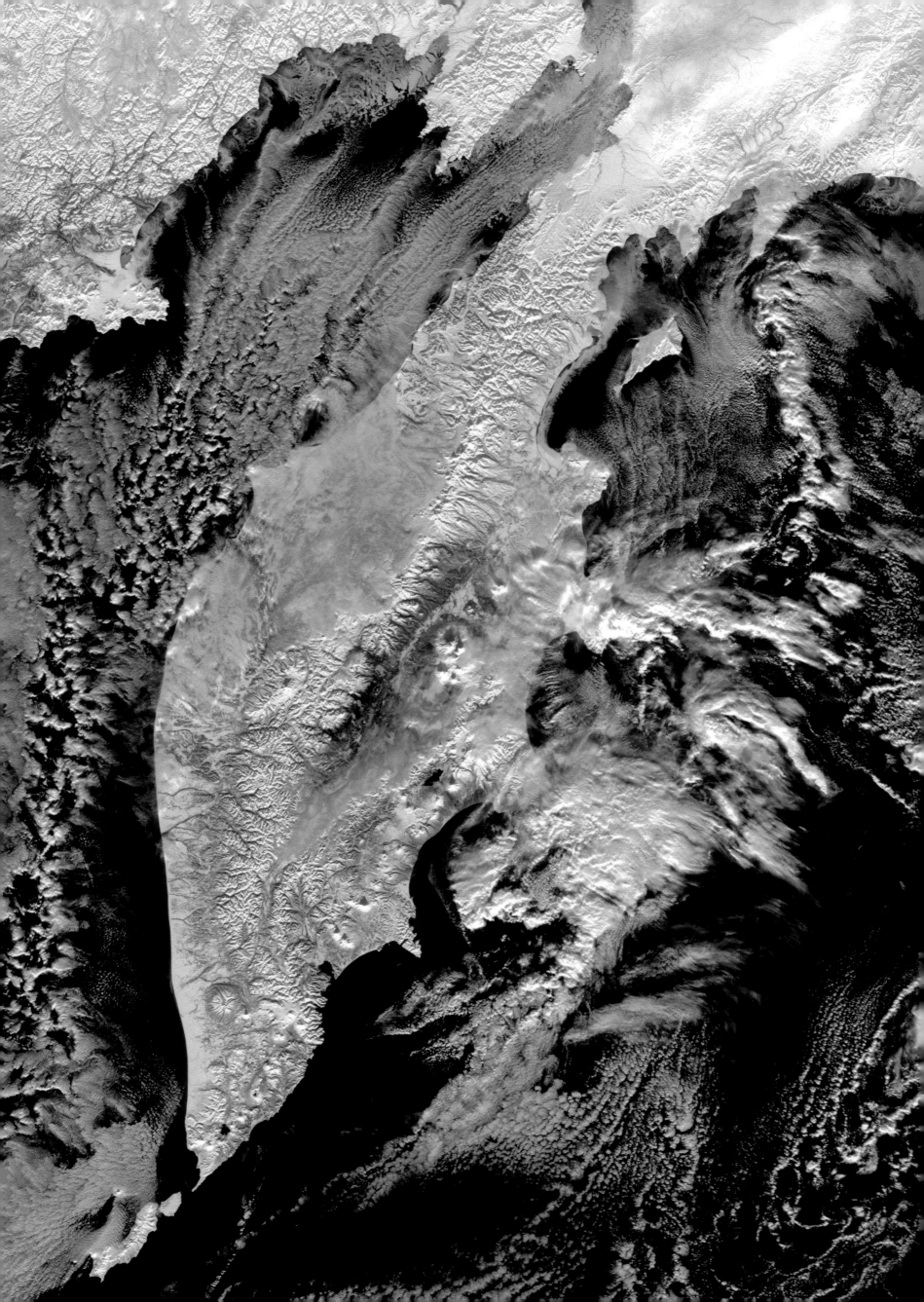

The Kamchatka Volcanoes
RUSSIAN FEDERATION

KAMCHATKA PENINSULA
REGISTRATION: 1996, 2001
CRITERIA: N (I) (II) (III) (IV)

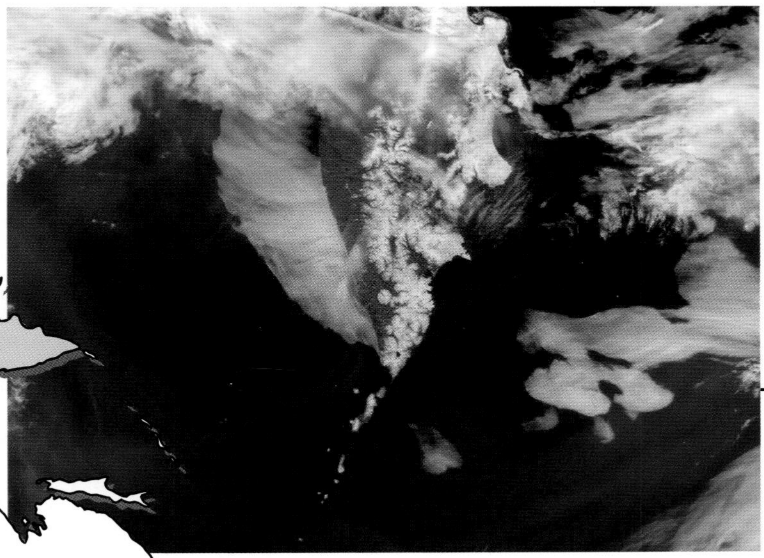

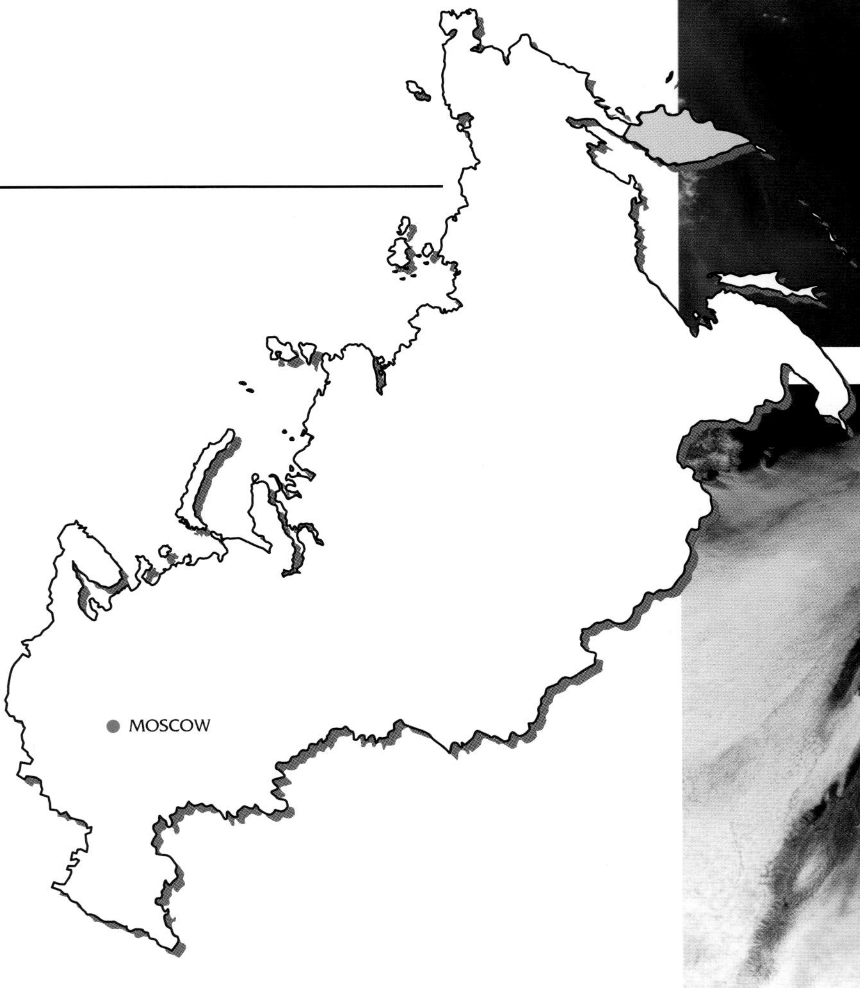

● MOSCOW

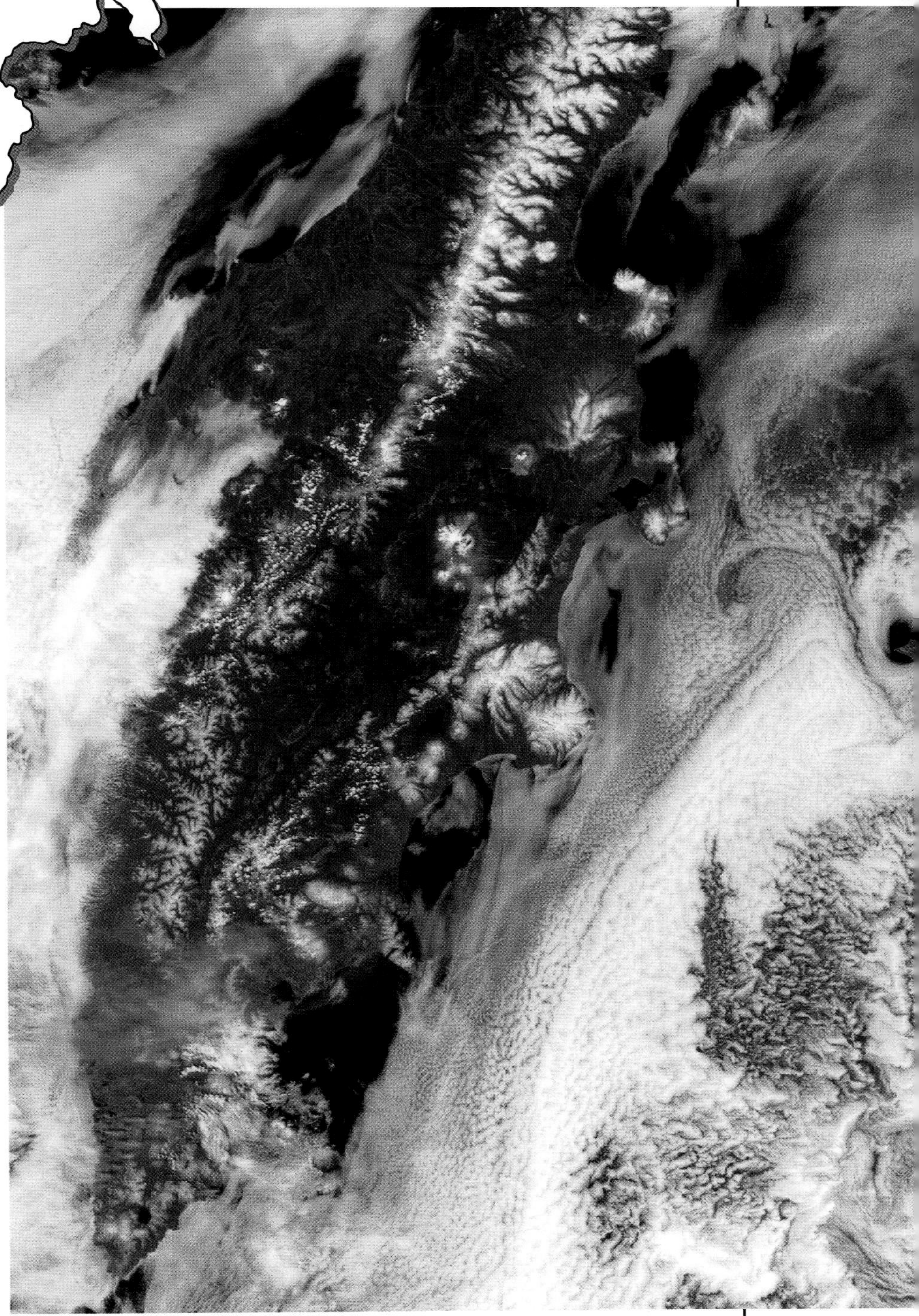

134 During winter Kamchatka is completely covered by ice, as is seen in this photograph taken from a NASA satellite of the valleys that slope down into Sredinnyyi Khrebet, the volcanic chain in the center of the peninsula.

135 top Photographed from space in 2001, we see a long plume of smoke streak the skies of Siberia.

135 bottom The 14,270 square miles of the Kamchatka Volcano Reserve covers 29 active volcanoes, 300 extinct volcanoes and 150 thermal springs.

At a height of 15,600 feet above sea level, the perfectly conical Mount Kluchevskoy is the highest active volcano in Eurasia; it and its sister mountains Kamen, Bezymyanny and Plosky Tolbackik, together form the volcanic complex of Kluchevskaya. Its first eruption to be recorded by man occurred in 1697 when the Russian explorer Vladimir Atlasov found himself before it for the first time. Since then, vulcanologists have noted at least one eruption every five years, but Kluchevskoy, like Kamchatka's other volcanoes, has never been a danger to the local people.

This is not the only attraction on the peninsula that stretches between the Sea of Okhotsk and the Bering Sea. The 11,575-foot high Mount Kronotsky is also a perfect cone though it is not so high. The Uzon Volcano, formed 40,000 years ago, is one of the most interesting geological phenomena in the area; it covers an area of 36 square miles and has a crater like an enormous bowl with walls between 650 and 2,600 feet high. A vast hydrothermal system has been formed inside in which minerals are in processes of constant production.

Included in the World Heritage list in 1996, the vast Kamchatka Volcano Reserve covers 14,270 square miles.

It is divided into six sections that offer a complete overview of the many volcanic activities that occur in the region. The peninsula lies on the meeting point of different circumpacific tectonic plates in an area subject to intense volcanic activity.

The reserve covers many of the 29 volcanoes still active in the peninsula, roughly 300 extinct volcanoes and over 150 thermal and mineral sources. Dozens of geysers, fumaroles and waterfalls line the sharply peaked mountains, on whose flanks turquoise lakes and fields of colored seaweed make the Geyser Valley a fairytale landscape.

The great variety of climates in the volcanic region has encouraged the development of an extremely rich and diverse vegetation, including vast expanses of tundra and taiga, and 1,168 species of giant grasses and wild berries, 10% of which are endemic to Kamchatka.

The fauna numbers 145 species of birds such as eagles, cormorants, puffins, geese, ducks, gulls and swans. The 33 mammals include brown bears, elk, gray wolves, caribou, mountain sheep and foxes. An endangered species is Steller's sea eagle (*Haliaetus pelagicus*), half of whose world population lives here in Kamchatka. Another animal under threat is the Kamchatka bear (*Ursus arctos*), which is a subspecies of the brown bear. It is also related to the 10,000 grizzly bears that make the peninsula their home.

The most extraordinary sight on Kamchatka occurs between the start of summer and winter when millions of salmon – belonging to the five species

136 top Taken from the Endeavor space shuttle on 30 September 1994, this photograph shows one of the most recent eruptions of Kluchevskoy, which, at 15,584 feet, is the highest active volcano in Asia.

136 center Lying on the meeting point of various tectonic plates, Kamchatka is one of the most intense volcanic areas on the ring that circles the Pacific Ocean.

136 bottom Inside the reserve there is a glacial lake that formed in the crater of an extinct volcano.

136-137 The perfect cone of most of the volcanoes in Kamchatka is a characteristic of their nature as stratovolcanoes, which means they have been formed over tens or hundreds of thousands of years by the accumulation of eruptive materials.

137 This aerial view of the Kliuchi group is dominated in the background by the cone of Kluchevskoy. The group includes the volcanoes Udina, Zimina, Bezymianny, Kaman and Tolbachik, which ring the highest peak.

138 top Geysers,
fumaroles, turquoise lakes
and fields of polychrome
algae make Geyser Valley a
unique sight. The remote
Kamchatka was explored by
Russians at the end of the
seventeenth century.

138-139 A close relation of
the American grizzly, the
Kamchatka bear is a
subspecies of Ursus arctos.
During hibernation – which
ends in May – it loses about
30% of its body weight.

of Pacific salmonids – tackle the currents of the many rivers to reach their place of birth and reproduction. In that period of the year, Kamchatka has the most crowded salmon population in the world.

The peninsula's recent opening up to tourism and mineral exploitation has created a serious risk to the delicate environmental balances.

A plan for gold mining a few miles from the Bystinsky Nature Park has not yet been approved by the government, simply because of a lack of sufficient funding. If the project does go ahead, it would inevitably affect one of the unspoilt ecosystems of the region.

139 top Around 10,000 Kamchatka bears live on the peninsula. After the mating season, these plantigrades spend most of their time solitarily.

139 center At the start of summer, millions of fish from the five species of Pacific salmon begin their journeys up the rivers, where the bears lie in wait for them.

139 bottom The fox (Alopex lagopus) is white in winter and tawny in summer. It does not hibernate and, during winter, feeds on carcasses or prey killed by other animals.

Lake Baikal

RUSSIAN FEDERATION

Autonomous republic of Buryat,
southeastern Siberia, region of Irkutsk
Registration: 1996
Criteria: N (i) (ii) (iii) (iv)

It must have been a surprise for the unbending establishment of the Soviet Union when, in 1957, public opinion in southeast Siberia suddenly voiced itself. Scientists, writers, fishermen and ordinary citizens broke 40 years of silent obedience to contest the decision of the distant government in Moscow to site a gigantic papermill on the shores of Lake Baikal.

During that period, public dissent did not receive much of a hearing and, at the start of the 1960s, the battle given by those pioneering environmentalists did not meet with success. The factory was built and almost 30 years were to pass before its opponents were able celebrate victory, following the decision of the Council of Ministers of the Soviet Union in 1987 to set up the Lake Baikal Coastal Protection Zone. This area covers the immense area of 34,000 square miles and, according to scientists who recently carried out research into the quality and properties of its waters, the habitat of the lake has not suffered excessively from the factory's temporary but damaging presence.

With a surface area of 12,162 square miles and a maximum depth of 5,370 feet, Baikal is the largest mass of freshwater on earth; icepacks apart, it contains 20% of the entire planet's

140 top The closest relations of the Baikal seal (Phoca sibirica) live in the Arctic regions: the most highly accredited theory has it that the first seals reached Baikal down the Lena River.

140 bottom The spring blooms enliven the south shore of Baikal with color. The local flora has 800 species of vascular plants whose distributions vary owing to the strongly asymmetrical climate.

141 bottom The Baikal seal can swim at a depth of 1,000 feet. Though small, it is voracious and eats at least 7 pounds of fish a day.

140-141 The largest island in the lake is called Okhlon. It points towards the deepest point in the lake, 5,370 feet below the surface.

141 top In addition to being the deepest lake in the world and containing the largest body of freshwater, Baikal is also the earth's oldest lake. It was formed 25 million years ago.

● MOSCOW

freshwater, has an estimated volume of 5,520 cubic miles and a catchment area of about 200,000 square miles of land. To fill this extraordinary bowl – it measures 398 miles north to south and an average of 30 miles wide – it would take almost a year for the Volga, Danube, Amazon and Nile together to fill it. The lake has 365 tributaries but only one emissary, the Angara.

Baikal is also the oldest lake in the world, having been formed around 25 million years ago, however, geologists are not all in agreement on its origins – some of whom believe it was created by

142 top The southeastern
section of Okhlon Island
has steppe vegetation and is
always swept by the
sarma, the strong wind
that crosses the lake.

142-143 The forests of
Pinus sibirica and the
taiga in the Khamar-
Daban mountains on the
west shore of the lake are
the kingdom of the brown
bear.

subduction of the earth's crust. Thanks
to its exceptional quantity of
zooplankton, Baikal's water is extremely
pure and has a mineral content of 25-
50% less than most lakes.

The body of water has a significant
influence on the local climate.
Although the average winter
temperature at the water surface is -
13°F and from January to May the ice
on the lake is 30-45 inches thick, the
temperature on the land around it
averages -6°F. Vice versa, in the summer
the land temperature is cooler than that
on the water surface.

This climatic and environmental
context has favored the development of
an unmatched biodiversity: over 1,000
species of aquatic flora have been
recorded, including algae and water
flowers, which alternate with the
seasons. On the lakeshores, roughly 800
species of vascular plants have been
found distributed unevenly owing to a
strongly asymmetrical climate.

In the western section of the

fauna. There are 1,500 species, of
which 80% are endemic: 255 species of
amphipods, a group of crustaceans, 80
species of flatworms (Phylum
Platyhelminthes) and a unique
mammal, the Baikal seal (Phoca
sibirica). Land fauna is less specific as it
is common to the vast region of
Siberia. In the north there are 243
species of birds and 39 mammals
(including marmots, flying squirrels,
foxes, elk, brown bears and animals
valued for their furs, such as otters and
sables. In the south, there are 260 birds
and 37 mammals, including roe deer,
boar, steppe skunk and lynx.

Innumerable archeological remains,
such as rock paintings and the ruins of
ancient settlements, reveal the
importance of Baikal in the development
of human civilization in northeast Asia.
Today roughly 100,000 people live in the
area, whose livelihoods are mostly
related to agriculture, fishing, animal
breeding and forest activities.

They belong to different ethnic

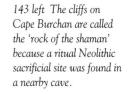

143 left The cliffs on
Cape Burchan are called
the 'rock of the shaman'
because a ritual Neolithic
sacrificial site was found in
a nearby cave.

143 right Rhododendrons
(Rhododendron
dahuricum) flowering in
the Baikalo-Lenski
Reserve, which is an
unspoilt area measuring
2,317 square miles.

catchment area, there are mainly forests
of conifers and mountain steppes, while
to the east there are pine forests. To the
north lie deciduous forests of larch (Larix
dahurica) and rhododendrons
(Rhododendron dahuricum).

At higher levels (the highest point in
the basin reaches 9,320 feet), there are
forests of beech (Abies sibirica) and
Siberian pine (Pinus sibirica) before the
vegetation gives way to tundra.

Even more surprising is the aquatic

groups, for instance, Buryat, Evenk and,
of course, Russian. The Russians arrived
to this area around the mid-seventeenth
century. The Kossacks under Kurbat
Ivanov arrived in 1643 and, 12 years
later, Awakum Petrov, a violent
archpriest was exiled to these parts. He
was evidently charmed by the nature of
Lake Baikal because he gave a touching
description of it in his biography, as a
result of which all of Russia came to
learn about the area.

Central Sikhote-Alin
RUSSIAN FEDERATION

REGION OF PRIMORSKI
REGISTRATION: 2001
CRITERIA: N (IV)

In February 2000, Peter Matthiessen, a journalist and writer, published *Tigers in the Snow*, a touching book in which he raised the alarm about the fate of one of the world's most fascinating big cats. At over 70 years of age, Matthiessen had gone in search of the last of the Amur, or Siberian, tigers (*Panthera tigris altaica*), the most majestic of the five subspecies and the one at most serious risk of extinction.

The Siberian tiger lives in the extreme eastern tip of Siberia that faces onto the Sea of Japan opposite Sakhalin Island. Back in the 1930s the government of Moscow had created the Sikhote-Alin Nature Reserve to protect the few animals that remained. At the end of the 1980s, however, the collapse of the Soviet Union and the poverty of the few local inhabitants encouraged the rise of smuggling operations into China and the countries of Southeast Asia, where the belief that an infusion of tiger restores sexual potency is widespread. And when the price of a tiger skin reaches 15,000 dollars on the black market, it is easy to understand how the slow repopulation of the tiger community has taken a rapid step backwards.

There are roughly 400 Siberian tigers left, but many live in such small and isolated groups that their number does not guarantee their survival. The only area in which the population of tigers might once again increase, given adequate protection, is Sikhote-Alin, where approximately 150 live.

Covering an area of 6,300 square miles, the Central Sikhote-Alin is divided into five reserves characterized by a series of mountain ridges, river valleys, depressions and plateaus that run from the coast inland up to an altitude of 6,200 feet. The formation originated at the end of the Tertiary period when basaltic and andesitic lava percolated down; later modeled during the Ice Age, its gullies contain the largest and most unusual temperate forest in the world. Depending on the altitude and degree of exposure, there

144 top The Siberian tiger (Panthera tigris altaica) proliferated for half a century thanks to the creation of the Central Sikhote-Alin Natural Reserve, but following the collapse of the Soviet Union, poaching has once again threatened its survival.

144 bottom left Two thirds of the reserve are unaffected by human presence, which allows 1,200 vascular plants to live unthreatened.

144 bottom right The roe deer (Capreolus capreolus) is a highly selective ruminant that mostly feeds on shoots in the abundant undergrowth.

145 Divided into bands of vegetation, the regional flora includes thick virgin forests of conifers and broadleaf trees, such as Betula ermanii, Pinus pumila and species of rhododendrons.

MOSCOW

are virgin forests of pines, broadleaf trees, conifers and high-altitude scrub in which birch, Siberian oak and rhododendrons predominate. Other ecosystems feature spruce, beech, larch and Korean pine (*Pinus koraiensis*).

In total there are more than 1,200 species of vascular plants recorded in the area, even though the biodiversity in the forests of Central Sikhote-Alin is diminishing, which puts remnant and rare endemic species in jeopardy. This is the case although the impact of man is practically non-existent as the area is relatively uninhabited compared to the rest of Siberia. The reduction in biodiversity could be damaging for the extraordinary fauna in the region. Of the 65 mammals in Central Sikhote-Alin there are species other than the tiger in danger, like the Manchurian deer (*Cervus elaphus xanthopygus*), which is the tigers' favorite prey, and the black bear (*Ursus thibetanus*). There are also otters, sable, squirrels, mink, weasels and roe deer, then 241 species of birds, including the Manchurian crane and hooded crane, eastern stork, black stork and Indian buzzard, all of which are endangered.

Although the climate of this region is one of the most hostile for man, archeologists have found traces of human settlements from the late Paleolithic. In the basin of the most important river in Sikhote-Alin – the Bikin – the temperature can reach -58°F, and the ground is covered with permafrost for nine months of the year.

146 top left The otter (Lutra lutra) has highly developed senses and is a very sociable animal. It spends much time at play, which is its favorite pastime after hunting and swimming.

146 top right The largest population of brown bears (Ursus arctos) in Eurasia lives in Russia. This omnivorous, plantigrade animal rarely hunts animals larger than itself.

146-147 Fires lit for agricultural purposes sometimes affect the protected area, as the remains of this subalpine forest area show.

147 top The lower stretch of the Bikin (the most well-preserved river in the region) is home to several hundreds of the rare Manchurian crane (Grus japonensis).

147 center and bottom The most representative area of the reserve is the mid and upper stretches of the Bolshaya Ussurka River. Central Sikhote-Alin has large areas of taiga typical of the Ussuri, including Korean pine.

148-149 The Siberian, or Amur, tiger is the largest cat in the world. It creates strong bonds within the pair but when the cubs turn adult, aggression breaks out and the weakest are isolated.

The Golden Mountains of Altai

RUSSIAN FEDERATION

REPUBLIC OF ALTAI

REGISTRATION: 1998

CRITERIA: N (IV)

150 Like the peregrine falcon, the golden eagle (Aquila chrysaetos) prefers to nest among the rock pinnacles on the peaks of Katunksy Zapovednik. The imperial eagle (Aquila heliaca) instead favors moderate heights and semi-open terrain.

Remote and unknown to most, the Republic of Altai, on the Russian borders with China and Kazakhstan, is the principal source of agricultural products in Russia. Over 27,000 square miles of its territory (27% of the agricultural land in Asiatic Russia) is used for cultivation – mostly cereals. The reasons for this enormous percentage are the fertility of the soil and the abundance of water from the huge Altai mountain chain, which measures 400 miles long and 480 miles wide. The Golden Mountains is the name they are given here. They are considered so important that they are protected by strict environmental laws that allow access only to scientists for research purposes in much of the territory.

Divided into the Altaisky Zapovednik Nature Reserve (3,730 square miles), the Katunsky Zapovednik Nature Reserve (1,517 square miles) and the Ukok Highland Nature Reserve (980 square miles), the area of the Golden Mountains is the highest point of the Arctic Ocean hydrological basin and encloses the upper course of the Ob, the largest river in Siberia and one of the largest in the world. The highest mountain, the Belukha, is 14,783 feet high and its north wall, the Akkemsky, is a spectacular rock face 3,280 feet in height. Most of the range's peaks exceed 13,100 feet and are interspersed with 1,500 glaciers that together cover an area of 350 square miles. The many valleys – some steep and deep, others gentle and open – are furrowed by streams and waterfalls or enclose lakes. In total there are 1,274 lakes, the largest of which, Lake Teletskoe, contains 51 billion cubic yards of water, is 1,066 feet deep and extraordinarily clear.

This varied landscape supports a flora of over 2,000 species, of which 17 are remnants and 212 are endemic. At low levels there are the steppes, which slowly give way to forests of conifers as the altitude increases. Forests of fir and Siberian pine are mixed with forests of aspen, birch and a species of alder that only grows in the Altai. At a height of 6,200 feet, the trees are replaced by tundra, at first alpine with herbaceous plants of *Carex altaicus* and *Festuca krylovus*, then glacial, characterized by mosses and lichens.

The difficulty of entering these mountains – not just because access is forbidden officially, but also owing to the morphology of the terrain – has

● MOSCOW

150-151 An opportunistic predator capable of killing animals up to three times its size, the snow leopard (Uncia uncia) prefers small mammals in the high Altai Mountains such as the alpine pika (Ochotona alpina).

151 top Lake Poperechnaya in the high Katunsky Zapovednik massif begins to be covered with snow in September. Almost 1,300 lakes are formed by the 1,500 glaciers in the Golden Mountains, which cover an area of 350 square miles.

151 right Unlike the snow leopard, the fox (Vulpes vulpes) lives in the alpine tundra and low level forests. It is another of the many predators in the area, along with the wolf (Canis lupus), wolverine (Gulo gulo) and lynx (Lynx lynx).

151 bottom Recently, the Russian government has financed many studies of the population of the snow leopard, which finds one of its last refuges in the high Altai. The residual population across central Asia is estimated to be between 4,500 and 7,000.

152 top left Dominated at low quotas by the Siberian steppes, the Golden Mountains are mostly covered by vast conifer forests of fir, larch, Siberian pine, birch and aspen.

152 top right The 'Shumy' rapids separate the upper and middle section of Lake Multinskie, two of the many bodies of water that have this name. They are all connected by short, fast-running stretches of river.

152-153 A golden eagle helps its chick in the nest. At around 30 days of age the chick is able to eat on its own the prey brought by its parents, and it flies for the first time at around nine weeks.

preserved alpine flowers, including several species of gentian that are now extinct elsewhere in the world. But it is above all the fauna that benefits from the isolation. The Altai is one of the last sanctuaries of the snow leopard (*Uncia uncia*). No census has been taken but zoologists have found many traces of the species, for example, the remains of its prey. Overall, the Golden Mountains contain 60 or so mammals, including the Mongolian gazelle, the Arctic squirrel, the alpine pika and the sable. There are over 300 species of birds (13 of which are in danger of extinction), 11 reptiles and 20 or so fish.

Although there are no human settlements even on the edges of the protected area, and the entire Republic of Altai has a population of just 200,000 people, the mountains have revealed a surprising series of archeological remains. In the Ukok reserve alone there are a hundred or so mounds dating to the fifth century BC built by the Pazyryk people. Some of the artifacts found in the tombs of the tribal chiefs today occupy a room in the Hermitage Museum in St. Petersburg.

153 top The lakes, rivers and torrents in the 6,200 square miles of the Golden Mountains are part of the hydrological basin of the Ob River. The Ob is the largest river in western Siberia and one of the longest in the world.

153 center The Arctic squirrel (Eutamias sibiricus) is a small tree-dwelling rodent that lives in large colonies. However, it is a very territorial animal and each one occupies a well-defined area inside the colony.

153 bottom The brown bear (Ursus arctos) of the Altai tends to change its territory with the seasons. It wanders around Lake Teletskoye during spring and moves gradually higher with the start of summer until it reaches the snowline.

Huanglong and Jiuzhaigou
CHINA

PROVINCE OF SICHUAN
REGISTRATION: 1992
CRITERIA: N (III)

It cannot be said that the Chinese are not trying everything possible to save the giant panda (*Ailuropoda melanoleuca*), which, for more than 40 years, has been the emblem of the World Wildlife Fund and the symbol of all species threatened by extinction, for, in addition to protecting the fragile habitat in which this mammal lives (though in a rather disjointed and reluctant manner), they have tried to stimulate the apparent reduction in sexual desire of the pandas, using pornographic films and Viagra, and have even made a weak attempt at cloning.

The situation is not rosy but artificial insemination has produced some results. In Wulong, for example, the population of the pandas has risen to 55 compared to 20 in 1998. Fewer in number are the pandas in the Jiuzhaigou Valley, which were estimated to be just 17 in 1996, while in the adjacent reserve of Huanglong four communities have been recorded in the five areas able to provide them with a habitat. They are not many and

their proximity to Wanglang Reserve heightens their chances of survival.

Situated in northern Sichuan – China's gateway to inland Asia – the histories of the Huanglong and Jiuzhaigou Valleys run in parallel. Created at the end of the 1970s, they have respective areas of 270 and 278 square miles. They lie in a mountainous area of complicated tectonic development where the peaks reach 16,400 feet. Both sites are crossed by fault lines that produce intense and frequent seismic activity. From a geological standpoint, both are characterized by Paleozoic carbonate rock covered by recent deposits of alluvial gravel and glacial moraines. On these lie deposits of calcite that form huge areas of travertine and limestone, which give rise to karstic phenomena. There are many glacial lakes at high levels and the landscape is strongly characterized by ravines and precipices; in fact, the name Jiuzhaigou means 'the valley of the nine ravines'.

The contiguity of the two areas is also reflected in their fairly uniform vegetation. At low levels, between 5,500 and 7,500 feet, there is a strip of forest dominated by Chinese fir (*Picea asperata*) and maples (*Acer yiu, Acer*

154 top The protected area of Huanglong lies in the climatic transition zone between the Himalayan, sub-tropical and tropical regions in the Northern Hemisphere. The temperatures range from -11 to +86°F.

*154 bottom Huanglong's surface is 65.8% covered by forest. At low levels (between 5,600 and 7,500 feet) the predominant species are Chinese fir (*Picea asperata*) and three species of maple.*

154-155 The area of Huanglong is renowned for the number of water sources with high mineral levels that appear to have curative properties. The water that gushes from Zhuzhuhu hydrothermal has a temperature of 70°F and forms a series of natural swimming pools.

155 top Chosen by the
World Wildlife Fund as the
symbol of nature
conservation, the giant
panda (Ailuropoda
melanoleuca) now only
lives in the mountains of
Sichuan. Despite attempts
by scientists, its population
is dropping rapidly and
attempts to encourage
reproduction in captivity
have produced very
poor results.

BEIJING

156 top left Jiuzhaigou is a complex hydrological system: its main rivers all flow into the Jialing which, in turn, feeds into the immense river system of the Yangtze.

156 top right The bottom of Lake Wolonghai has a curious limestone formation that the locals consider to be a dragon. Traditional legends – and recent belief – has it that monsters live in the lakes of Jiuzhaigou, a claim that some scientists are taking seriously.

156 bottom The 19 lakes in Shuzeng and 18 in Nuorilang all lie in the protected area of Jiuzhaigou. They are like water terraces separated by formations of travertine that resemble small dikes.

erianthum and Acer davidii). Higher up there are conifers with various species of fir, larch and birch, while at heights of 12,000-13,800 feet the land develops into large alpine meadows of grass and shrubs. The many botanical species in both sites (101 in Huanglong and 92 in Jiuzhaigou) are considered to be of extreme interest for the rate of endemics, their ornamental value and for their use in traditional Chinese medicine.

Besides the giant panda, the fauna includes 59 mammals in Huanglong but only 10 or so in Jiuzhaigou, though these figures are the result of unsystematic research. The most interesting mammals are the snub-nosed langur (Pygatrix roxellanae), which is also under threat owing to reduction of its natural habitat, the lesser panda (Ailurus fulgens), the Asiatic black bear (Selenarctos

thibetanus) and the takin (Budorcas taxicolor thibetana).

Although wrapped in legend for the role they have played in Tibetan religion and tradition, the inaccessibility of these mountains has made them unsuitable for human settlement and the two valleys of Huanglong and Jiuzhaigou are only inhabited by small villages with a total population of just 1,500. Yet that does not mean that no threat from man exists to the areas; indeed their conservation is a worrying task. A massive government campaign to encourage tourism in internal China has increased the number of visitors to the zone enormously, which have now reached 300,000 a year. In addition, large sections of the forest have been cut down for agricultural use by the surrounding populations and fires and pollution have also added to the threats to the pandas.

156-157 Zhengshutan
Waterfall is the one that
attracts most attention of
the many in Jiuzhaigou. Its
is 1,017 feet wide and has
an average drop of 92 feet
over a travertine hill.
Formations of this nature,
in continual evolution, are
as common in this area as
in Huanglong.

157 top 2.2 miles long,
the spectacular
Huanglonggou ('Throat
of the Yellow Dragon') is
a series of travertine pools
in which algae tint the
water with extraordinary
purity, giving hues of
yellow, green and blue.

Huangshan
CHINA

PROVINCE OF ANHUI
REGISTRATION: 1990
CRITERIA: C (II); N (III) (IV)

The Chinese think Huangshan is the most beautiful mountain in the world. An ancient saying tells that it is endowed with 'the magnificence of Taishan, the perilous peaks of Huashan, the white clouds of Hengshan, the thunderous waterfalls of Lushan and the elegance of Emei', in other words, all the characteristics that have made the five sacred mountains of China famous. Roughly 20,000 poems have been composed over 12 centuries of history that have Mount Huang as its protagonist, and innumerable paintings and drawings illustrate its natural marvels. In fact, the Shansui school of painting that flourished in the sixteenth century codified the forms of the mountain as the classic model for landscape art.

Since 1982, Huangshan (the 'Yellow Mountain', a name ratified on 17 June 747 during the Tang Dynasty by a decree from emperor Tiang Bao as a tribute to the sacred color of the dynasty) has been protected by the Counsel of State of the People's Republic of China as a place of historic and scenic interest. The area of the Huang Mountains covers 60 square miles and numbers many peaks, 77 of which exceed 3,280 feet. The highest, Lianhua Feng ('Lotus Peak') is 6,115 feet high and, as its name suggests, is shaped like the flower in bud. Other mountains are equally famous, for example, Guangming Ding ('Luminous Peak') and Tiandu Feng ('Peak of the Celestial Capital'). Overall, Huangshan is a granite massif composed of feldspar, diorite, quartz and yellow and black mica, and formed during the Mesozoic era by tectonic shifts followed by the withdrawal

of the Yangtse Sea.

However, it was during the last Ice Age that this landscape was modeled into a series of picturesque rocks and masses, caverns, natural bridges, ravines, precipices and valleys that have, over the centuries, been given such imaginative names as 'The monkey that eats the melon' or 'The immoral man who shows the path'.

Water too has contributed to create the myth of Huangshan. Of its many waterfalls, the most admired is Renzi near the Peak of the Purple Clouds. The water is divided into two streams that drop into a crystal pool to create what tradition

identifies as the ideogram that signifies 'person'. The best-known hot spring is Tangchi where approximately 50 tons of water bubble to the surface each hour.

There are 300 species of fauna, of which 48 are mammals and 170 are birds. But an equal marvel of Huangshan is its vegetation: 56% of the territory is covered by pines, in particular *Pinus massoniana* and *Pinus huanshanensis*. Although the flora is more famous for its esthetic value – there are examples of *Pinus huanshanensis* and *Gingko biloba* that are centuries old – it is also of notable scientific interest thanks to the number of its endemic species. There are 240 species

158 top left The forests of Pinus massoniana and Pinus huangshanensis are distributed at altitudes between 2,625 and 5,900 feet and cover 56% of the entire protected area.

158 top right There are 77 peaks in Huangshan that exceed 3,280 feet in height. Many of these have been given picturesque names by literature and popular tradition, inspired by the rock forms or knotty trees that grow near the summits.

of bryophytes, which represent one third of all those in the whole of China. Huangshan is also home to plants in danger of extinction, like *Buckleya henryi*, and rare species used in traditional Chinese medicine, like *Inula iinariaefolia* and *Captis Chinensis*. The richness of the flora is owing to the high level of humidity in Huangshan: for 200 days each year the territory is covered by a thick layer of cloud from which only the highest peaks protrude. It is the sight of these summits above the clouds, like islands in the air, that has earned Huangshan the name 'First Mountain Below the Sky'.

158-159 Considered 'the most beautiful mountain in the world', Huangshan was chosen by artists in the Ming Dynasty as the classic model of the landscape. In 12 centuries, it has inspired more than 20,000 songs and poems.

159 top and bottom An average humidity of 75% and 94 inches of annual rainfall, mostly concentrated in July, are responsible for Huangshan's 'mystery', creating veils of mist and almost perennial layers of cloud.

Wulingyuan
CHINA

PROVINCE OF HUNAN
REGISTRATION: 1992
CRITERIA: N (III)

BEIJING

*T*ianqiashengkong means 'bridge across the sky' and is the name given by the population of Zhangjianjie village to what is considered the largest natural bridge in the world. It measures 130 feet long, 33 feet wide and 50 feet thick and is protected by two hills that rise 1,150 feet from the bottom of the valley. Yet Tianqiashengkong is only one of the unusual attractions in Wulingyuan, which is an area of such singularity that it is called the 'Labyrinth of Nature'.

It covers 102 square miles around the drainage basin of the Suoxi Torrent.

It is a mountainous area of between 1,500-4,150 feet that is threaded by 60 or so torrents and streams. With the passing of the centuries, erosion by surface water and the abundant rainfall have produced an extraordinary forest of over 3,000 spires of quartzite that stand over 650 feet high and whose composition is 75-95% pure quartz. Running between these spires are picturesque gorges and precipices with waterfalls, pools and lakes.

In the site – named an 'area of historic and landscape interest' by the Chinese government's Council of State in 1988 – there are also vast karstic formations of calcareous rock. In particular, there are roughly 40 caves along the banks of the Suoxi and on the southeast face of Mount Tianzi. Huanglong, or the 'Cave of the Yellow Dragon', is one of the largest in all China; its length of nearly 7 miles contains spectacular deposits of calcite and a waterfall 164 feet high.

160 top The Chinese water deer (Hydropotes inermis) is the only species of deer in which neither males nor females have antlers. Instead the females have long teeth rather like tusks.

Situated in the extreme northeast of the province of Hunan, Wulingyuan has no long history of human settlement, unlike many other areas in China.

In antiquity it was considered a remote and inaccessible place and popular legends tell of a noble of the Han Dynasty who withdrew there to live a life of asceticism. It was only during the Ming Dynasty that the area was cited regularly in official registers and that many descriptions of its beauty and references to its plant life were made in literature.

Wulingyuan is part of the botanical region in central China that is home to roughly 3,000 species, including 600 trees belonging to 252 genera and 94 families, which are equally divided between tropical, subtropical and temperate species. Below 2,200 feet, a community of broadleaf evergreens prevails, with oak, maple and chestnut. As the altitude increases, conifers and deciduous broadleaf trees take over.

The fauna of Wulingyuan officially numbers 116 species of vertebrates, including 12 amphibians, 17 reptiles, 53 birds and 34 mammals, but recent studies indicate these numbers may be too low. Several of these species are threatened by global extinction: the dhole (*Cuon alpinus*), Asiatic black bear (*Selenarctos thibetanus*), Chinese water deer (*Hydropotes inermis*) and the clouded leopard (*Neofelis nebulosa*).

In grave danger is the Chinese giant salamander (*Andrias davidianus*).

To create a habitat to aid its survival, the Chinese authorities built a dam on a branch of the Suoxi to create Lake Baojeng – but today its waters are enjoyed by the many tourists who come here for a day out on a boat.

160-161 Wulingyuan's spectacular landscape is formed by 3,000 quartzite pinnacles more than 650 feet tall that have been sculpted by surface water and the abundant rains that affect the region.

160 bottom Increasingly rare, the Asian black bear (Selenarctos thibetanus) is essentially a carnivore although it has adapted to eating vegetation. An adult male can weigh 400 pounds.

161 top Wulingyuan is known popularly as the 'land of the 800 streams'. In fact there are only 60, most of which flow into the Suoxi River.

161 bottom Although it has the status of a protected animal in China, the clouded leopard (Neofelis nebulosa) is threatened by hunters for its splendid fur and for its bones, which are used in traditional Chinese medicine.

Shirakami-Sanchi

JAPAN

PREFECTURE OF AOMORI AND AKIRA,
REGION OF HONSHU
REGISTRATION: 1993
CRITERIA: N (II)

Respect for the past, for ancestors and tradition is a characteristic of the Japanese and this is why the last beech forest to have survived in the country is looked after with such care and strict conservation regulations. These beech trees, of the species *Fagus crenata*, grow in the Shirakami Mountains in northern Honshu.

The forest is called Shirakami-Sanchi and has been protected since 1992. It is 65 square miles in size and lies in a remote area at between 3,280-3,940 feet in altitude. It suffers cold, snowy winters owing to its proximity to the Sea of Japan and the masses of cold air that arrive from Siberia. From a geomorphological viewpoint, the Shirakami Mountains are formed by sedimentary rocks over a base of granite and were created following strong telluric movements during the Quarternary period. The landscape is a dizzying sequence of ravines and slopes, most of which are steeper than 30 degrees. The rare paths often disappear between the rocks, as there is almost no trace of human presence despite ancient documents alluding to mining during the Daido period at the start of the ninth century. It even seems that the famous statue of the Giant Buddha of Nara was fused using copper mined at Shirakami. The villagers at the foot of the mountains occasionally climb up to the forest to collect mushrooms and medicinal plants, and each year roughly 3,000 sportsmen and hunters climb Mount Huatsamori on the edge of the protected area to perpetuate an ancient bear-hunting ceremony called *Matagi*.

In addition to the beech trees, Shirakami-Sanchi forest has 500 vegetal species. This number is not particularly high if compared to other Japanese mountain areas, but the flora is of great interest for its endemic species, for several plants considered to be in global danger, such as *Hylotelephim tsugaruense* and *Poa ogamontana*, and for unusual varieties of orchids such as *Calanthe discolor*, *Cypripedium yatabeanum* and *Tipularia japonica*.

The trees and rocky spurs are the favorite nesting places of the birds. Of the 87 species that have made the forest their home, some – like the black woodpecker (*Dryocopus martius*), golden eagle (*Aquila chrysaetos*) and hawk eagle (*Spizaetus nipalensis*) – are on the International Union for the Conservation of Nature's Red List and have been awarded the status of National Monument in Japan. This title has also been conferred upon two mammals that live in Shirakami: the serow (*Capricornis crispus*), a large primitive looking herbivore, and the Japanese dormouse (*Glirulus japonicus*), which is a nocturnal rodent that hibernates in the hollows of trees, rolled up into a ball.

Considering animals and plants as National Monuments (on a level with the pagodas of Kyoto) is an attitude explained by the philosophies of the Far East. Their protection is, for the Japanese, imperative and is instilled in the conscience of each individual. So much so that in 1981, well before the protected area was set up, a battle was won by the local population against the authorities that had approved the construction of a road to join the prefectures of Aomori and Akira, but which would most certainly have endangered the environmental balance.

TOKYO

162 left The beech trees of the Fagus crenata species dominate typical Japanese temperate forests. Unfortunately, the 65 square miles of Shirakami-Sanchi are the last remaining shred of primary forest in the country.

162 top right A recent discovery is that the Harlequin duck (Histrionicus histrionicus), a multicolored sea duck, nests on the Akaishi River in the Shirakami Mountains.

163 Having adapted to living in cold climates, the population of the Japanese macaque (Macaca fuscata) has been decimated over the last few decades by deforestation and illegal hunting and the creature is now on the IUCN's Red List.

Royal Chitwan National Park

NEPAL

TERAI
REGISTRATION: 1984
CRITERIA: N (II) (III) (IV)

164 bottom A female Asian rhinoceros in the tall grass with her offspring. Pregnancy lasts 480 days for this species and a baby rhino weighs 150 pounds at birth. Females reach sexual maturity at four years of age and the males at nine.

164-165 Covering 360 square miles of southwest Nepal on the border with India, Chitwan National Park was for centuries a hunting reserve for the exclusive use of the Nepalese monarchs. Today it is home to wildlife that is rare in the rest of Asia.

Rhinoceros unicornis is the scientific name of the one-horned Asiatic rhinoceros, a species of which only 1,800 remain. Around 450 of these live south of the Rapti River on the Terai Plain in Nepal. This area was declared a protected area in 1963 on the initiative of Mahendra, the king of Nepal. Ten years later, the refuge of the rhinoceros was included in the first Nepalese national park, the Royal Chitwan.

In addition to Nepal, this large mammal lives in the Indian states of Bengal and Assam. It can reach a length of 14 feet, a height of nearly 7 feet and have a weight of nearly 9,000 pounds. Its very size made it the most highly prized trophy during big game hunting by the Nepalese sovereigns and their court. In fact, the area of the Royal Chitwan – which covers 360 square miles and is bounded by the

Churia Hills and the Rapit, Reu and Narayani Rivers – was for centuries reserved exclusively for the hunting pleasure of the royal family in Katmandu.

The Royal Chitwan National Park (*chitwan* is the Newari word for 'in the heart of the forest') has a subtropical monsoon climate. Nearly three quarters is covered by deciduous forests of sal trees (*Shorea robusta*) and another fifth by grasslands where roughly 50 species of herbaceous plants grow. The most common are elephant grasses (*Saccharum spontaneum* and *Saccharum bengalensis*), which can reach a height of 26 feet, and species of a rather smaller size in the genus *Imperata*, which are largely used by the local peoples to build roofs, mats and paper. Along the banks of the rivers abound *Trewia nudiflora*, *Bombax cieba*, *Dalbergia sissoo* and *Acacia catechu*,

KATHMANDU

165 top left The single horn on the Asian rhino (Rhinoceros unicornis) measures up to 21 inches in length.

165 top right There are roughly 450 rhinos in Nepal. To protect them from poaching, the government has employed 700 armed rangers.

165 bottom The quiet waters of the Rapti are disturbed by the backs of two rhinos. These mammals love to live in solitude and can become aggressive. Despite their human protection, a frequent cause of death is the fights held between males in high density areas.

166 top Common in
Nepal, India, Myanmar,
Bhutan and Bangladesh,
the entello
(Semnopithecus
entellus) also lives in
urbanized areas. It is also
called the Hanuman after
the Hindu monkey god.

166 bottom left
The sambar (Cervus
unicolor) is the most
magnificent deer in the
subcontinent, as well as
being the favorite prey of the
Bengal tiger. The males
have impressive antlers that
can reach 3 feet in length.

while on the tops of the Churia Hills
there are forests of sal and *Pinus
roxburghii.*

Besides the Asian rhinoceros, the
Royal Chitwan offers refuge to another
mammal on the Red List of species in
danger drawn up by the International
Union for the Conservation of Nature,
the famous Bengal tiger (*Panthera tigris
tigris*). About 100 of reproduction age
live in the park, which represent a
quarter of the continental total.

The Royal Chitwan is also home to
about 50 species of mammals,
including the Indian elephant (*Elephas
maximus*), the gaur (*Bos gaurus*), the
susu (*Platanista gangetica*) and five

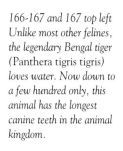

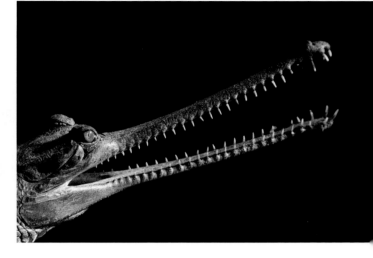

species of antelope. There are also 500 types of bird and 45 amphibians and reptiles. The latter include the gavial (*Gavialis gangeticus*), which is also considered threatened with extinction.

The Royal Chitwan is one of the most closely studied natural areas in Asia. Since it was instituted, and the consequent ban on hunting, the population of rhinoceroses and tigers has quadrupled and their territory has become the center of many studies and monitoring projects. Nonetheless, the growing demographic pressure on the Terai Plain and the industrialization that Nepal is undergoing threatens the unity of the park.

On one hand, a dangerous interaction has developed between man and wandering animals like the elephant; on the other, industrial waste has caused pollution that has caused the extinction of the susu in the Narayani River and a notable reduction in its numbers in other water courses. Conservation of the Royal Chitwan therefore looks like it is becoming a difficult challenge.

Sagarmatha National Park

NEPAL

KHUMBU
REGISTRATION: 1979
CRITERIA: N (III)

They walk barefoot in the snow and are amazingly strong and adapted to the inclement climate. They enjoy long lives and are a peaceful, pragmatic people who follow the philosophy of Tibetan Buddhism to the letter. They are the Sherpa, the 'people who came from the east', who live in the Nepalese region of Khumbu on the slopes of the world's highest mountain, Everest. They arrived here from Kham in eastern Tibet at the end of the sixteenth century, having crossed Nangpa La pass at a height of 19,350 feet.

To the Sherpa, mountains are sacred and in ancient times they considered climbing them a blasphemous act. Everest – at 29,029 feet high – in their language was called *Chomolangma*, the 'mother-goddess', to whom was attributed the role of supreme deity in the Himalayas. The region of Khumbu, most of which lies in Sagarmatha National Park (the Nepalese name for Everest), encloses three mountains over the magic figure of 26,246 feet: they are Lhotse (27,940 feet), Cho Oyu (29,906 feet) and of course Everest itself.

About 3,500 Sherpa live within the boundaries of the world's highest park and their livelihood has been increasingly dependent on mountain tourism since 1953, when Everest was first climbed by the New Zealander Edmund Hillary and Tenzing Norgay, the first Sherpa to violate the sacred mountain. Forty years later, the first woman to reach the summit was Pasang Lhamu.

Sagarmatha National Park covers an area of 443 square miles. It contains glaciers, ravines, wide valleys and the sources of two rivers (the Dudh Kosi and the Bhote Kosi). The lowest point in the park is at a height of 9,343 feet and traveling from there up to the peaks one passes through four different climatic zones. In the first grow juniper, birch, fir, bamboo and rhododendrons that grow up to 30 feet in height. The blooming of the rhododendrons in March and April is one of the most spectacular sights in the region. The second climatic zone is dominated by dwarf trees and bushes, then higher up plant life is restricted to mosses and lichen before disappearing altogether around 18,700 feet where lies the permanent snowline.

The lowest section of Sagarmatha offers an ideal habitat to 118 species of birds and many mammals. Common are the musk deer (*Moschus moschiferus*) and the tahr (*Hemitragus jemlahicus*), which is a beardless mountain goat with short horns that curve backwards. But

Sagarmatha is not really a park for observation purposes. Many of its most interesting inhabitants are both rare and shy, like the snow leopard (*Felis uncia*), the Himalayan black bear (*Selenarctos tibetanus*) and a species of panda with tawny fur (*Ailurus fulgens*). With the arrival of the monsoon season, the park is populated by 26 species of butterfly.

In recent years, even the paradise that surrounds the roof of the world has suffered from environmental problems. Although the Sherpa are very respectful of their land, the many climbing expeditions have left behind them tons of waste that have attracted the attention and protests of ecological groups. Various clean-up campaigns have been conducted and an annual limit on the number of expeditions is being considered, but there is another threat lying in wait: the shrinking of the glaciers caused by global climate change will not spare even the sacred mountains of the Himalayas.

168 left The snow leopard (Leo uncia) is the shyest feline in the world. It is estimated that there are now only 4,000 living wild. The most serious problems to its survival are the progressive reduction of its habitat and consequent diminution in the number of its prey.

168-169 The sacredness of the highest points on the planet is represented by chorten, which are the Tibetan and Nepalese equivalents of the Indian stupa. Prayer flags are tied to the chorten so that the wind can spread their invocations across the world.

169 top A little to the south of Mount Everest, Mount Lhotse is a worthy neighbor of the giant. At a height of 27,939 feet, it is the third tallest mountain in the world and one of the most difficult to climb.

169 bottom Seen here from Kala Pattar (18,448 feet), the unmistakable, pyramidal summit of Everest is seen blazing in the dawn light.

Nanda Devi National Park

INDIA

UTTAR PRADESH
REGISTRATION: 1988
CRITERIA: N (III) (IV)

More important than the fact that it is the second highest mountain in India, to the country's inhabitants, Nanda Devi is the earthly manifestation of the goddess Parvati, Shiva's consort. Hindus in the Himalayan region of Gharwal have worshiped this mountain since the twelfth century and to climb it is an act of sacrilege. However, to the more pragmatic British, at 25,646 feet Nanda Devi had the role of being the Empire's tallest mountain and, as such, it had a particular fascination for explorers.

Since the end of the nineteenth century, many attempts have been made

DELHI

170 top and bottom Nanda Devi East (24,390 feet) and another dozen or so peaks over 19,700 feet form a crown of mountains with a circumference of 80 miles.

170-171 Since 1987 the park has been included in the Indian government's plans to safeguard the snow leopard (Panthera uncial), which, according to the local people, is actually very common.

to force a path over the crown of mountains (almost all over 19,600 feet) that forms a ring around Nanda Devi of roughly 80 miles. But these attempts were in vain; it seemed that the legend of its inviolability was actually of divine origin. Almost four decades passed from the first attempt until the Englishmen Bill Tilman and Eric Shipton found a path near the base of the mountain through the narrow gorge of the Rishi Ganga River. Two years later, in 1936, Tilman managed to reach the top accompanied by Noel Odell. For 14 years, Tilman and Odell could claim to

be the humans to have climbed highest on earth, until Annapurna in Nepal was climbed in 1950. Worried about the impact of man on the environment in the area of Nanda Devi, in 1982 the Indian government instituted the Nanda Devi National Park, thereby putting an end to the indiscriminate use of the mountain as a gym for extreme sports.

Measuring 243 square miles, this park is today considered one of the most dramatic and wildest environments in the entire Himalayan chain. It encloses the huge glacial basin of the Rishi Ganga that is divided into a series of mountain crests that run north to south. Some of these form the Nanda Devi crown: they are Dunagiri (23,182 feet), Changbang (22,520 feet) and Trisul (23,359 feet). The upper Rishi Valley, also known as the Inner Sanctuary, contains four glaciers and is separated by Nanda Devi

of birch (*Betula utilis*) leads into communities of low alpine vegetation and, at the entrance to the Inner Sanctuary, junipers (*Juniperus pseudosabina*) predominate before being replaced by herbaceous plants, mosses and lichens.

from the lower Rishi Valley (the Outer Sanctuary).

The highest parts of the Rishi basin are entirely covered by snow for six months of the year and, in the lower sections, the protection provided by the mountains has created an unusually humid microclimate that has given rise to a rich and varied vegetation. Close to the gorge there is an area of fir forest (*Abies pindrow*) and rhododendrons (*Rhododendron campanulatum*) that rise to a height of 11,000 feet. From here a belt

The park's fauna has not yet been studied systematically. There are many birds and among the mammals, hoofed animals predominate. It is supposed there is a strong community of Himalayan oxen and brown bears. And, most importantly, people living at the edges of the protected area report that the rarely seen snow leopard is 'very common'. For this reason, since 1987, Nanda Devi National Park has been included in the government project to safeguard this animal.

171 top Included in the IUCN's Red List of endangered species, the tahr (Hemiotragus jemlahicus) is on the increase in Nanda Devi thanks to the park's ban on human activities.

171 bottom Nanda Devi has an abundance of hoofed animals. One of these is the rare bharal (Pseudois nayaur), of which there are about 1,000.

Kaziranga National Park

INDIA

ASSAM
REGISTRATION: 1985
CRITERIA: N (II) (IV)

The Brahmaputra is one of the great rivers of Asia. It begins its 1,864-mile journey towards the Gulf of Bengal on Mount Kailash in western Tibet. Kailash is the mountain that Buddhists and Hindus worship as the incarnation of Meru, the mystical mountain at the center of the universe. At the start of its course, the river rushes impetuously through the Himalayan Plateau forging gorges and dividing into myriad streams that meet up again in the great plain.

For the state of Assam, one of the most remote in India, the Brahmaputra represents both life and death. It is so powerful that it is capable of altering the morphology of the landscape, bringing destruction during the monsoon season (from May to September) and bringing fertility to the soil during the dry season. Its basin and vast sandy areas are in continual evolution and are among the last habitats for species at risk like the Asiatic rhinoceros and the Bengal tiger.

In order to safeguard this fauna, in 1975 the government of Assam instituted Kaziranga National Park, which is considered one of the last untouched areas on the subcontinent owing to the total absence of human settlements within its boundaries – an oddity given the overpopulation in India as a whole. When it was founded, Kaziranga covered 166 square miles but, according to recent estimates, the action of the river has reduced the surface area to 146 square miles. During the summer monsoon, there is an average of 86 inches of rainfall, causing floods and subsequent huge green areas. The fauna is able to survive these events by taking refuge in the Miri Hills or on the Karbi Plateau. But in exceptional years, the floods put the wildlife's existence at risk. During the last floods, in 1998, in just a few hours 70% of the park was covered with water, drowning 38 rhinoceroses, 1000 antelope, three baby elephants, two tigers and many other animals.

Nonetheless, there is optimism regarding the number and the composition of the animal populations in Kaziranga. Today, there are 1,250 rhinos. This is a great success, considering that in 1908, the year in which hunting was banned in this area, there were just a few dozen. There are also 1,100 Indian elephants and 86 tigers, besides a great number of ungulates, primates and reptiles. The birdlife includes 300 species; one third of these are migratory birds that arrive during the winter from as far as away as Siberia to populate the areas around the alluvial pools that teem with fish and insects.

Rainforests cover 29% of the park; the rest is covered by sand, water (12% during the dry season) and huge grassy areas as a result of thousands of years of flooding. The grassy areas are kept healthy partly by controlled fires started

172 top left The wet tropical forest is one of the three principal ecosystems in the park and covers 29% of the park's surface.

172 center The park is home to the world's largest population of rhinos (Rhinoceros unicornis), with 1,250 individuals.

by the Kaziranga staff.

These people have recently been praised by the Indian government and non-governmental organizations that monitor the protected area. With a great many belonging to the Mikir people, who have always lived around this ecosystem, they are utterly committed to the protection of the fauna, organizing spontaneous patrols to flush out rhinoceros poachers. And this despite the very low pay they receive and the scarce interest of the local authorities, who are more involved in the consequences of the war of independence waged by various ethnic groups against the state of Assam.

172 bottom With the arrival of the monsoon, the elephants head towards the hills to escape the flooding of the Brahmaputra Plain.

172-173 Kaziranga has a population of 700 water buffalo (Bubalus bubalis). Hunting was banned in the park in 1908.

172 bottom left An egret from the species Bubulcus ibis has chosen the nose of a large male sambar (Cervus unicolor) as a perch.

172 bottom right The Assam macaque (Macaca assamensis) is common in India, Nepal, Bhutan and southeast Asia. It generally lives in groups of 10-50 and has complex social behavior.

Manas Wildlife Sanctuary

INDIA

ASSAM
REGISTRATION: 1985
INSCRIPTION IN THE WORLD HERITAGE IN
DANGER LIST: 1992
CRITERIA: N (II) (III) (IV)

174 left The habitat of the golden langur (Presbyis geei) is restricted to the Manas Wildlife Sanctuary and its adjacent zones in Bhutan. The last census, taken in 1980, estimated the population to be about 300.

DELHI

Since the end of the 1980s, the state of Assam has fought to obtain independence from the Indian government. This is one of the world's many forgotten guerrilla wars, accounts of which are only published in the subcontinent. However, the terrorist actions of the various armed factions of the Bodo (the largest ethnic group in Assam) have produced many civilian victims, as have the counteractions of the Indian army, and have undermined the fragile economy of that remote area.

Another victim of the war is the Manas Wildlife Sanctuary. This protected area covers 193 square miles and lies at the heart of the vast territory covered by Project Tiger. This is an initiative taken by the Indian government and the World Wildlife Fund to save the tiger.

The Bodo guerrillas have carried out sabotage on the territory, including poaching, starting fires and murdering park rangers. For this reason, UNESCO voted to place Manas on the World Heritage in Danger list in 1992. In 1997,

the Indian government set aside 2.35 million dollars in a plan to rehabilitate the area, which currently is producing satisfactory results although the area beyond its boundaries is still being exploited by the population at an unsustainable level.

Created in 1928, the Manas Wildlife Sanctuary is the place in India that contains the highest number of species on the International Union for the Conservation of Nature's Red List. Besides the tiger (*Panthera tigris*), there are 55 species of mammals, including many felines typical of the wetlands of Southeast Asia and a variety of monkeys. The latter number just a few hundred of an endemic species of langur (*Presbytis geei*) and the hoolock gibbon (*Hylobates hoolock*). Also of interest from a conservation viewpoint is the dwarf pig (*Sus salvanius*) and the Asian rhinoceros (*Rhinocerus unicornis*); while it has been estimated that the area is a stable home to roughly 1,000 elephants, as well as to the 2,000 that periodically cross into the sanctuary from the adjacent Royal Manas National Park in Bhutan. The inventory of the species also includes various snakes, amphibians and 450 species of birds, one of which is the highly rare hornbill.

This wealth of fauna is made possible

by the dynamic flora in Manas, despite the dangers offered by man. Situated in the pre-Himalayan plain, the territory receives abundant rainfall and has an average humidity index of 76% year round. The land is in continual evolution owing to the mass of mud and detritus carried by the Manas River (which divides Assam from Bhutan and then flows into the Brahmaputra about 40 miles downstream from the protected area) and by the other torrential watercourses that also create a number of pools. Around 55% of the zone is covered by grass and the rest by an

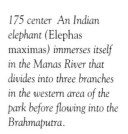

evergreen tropical forest and wet and dry deciduous tropical forests. These latter are dominated by trees like Bombax *ceiba* and *Sterculia villosa*, while luxuriant aquatic flora lines the banks of the rivers and pools. In all, 393 species of dicotyledons have been identified in Manas, including 197 forest trees and 98 species of monocotyledons.

174-175 In the past distributed as far west as the Khyber Pass, the Indian rhinoceros (Rhinoceros unicornis) now has its only refuges in certain areas of Nepal and India. It is thought that there are no more than a dozen in Manas Wildlife Sanctuary.

175 top This unusual species of fig, with a bark similar to the wrinkly skin of the elephant, clings to other trees for support, strangling them to death.

175 center An Indian elephant (Elephas maximas) immerses itself in the Manas River that divides into three branches in the western area of the park before flowing into the Brahmaputra.

175 bottom A solitary hunter and feared man-eater, and for this latter reason hunted ruthlessly down to about 80 individuals in Manas, the Bengal tiger (Panthera tigris tigris) is the subject of a large conservation program launched by the World Wildlife Fund and Indian government.

Keoladeo National Park

INDIA

BHARATPUR, RAJASTHAN
REGISTRATION: 1985
CRITERIA: N (IV)

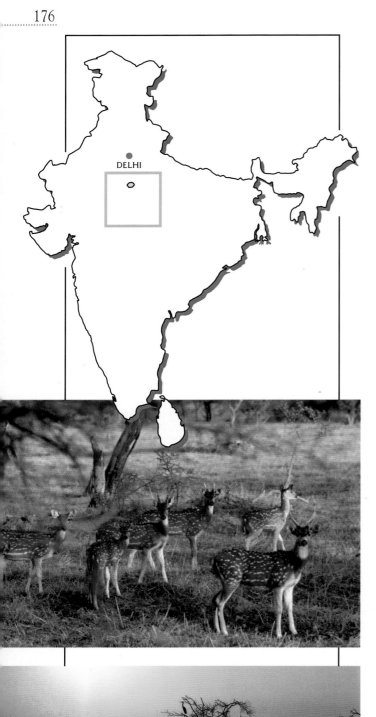

Unsurprisingly, it was the ancient temple of Keoladeo dedicated to Shiva, the Hindu god that creates and destroys, after which one of the most extraordinary protected areas in the subcontinent was named, as it was brought back to life following destructive modifications made to the landscape by man. Now its 11 square miles are a favorite stopping area for migrating birds.

Keoladeo National Park lies close to the edge of the Rajasthan city of Bharatpur and is not a 'natural environment' in the strict sense. Man has molded the countryside in an attempt to save Bharatpur from flooding caused by the monsoons. As early as 1760, the local maharajah had a dam built at Ajan on the edge of a depression in the land to create a lake. Then, at the start of the twentieth century a system of dikes and locks was added to allow the level of the water in the different sections of the lake to be controlled.

These building projects transformed the area into a series of bogs, marshes and meadowland that became a refuge for many species of birds. In consequence, the maharajahs of Bharatpur decreed the zone a duck shooting reserve that attracted famous foreign guests, for example, the British viceroy Lord Curzon. When India gained independence in 1948, Keoladeo became a bird sanctuary but the maharajahs retained shooting rights until 1972. In 1981 Keoladeo was finally awarded the status of a national park.

From September to February the reserve is home to approximately 1 million birds of over 360 migrating

176 top left The axis deer (Cervus axix) with its white-spotted fawn coat, is one of the world's loveliest deer.

176 bottom left Keoladeo is a mosaic of marshes created by man in the eighteenth century.

176 top right The rhesus monkey (Macaca mulatta) is one of the two primate species found in the park.

176 bottom right The trees in Keoladeo are always crowded with birds such as ibis, cormorants and cranes.

177 The water meadows in the park are inhabited by babul trees (Acacia nilotica) and many aquatic plants that form the basis of the diet of many birds.

species, from the gigantic Dalmatian pelican (*Pelecanus crispus*) – which has a wingspan of over 6 feet – to the minuscule Siberian chiffchaff (*Phylloscopus collybita tristis*), which is no longer than a small finger.

Cormorants, egrets, ibises, ducks and cranes arrive from Russia, Europe, China, Mongolia and the plains of Siberia.

A special attraction in the Park is the Siberian crane (*Grus leucogeranus*) – one of the rarest birds on the planet – of

which there are now just a few hundred in existence. To spend the winter here, it flies 425 miles over Afghanistan and Pakistan from the basin of the Ob River.

The park's wealth of microfauna, fish and aquatic flora (such as lotus plants and water lilies) also attracts numerous species of non-migratory birds, like the kingfisher, woodpecker, golden oriole and several species of pigeon.

With the arrival of the summer monsoons, another great spectacle begins in Keoladeo: the nesting of 17 species of heron, which collect in a very restricted area where the *babul* tree (*Acacia nilotica*) is prevalent. Up to 100 nests belonging to several different species will be built in each tree; the pairs choose to live so

close together to unite their forces to defend their young against predators like the peregrine falcon and imperial eagle.

Life in the park is not limited to its birds. Keoladeo is also home to mammals of naturalistic interest like the Bengal fox (*Vulpes bengalensis*), the golden jackal (*Canis aureus*), the boar (*Sus scrofa*) and the black buck (*Antilope cervicapra*). Among the reptiles, there is also an abundant population of pythons.

Being such a superb birdwatching site, Keoladeo receives hundreds of thousands of visitors each year, who represent an important source of income to the local inhabitants.

Of the many varied services offered, visitors can enjoy birdwatching excursions in a traditional rickshaw.

178 top The sarus crane (Grus antigone) is featherless on the upper part of its neck and red head, and is renowned for its complicated courting ritual.

178 bottom The painted stork (Mycteria leucocephala) is one of the many species of waders that live in the park. Another is the Siberian crane, one of the most rare birds on the planet.

178-179 Seen on top of a tree with their wings spread are two painted storks in all their beauty.

179 bottom A visitor to Keoladeo in the winter months, the bar-headed goose (Anser indicus) spends the rest of the year in the Himalayas where it has been seen flying even over Mount Everest.

Sinharaja Forest Reserve

SRI LANKA

PROVINCE OF SABARAGAMUWA AND
SOUTHERN PROVINCE
REGISTRATION: 1988
CRITERIA: N (II) (IV)

COLOMBO

In the *Enumeratio plantarum Zelaniae*, published around 1860, George Henry Thwaites illustrated the results of a decade of study of the innumerable botanical species he had recorded during his stay on the island that was then called Ceylon. About 20 years later, the soldier and ornithologist Vincent Legge published the book 'The History of the Birds of Ceylon'. Both often referred to the forest of Sinharaja, the last tropical rainforest on the island where they found respectively plants and birds that had never been described elsewhere.

The name, Sinharaja, of what in 1875 had already been registered as a forest reserve belonging to the British Crown, means 'the Lion King'. The local people still pass down a legend in which a lion that lived in a cave on Mount Sinhagala (the highest peak in the region) ruled over a huge territory until a giant managed to kill it, thereby releasing the local inhabitants from a terrible threat, though in fact Sinhagala does not have caves and lions have never been seen in Sri Lanka.

The Sinharaja Forest Reserve is not quite 30 square miles in size and is exceptional for its biodiversity. It is composed of a thin band of hills and valleys that range in height between 980 and 3,800 feet, between which flows an intricate network of streams that run into the Gin Ganga River, to the south, and the Kalu Ganga River, to the north. Over the last 60 years, the registered rainfall has never been less than 143 inches and has reached a maximum of 196 inches.

Isolation from the subcontinent has undoubtedly provided Sri Lanka with its own evolutionary processes, traces of which are evident in the incredible vegetation of Sinharaja. There are two separate communities: at the lower altitudes there are forests of *Dipterocarpus*, while up on the hills the slopes are covered by species of the genus Shorea. Of the island's 217 endemic species, this area contains 139; they are often limited to very restricted areas, as is *Atalantia rotundifolia* or the palm *Loxococcus rupicola*. The variety of flowers is extensive, particularly the orchids, including *Arundina graminifolia* and two species of carnivorous *bandura*.

Of 20 birds, 19 are to be found in Sri Lanka only. And even among the mammals and butterflies the endemic species exceed 50%. Endangered mammals include the leopard (*Panthera pardus*), Indian elephant (*Elephas maximus*) and an endemic primate, the red-nosed langur (*Presbytis senex*), known as 'kola wandura'.

The following are endangered or rare birds: the Sri Lankan pigeon (*Columba*

180 *A gecko (*Cnemaspis kandianus*) merges perfectly with the trunk of a tree. Of the 45 reptiles in Sinharaja, 21 are endemic.*

181 *top Another endemic species is the dangerous tree-dwelling viper* Trimeresurus trigonocephalus. *It can be recognized by its green, yellow and black spotted skin that allows it to hide very effectively among leaves and branches.*

181 *bottom Dominated at low levels by* Dipterocarpus zeylanicus *and* Dipterocarpus hispidus, *and by species of the Shorea genus higher up, Sinharaja is the last strip of primary tropical forest left in Sri Lanka. The park contains 139 endemic botanical species.*

182 top A colony of fungi grows on a tree stump in the undergrowth of Sinharaja. Leaves, fruit, seeds and fungi are some of the most exploited food resources by the inhabitants of nearby villages.

182 center right Five of the eight species of lizard in Sri Lanka are endemic and two of these form their own genus.

182 center left Widespread in India, China, Malaysia, Indonesia and Sri Lanka, the atlas moth (Attacus atlas) is the largest moth in the world.

182 bottom left Nepenthes distillatoria is the more common of the two carnivorous plants in Sinharaja. The insects the plant feeds on get trapped in leaves formed like a sac.

torringtoni), the green coucal (Centropus chlororhynchus), the white-faced starling (Sturnus senex), the Ceylon blue magpie (Cissa ornata) and the red-faced cuckoo (Phaenicophaeus pyrrhocephalus). There are also many endemic or endangered species among the reptiles, amphibians and butterflies.

The greatest threat posed to the forest's fragile habitat is not tourism, as holiday-makers prefer the island's beaches, but the poverty of the roughly 5,000 local inhabitants of the protected area and its immediate surroundings. For them, Sinharaja is an essential source of subsistance. From the coconut palm kitul (Caryota urens) they extract a sugar substitute, the flexible Calamus rushes are exploited as a textile, cardamom (Elattaria ensal) is a spice that is greatly used in local cooking, the Shorea is used to make flour and Coscinium fenestratum is used in traditional medicine. However, the forest reserve suffers mostly from the cutting down of trees for firewood, which may put rare species of inestimable value at risk.

182 bottom right A spring trickles among the ferns in the rainforest. Sinharaja has many surface water resources and streams that all flow into the Gin Ganga or Kalu Ganga Rivers.

183 The bright chrome yellow 'net' of a Dictyophora fungus stands out in the thick forest in Sinharaja.

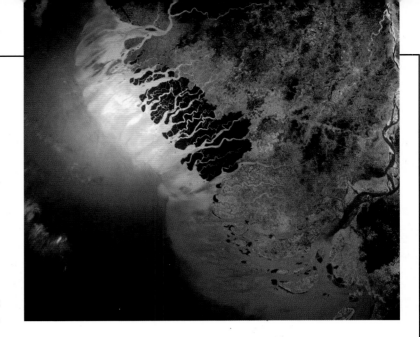

184 top *Photographed from the Columbia space shuttle, this view of the Ganges Delta shows the mangrove forest in the Sundarbans Biosphere Reserve in the darkest area at the center of the picture.*

DHAKA

184-185 *The jaws of a crocodile appear as it suddenly emerges from the brackish waters of the delta; this is the tactic this deceptively slow and lazy creature uses to attack.*

184 bottom *Sundarbans is the name of the largest mangrove forest in the world and is derived from sundri (Heritiera fomes), which is the local name for the species.*

Sundarbans

BANGLADESH

DISTRICT OF KHULNA
REGISTRATION: 1997
CRITERIA: N (II) (IV)

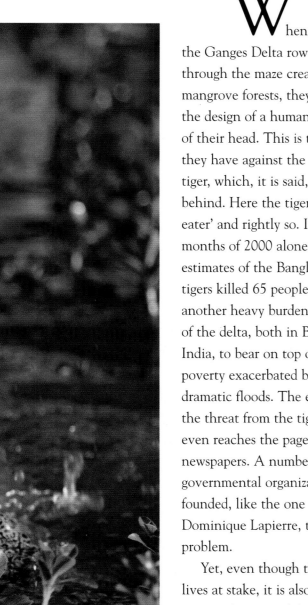

When the fishermen in the Ganges Delta row their wooden boats through the maze created by the mangrove forests, they wear a mask with the design of a human face on the back of their head. This is the only 'defense' they have against the ferocious Bengal tiger, which, it is said, only attacks from behind. Here the tiger is called the 'man-eater' and rightly so. In the first four months of 2000 alone, according to the estimates of the Bangladeshi government, tigers killed 65 people. The danger is yet another heavy burden for the inhabitants of the delta, both in Bangladesh and India, to bear on top of their unrelenting poverty exacerbated by frequent and dramatic floods. The extent and drama of the threat from the tigers is such that it even reaches the pages of foreign newspapers. A number of non-governmental organizations have been founded, like the one by the writer Dominique Lapierre, to grapple with the problem.

Yet, even though there are human lives at stake, it is also necessary to protect this animal for which the Ganges Delta is its last enclave. Zoologists have estimated that in the section of the delta in the state of Bangladesh – of which 540 square miles have been protected by environmental laws since 1977 – 450 tigers are left, and this means that the Bengal tiger is included on the International Union for the Conservation of Nature's list of endangered species. The only way that the threat to man can be diminished is to maintain the balance of the ecosystem and to prevent further portions of the wilderness being transformed into agricultural land.

The Ganges Delta, into which the waters of the Brahmaputra and Meghna Rivers flow to form the Bengal Basin in Bangladesh, is the largest delta on earth. The sandy islands divided by thousands of channels, whose flow depends on the tide and season, provide the location for the largest mangrove forest in the world. The forest is called Sundarbans, from the word sundri, which is the name of the most common species of mangrove (*Heritiera fomes*) in the delta.

The tropical climate is very humid in the Sundarbans. The annual rainfall is 110 inches, most of which falls in the monsoon season from June to October, but it is the cause of a wide biodiversity of 334 arboreal and herbaceous plants belonging to 245 genera (excluding the mangroves). The zone also has an outstanding assortment of wildlife, the largest in the Bengal Basin. Though the

185 top The species of mangroves in the forest vary depending on the salinity of the water. Overall 334 species have been recorded, which represent 245 genera.

185 bottom Below the surface of the water, the roots of the mangroves nourish a complex ecosystem that includes small fish and the larvae of many marine animals.

186 top Only 700 estuary crocodiles (Crocodylus porosus) remain in the Sundarbans Biosphere Reserve. Although the government has slowed illegal hunting, the population shows no sign of recovery.

186 bottom A green egret (Butorides virescens) waits for its meal in shallow water. The bird population in Sundarbans numbers 315 species, 95 of which are aquatic and 38 are birds of prey.

Javan rhinoceros, water buffalo and gaur disappeared from the Sundarbans at the start of the twentieth century, the area has 50 species of mammals, including 60,000 rhesus monkeys (Macaca mulatta), 80,000 spotted deer (Cervus axis) and 20,000 boar, which are the tiger's main prey. There are also three species of wild cat and three types of otter; the otters are trained by the fishermen to help them chase fish into their nets.

Sundarbans is also a bird sanctuary with 315 species, of which 95 are aquatic; there are also large varieties of amphibians and reptiles, of which 19 are snakes. However, what provides the most interest for the 2.5 million inhabitants who live around the protected area is the marine life, as fishing supplies their principal source of food. In addition to the 120 species of fish, there are also a great number of crustaceans, of which the crabs, with a biomass of 155 thousand tons, represent the highest proportion of the Sundarbans total animal biomass. Consequently, the sale of crabs, prawns and lobsters are top of the list of commercial activities in the nearby coastal city of Chittagong.

186-187 With 450 Bengal tigers (Panthera tigris tigris), Sundarbans has the largest population of the creature in the world, but the continual reduction of its habitat puts its future at severe risk.

187 top The Indian python (Python molurus) can reach 21 feet in length; it is one of the 53 species of reptile that live in the park.

Thung Yai and Huai Kha Khaeng
THAILAND

PROVINCES OF KANCHANABURI, TAK AND UTHAI THANI
REGISTRATION: 1991
CRITERIA: N (II) (III) (IV)

In 1988 the footprint of a Javan rhinoceros (*Rhinocerus sondaicus*) was photographed, thereby doing away with the assumption that the large mammal had become extinct in these regions. And recently, a group of 50 banteng (the large bovine *Bos javanicus*) was sighted, which was previously thought to live only on the island of Java, as well as 24 wild water buffalo (*Bufalus arnee*), also a species whose existence was unsuspected. Scientists assure us that new and interesting surprises still lie in store.

Although Thailand is the most developed country in Southeast Asia and is experiencing an economic boom that has led to a dizzying increase in urban and industrial areas, the strip of land along the border with Myanmar (or Burma as it used to be known) is one of the least explored and studied areas in this part of the continent. This virgin land of 2,402 square miles – divided into the Thung Yai Wildlife Sanctuary and the adjacent Huai Kha Khaeng Wildlife Sanctuary – forms the largest protected zone in Thailand.

BANGKOK

188 top With an area of over 2,400 square miles, the natural reserves of Thung Yai and Huai Kha Khaeng together form the largest protected area in Thailand.

188 bottom
The Indochinese tiger (Panthera tigris corbetti) is one of the eight subspecies of this large cat. Its population in the Thai parks is estimated to be around 400-600.

Although recording of the fauna is still at a very early stage, scientists are agreed that the two sanctuaries are the point of contact between Sundaic, Indo-Chinese, Indo-Burmese and Sino-Himalayan species, and that, from a faunal standpoint, the zone is one of the world's most important examples of how the Pleistocene epoch had an impact on the distribution of Asian species. It is thought that Thung Yai and Huai Kha Khaeng are sufficiently large enough to support an increase in the number of rare large mammals such as the Javan rhinoceros, tiger (*Panthera tigris*), leopard (*Pardus pardus*), Asian elephant (*Elephas maximus*), tapir (*Tapirus indicus*) and gaur (*Bos gaurus*).

At the moment the list of animals contains 120 species of mammals, 400 birds, 96 reptiles, 43 amphibians and 113 fish. The fish live in the four rivers of the area – the Mae Khlong, Kwai Yai,

principally dipterocarps. In the southwestern sector and Huai Kha Khaeng there is a greater degree of biodiversity with at least four types of evergreen forest, whose composition varies depending on altitude; the height of the park ranges from 820 feet to the 5,940 feet of Khao Thai Par, the highest point in the protected area.

The Karen people, an ethnic group that has lived in the area for over 300

Mae Kasart and Mae Suriat – as well as the many torrents that flow through the narrow valleys and over the alluvial plains, creating small lakes, pools and marshes. Water is responsible for the creation of deposits of mineral salts that are used as a source of nourishment by many animal species.

The vegetation in Thung Yai (the name is Thai for 'large field') is characterized by herbaceous plants and forests of bamboo and deciduous trees,

years, has developed considerable understanding of the ecosystem and is able to interact with it without damaging it. Nonetheless, soon after the establishment of Thung Yai, the Karen were 'invited' to leave the area by the Thai government. The World Wildlife Fund, on the other hand, launched the Thung Yai Ecology Project, according to which the Karen are fundamental to the study of new species and to future involvement in conservation operations.

Ha Long Bay

VIETNAM

GULF OF TONGKING
REGISTRATION: 1994, 2000
CRITERIA: N (I) (III)

190 top and center Between the Miocene and Pleistocene epochs, intense erosion modelled a huge sandstone plateau into bizarrely shaped pinnacles. At the end of the last Ice Age, the sea invaded the plateau and created the bay of Ha Long.

190 bottom 1,400 yards long and named the 'Tunnel' during the colonial era, Quang Hanh is the largest cave in Ha Long.

The literal translation of Ha Long is 'the place the Dragon entered the sea'. The legend, which was handed down orally until the nineteenth century, says that Ha Long Bay was created during a naval battle between the Viet people and their enemies who sailed down the coast from the north. The Viet were about to lose the battle when the Jade Emperor sent the Mother of all Dragons and one of her young sons to their aid. A huge number of pearls flowed from the dragons' mouths that, on contact with the water, were transformed into beautiful islands that the boats of the enemy ran into and broke upon. And, as the bay was so beautiful, the dragons remained there to live. This story is so rooted in local tradition that fishermen still talk about a giant sea creature that occasionally appears on the surface of the sea.

Human history in this superb bay is given by archeological studies in the caves that have revealed evidence of the first settlements, dating from 25,000 years ago, in what is today Vietnam.

Ha Long is often described as a natural work of art and has inspired verses by many poets. An area of 580 square miles is dotted with 1,969 islands that range in height from 160 to 640 feet, 989 of these islands have been given names that refer to their picturesque morphology, for example, fighting cocks, pairs of swans, human heads and so forth. And many of the islands have underground caves and hollows that provide the habitat for extremely rare species.

Leaving aside the legend, the geological history of Ha Long Bay began around 500 million years ago with orogenetic processes and tectonic shifts. It continued through the Carboniferous and Permian periods (350-240 million years ago) when the zone was occupied by a sea, the bottom of which was formed by a layer of sandstone up to 1,100 yards thick. Over a period of 20 million years from the Miocene to Pleistocene epochs, strong erosion of the sandstone table (which by then had become a coastal plain) gave origin to the formations of schist and sandstone that today emerge in the bay. The return of the water occurred at the end of the last Ice Age around 10,000 years ago.

Ha Long's biodiversity can be divided into three main ecosystems: the tropical

forest and the coastal and marine habitats. The first is typified by an extraordinary variety of botanical species; seven of have been identified by the International Union for the Conservation of Nature as unique in this environment. The forest has 477 species of magnoliophytes, four species of amphibians, eight reptiles, 40 birds and 14 small mammals. The coastal habitat is characterized by 20 varieties of mangrove, whose branches provide shelter to 200 species of birds. And the marine habitat is also very fertile: it contains 170 species of coral (mostly of the genus *Scleractinia*) and 91 algae. The animals include 81 species of gastropods, 130 bivalves, nine crustaceans and 313 fish that feed principally on phytoplankton and zooplankton.

Ha Long's natural ecosystems have recently been joined by an artificial one – fish-breeding – which has caused the destruction of huge areas of mangrove swamp and threatens to alter the biological balance of the bay. And the headlong economic development of Vietnam is exploiting its tourist potential: plans have been made for the construction of a 100 million dollar hotel complex on the island of Tuan Chau.

190-191 There are almost 2,000 islands that range between 160 and 650 feet in height in spectacular Ha Long Bay. Their unusual shapes – with caves hollowed out by sea and rain water – have resulted in their being given traditional picturesque Eastern names.

Tubbataha Reef Marine Park

PHILIPPINES

Palawan Province,
Municipality of Cagayancillo
Registration: 1993
Criteria: N (II) (III) (IV)

MANILA

In February 2002, the coast guards of Puerto Princesa arrested 52 Chinese and nine Philippine poachers on four boats inside the Tubbataha Reef National Park. They also confiscated more than 200 giant mollusks, 54 turtles and a large quantity of dynamite and cyanide. This was only one of an endless stream of poaching episodes that over the last 20 years have placed the habitat of the park in great difficulty. And yet, over the last two years, a growth of 40% has been recorded in the coral reef thanks to the feverish activity of the Philippines World Wildlife Fund and other organizations that have aided in patrolling the protected area.

Seen from the sea, Tubbataha is not much to look at. In all its 12,818 square miles, only two small islands emerge from the surface, though they are surrounded by white sands and fragments of coral. Nor is

there a trace of a human presence. It is underwater, however, that the area is transformed into a world of rare beauty with a biodiversity that places it among the richest environments of marine fauna.

Separated by a canal 5 miles long in the Sulu Sea, the North and South Reefs are the only atolls in the Philippine Archipelago. The first is a coral platform, oblong in shape, that measures 10 miles long by 2.75 miles wide, and which encloses a sandy lagoon that is 78 feet deep. The main strip of land is the North Islet, just 3,500 square yards of coral sand where marine birds and turtles lay their eggs. The South Reef is triangular in shape, about a mile wide, with a lagoon

inside it so shallow that large sections emerge during low tide.

The terrestrial vegetation is limited to a few species but the reef is inhabited by 45 species of benthic macroalgae and by extensive beds of aquatic grasses on the less shallow stretches of the lagoon. On the islands 46 species of birds have been sighted, including two gannets (*Sula leucogaster* and *Sula sula*), the sooty tern (*Sterna fuscata*), the great crested tern (*Sterna bergii*) and the common noddy (*Anous stolidus*). There are also two species of turtle, the green turtle (*Chelonia mydas*) and the hawksbill turtle (*Eretmochelys imbricata*). The reef has an extraordinary diversity, with 300 species of coral belonging to 46 genera that exist at different depths. In deeper water the main platforms are of genera *Pachyseris*, *Leptoseris* and *Montipora*. At depths between 40 and 66 feet, one can observe *Diploastrea*, *Platygyra* and *Porites*, whereas the edge of the reef is formed by *Acropora*.

Equally impressive is the marine fauna, with 379 species belonging to at least 40 families. Divers – who are allowed to enter the park but of course not to hunt or fish – can easily see blacktipped and whitetipped reef sharks (*Carcharinus melanopterus* and *Triaenovon abesus respectively*) and eagle rays and devil rays (*Mobula diabolus*). Particularly numerous are the mollusks with several species of giant clams.

According to conservation experts, who are currently satisfied with the state of the park, Tubbataha coral forest has such a variety of aquatic microorganisms that it plays a fundamental role in the feeding habits of marine fauna in the oceanic area of Palawan Province, and, therefore, in the economy of the entire region.

192-193 It is not rare for the diver in the waters of Tubbatha to be attracted by the bright colors of the frogfish (red in this case but the many species are very varied in hue). They belong to the antennarid family.

192 bottom left A shoal of small catfish (Plotusus lineatus) vibrates with life. The ecosystem on Tubbataha Reef is considered by experts to be vital to all the ocean area in the province of Palawan.

192 bottom right The largest section of the park above sea level is represented by a small island of coral sand that covers just 3,600 square yards. Birds and turtles nest here.

193 top A colony of sea-fans extends delicate ramifications into the current. Tubbataha reef is home to a recorded 46 species of coral.

193 bottom A large barrel sponge is surrounded by cobra fish (Pterois antennata). With 379 species belonging to at least 40 families and 300 species of coral, the biodiversity gives Tubbataha one of the richest oceanic ecosystems in the world.

Kinabalu National Park

MALAYSIA

BORNEO, STATE OF SABAH
REGISTRATION: 2000
CRITERIA: N (II) (IV)

194 top Weighing 20 pounds and 4.5 feet in diameter, Rafflesia arnoldii is the largest flower on the planet.

'A Hollywood creation' is the term most commonly associated with *Rafflesia arnoldii*, the largest flower in nature. It has a bright red fleshy mass , reaches 3 feet in diameter, can weigh 20 pounds and does not have a pleasant smell. To see it in all its splendor is not an easy task as *Rafflesia arnoldii* is a parasite, without roots or leaves, and can only germinate at the base of Tetrasigma, a woody stem of the vine family. It grows for an entire year and then blooms during a single rainy night, lasting just one week before withering.

The flower was named as a tribute to Sir Thomas Stanford Raffles (1781-

1826), the enterprising Englishman who founded the city of Singapore. It was, however, discovered by the botanist Joseph Arnold, who accompanied Raffles on many expeditions to the island of Borneo.

It is easy to imagine his amazement on finding this extraordinary plant in the jungle on the slopes of Mount Kinabalu, and time has not diminished its interest to scientists. Today 16 species of *Rafflesia* have been identified, the last of which was in 1988. Apart from the occasional example found on Sumatra, *Rafflesia* is considered native to Borneo.

This is the location of Mount

Kinabalu, the highest mountain in Southeast Asia at 13,435 feet.

Its morphology is the result of volcanic and tectonic activity that took place about 1.5 million years ago, sedimentary processes during the Tertiary period and erosion from glaciation. If that were not enough, scientists have recently recorded a growth in the mountain of a fifth of an inch a year.

The national park that encloses Mounts Kinabalu, Tambuyukon (8,461 feet) and Templer (3,719 feet) and their surrounding countryside contains one of the most profuse ranges of flora on earth. In addition to giants like *Rafflesia arnoldii*

194 bottom left At 13,345 feet, Kinabalu is the highest mountain in Southeast Asia. Its slopes are lined with rainforests that are differentiated biologically depending on altitude.

194 bottom right The many botanical species on Kinabalu include nine carnivorous plants of the Nepenthes genus, 4 of which are endemic to the park.

195 top Langanan Waterfall in the center of the park makes seven leaps, the last of which is a spectacular 490 feet.

195 bottom The wrinkled summit of Kinabalu is deeply furrowed by erosion from ancient glaciers that created moraines, U-shaped valleys and cirques. According to geological estimates, the mountain is growing at a speed of four-tenths of an inch per year.

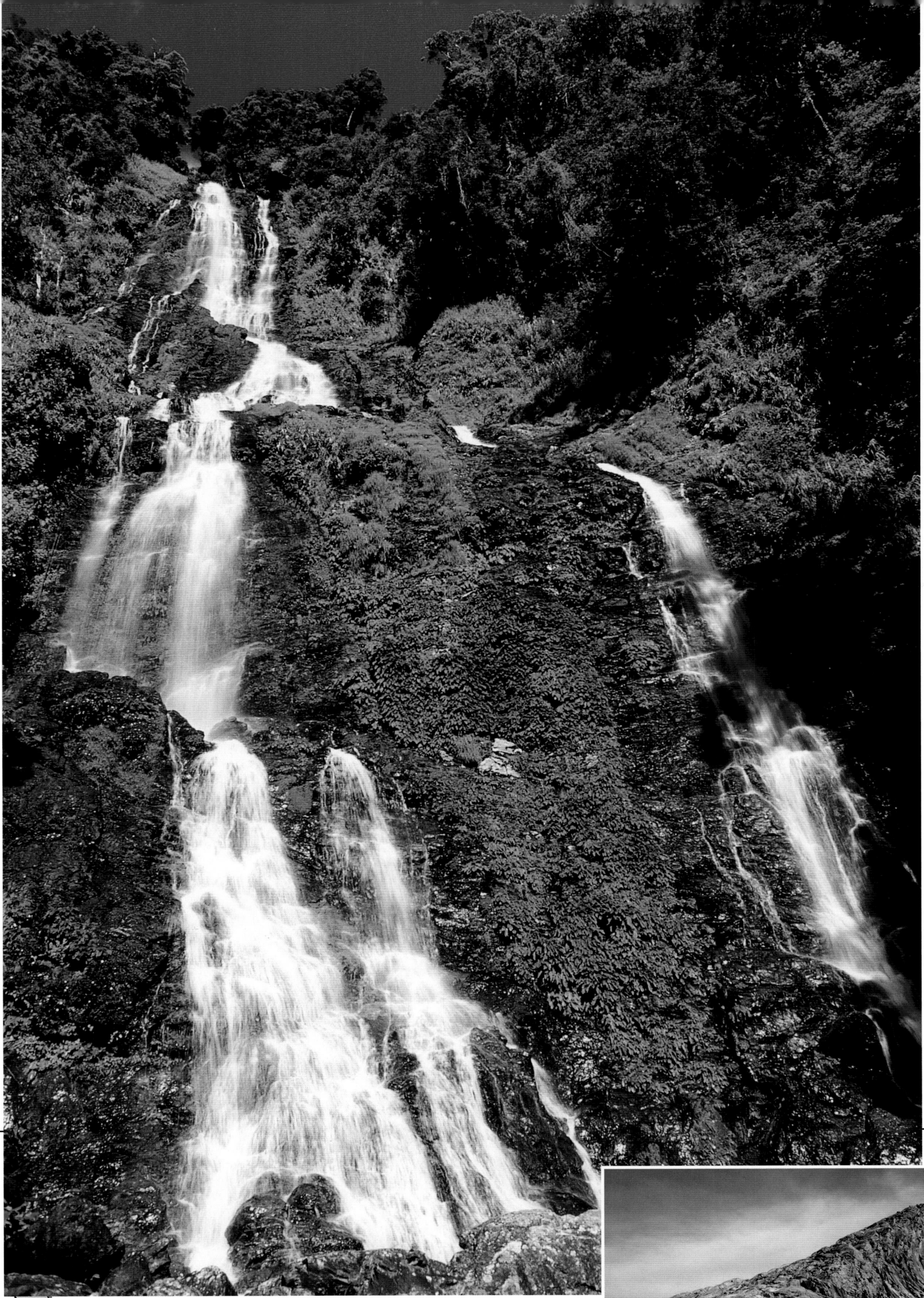

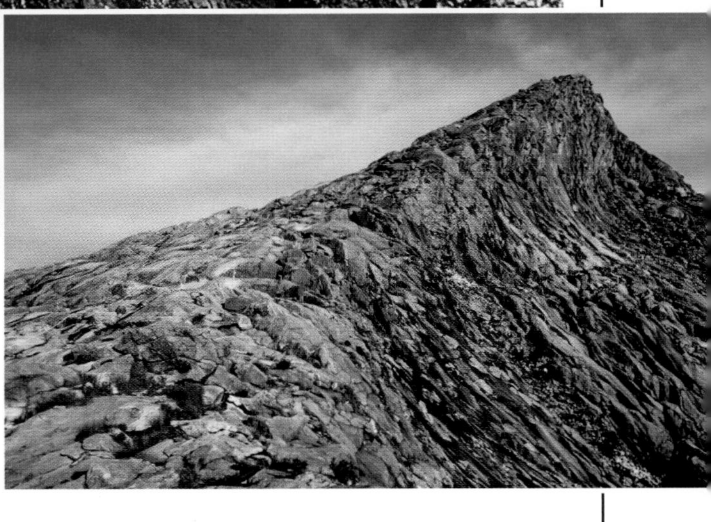

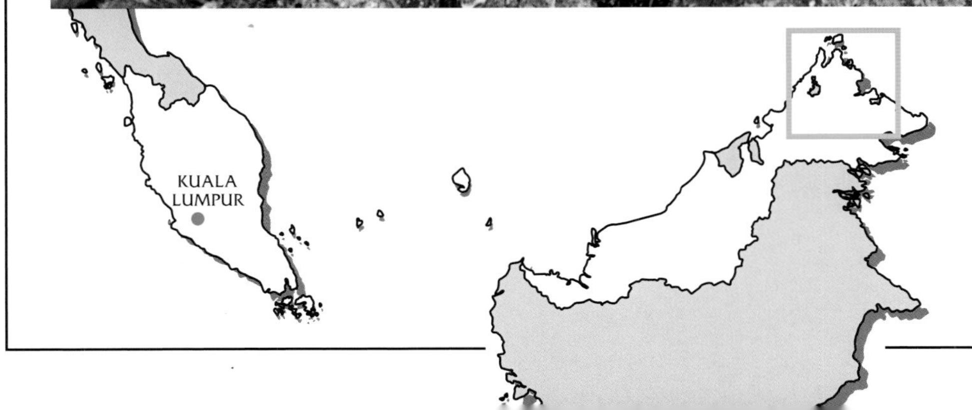
KUALA
LUMPUR

196 A colony of 120 orangutans (Simia satyrus) lives on Kinabalu. This number is all that remains after drastic reduction caused by fires (which devastated Borneo) and poaching.

197 top left A tree-dwelling primate that lives mainly on fleshy fruits, during periods of scarcity the orangutan gets by on tree bark.

197 top right Generally described as solitary primates, orangutans tend to socialize during the mating season and where there are large food resources.

197 bottom Territorial animals, orangutans occupy large areas (from 100 acres to 2.5 square miles) and the territory of each overlaps with that of others.

and the largest insect-eating plant in the world (Nepenthes rajah), roughly 6,000 species belonging to 200 families and 1,000 genera have been cataloged, with a high number of endemic plants. There are 1,000 types of orchid, 24 rhododendrons, 52 palms, 135 Ficus and 608 ferns. Botanists consider it a point of convergence of the genera of China and the Himalayas with those of Australia and New Zealand and even find affinities there with plants from the American continent.

Inside the park, six zones at levels between 500 feet and the top of Kinabalu contain a large variety of fauna. There are 90 species of mammal that live at low levels and 22 mountain species, including colonies of orangutan and other primates. The birds and butterflies are particularly profuse with 326 and 200 species respectively.

Kinabalu is also a sacred mountain to the Dusun and Kazadan peoples. Its name is derived from the Kazadan words Aki and Nabalu, which together mean 'the Sacred Place of the Dead'. This sanctuary was the theater of what was

sadly known as the Sandakan-Ranu march of death. In September 1944 the Japanese army made 2,400 British and Australian prisoners-of-war walk 150 miles through the jungle. Only six survived. On his return home, one of the survivors, Major Carter of the British army, founded the Kinabalu Memorial Committee. In the United Kingdom, interest for the area led to the organization of many naturalistic expeditions financed by the Royal Society, which, in 1964, resulted in the creation of the National Park.

Gunung Mulu National Park

MALAYSIA

BORNEO, STATE OF SARAWAK

REGISTRATION: 2000

CRITERIA: N (I) (II) (III) (IV)

KUALA
LUMPUR

T o provide an idea of the size of the Cave of the Deer, scientists do not simply give its dimensions – 1.25 miles long, 490 feet wide and between 260 and 394 feet high – instead they let their imaginations run free, calculating that it could easily accommodate five cathedrals or 20 Boeing 747s. The Cave of the Deer is the largest underground corridor in the world but its claims to fame do not end there: thanks to its wide opening in the side of the Gunung Api peak, the light that filters inside allows thick tropical vegetation to grow up to 546 yards from the surface; in addition it is home to a population of 3 million bats which, at dusk, fly out together into the forest in search of food, creating a spectacular black river that flows up into the sky uninterruptedly for about an hour.

If that were not enough, the nearby Cave of Good Fortune has a chamber

that measures 1,968 feet long, 1,361 wide and 262 high. In other words, it is the most capacious in the world. And then in the Cave of Clear Water – 67 miles long – there is an enormous stalactite in an unusual form owing to the influence of a constant subterranean breeze. In short, the Gunung Mulu massif is considered to be the mountain with the most cavities in the world. So far 183 miles of caves and tunnels have been explored and it is thought that these represent only one third of the total.

At 7,800 feet high, Gunung Mulu is the tallest peak in the massif (which includes the more modest Gunung Api and Gunung Benarat). It is composed of white and gray sandstone perforated by karstic phenomena that happened between 2 and 5 million years ago, and, on the exterior it appears like a forest of razor-sharp pinnacles caused by the erosive action of the tropical rains over

the millennia. However, the extraordinary geological and geomorphological features of Gunung Mulu are matched by its exceptional biodiversity, as a result of which in 1974 the Malaysian government turned the area into the Gunung Mulu National Park. The park covers 204 square miles and is divided into 17 vegetative zones in which 3,500 species of vascular plant grow. The thick forest that covers the mountainsides is one of the most fertile in Southeast Asia. In addition to its very many dipterocarpous trees, 1,700 species

of moss and lichen, and 4,000 species of fungi, this is the location of the largest collection of palms in the world, which consists of 111 species belonging to 20 genera. These include the extremely rare *Eugeissona utilis*, which grows on the steep slopes of Gunung Mulu, and *Licuala lanata*, which prefers the narrow alluvial valleys.

The fauna includes 81 species of mammals, 270 birds, 20,000 invertebrates, 55 reptiles, 76 amphibians and 48 fish. The most studied are the 200 species that inhabit the underground system. Besides the 28 species of bats, the world's largest colony of salamanders – several millions – lives in the lakes and rivers in the caves.

Ten years after its institution, Gunung Mulu National Park was opened to the public. Four caves have been equipped with artificial light and walkways, and 25 or so miles of walks have been laid out through the forest. Recently, a luxurious resort, only reachable by plane or traditional Sarawak canoe, has been built. But the 15,000 visitors to the park each year do not yet seem to have disturbed this outstanding ecosystem. The dangers to its integrity are more closely related to global climate change.

198 top Of the 20,000 species of invertebrates that inhabit the Gunung Mulu massif, several hundreds have adapted to living in the inhospitable caves – perhaps to avoid natural predators – thereby stimulating interesting speciation phenomena.

198-199 The slender karstic spires in Gunung Mulu are the result of thousands of years of erosion by the heavy tropical rains. In some points in the mountain range, these incredible limestone needles reach 150 feet in height.

198 bottom The fauna in Gunung Mulu National Park includes 23 species of lizard, one of which (Cyrtodactylus pubisculus) lives exclusively in the caves.

199 left Extraordinary organ pipe limestone formations exist in Lang Cave, the smallest of the four open to the public in Gunung Mulu. Lang was the name of the guide who discovered it in 1977.

199 right Several chambers in Gunung Mulu caves are vast; the park holds four world records for cave size, with roof heights of between 260 and 395 feet and corridors ranging from 490 to 1,475 feet in width.

Ujung Kulon National Park

INDONESIA

JAVA
REGISTRATION: 1991
CRITERIA: N (III) (IV)

201

200 top The banteng (Bos javanicus) is the most common ungulate in the park with a population of 700. Nonetheless it is included in the IUCN's Red List and zoologists suspect that it is in territorial competition with the Javan rhinoceros.

200-201 The most recent eruption of the ill-famed Krakatoa began in 1997 and is still in progress. During the massive eruption of 26 August 1883, the volcano expelled 5 cubic miles of rock and caused the death of at least 36,000 people.

201 top Ujung Kulon's low level rainforest is dotted with palms and dominated by Ficus and Dipterocarpaceae; it is the last scrap of primary forest in Java, one of the most densely inhabited areas in the world.

201 center Against the background of mangrove forest, this is the coast of Ujung Kulon covered with algae. The coastal reef is one of the richest and most diversified marine ecosystems in the Sonda Archipelago.

201 bottom Krakatoa and, in the foreground, Anak Krakatoa (the 'son of Krakatoa' that emerged in the eruption of 1883). A study center for botanists and geologists, the baby volcano has grown to a height of 593 feet above sea level since its volcanic activity in 1930.

At one time the Javan rhinoceros (*Rhinocerus sondaicus*) inhabited the vast region that stretches from Assam in eastern India, through Indochina, the Malaysian Peninsula, and Sumatra as far as Java but, sadly, these magnificent animals were slaughtered on a vast scale for their horn, which, being considered a powerful aphrodisiac, was a precious ingredient in many traditional Chinese medicines.

Hunted almost to extinction, this species is today probably the mammal most at risk in the world. In 2000, during the last census of the animal taken by the World Wildlife Fund, roughly 60 rhinos were counted in Ujong Kulon National Park, and this is the larger of its two groups. The only other population, about 10 in number, lives in the Cat Tien National Park in Vietnam. Despite attempts to increase its numbers, stability at least seems to have been achieved compared to the worrying figures of earlier years. Researchers suspect that the lack of increase is owing to interspecies competition with the population of banteng (*Bos javanicus*), which is a bovine creature also on the International Union for the Conservation of Nature's Red List. Perhaps, however, hunting continues to play a part because, although the number of rhinos has not increased, changes in the distribution of age have been noticed, which suggests that changes are probably taking place within the population.

Situated on a triangular peninsula at the southwest tip of Java (with 100 million people making it one of the most densely populated places on earth), Ujung Kulon National Park covers the last 463 square miles of rainforest to have survived man's impact, as well as the surrounding marine area, including the Krakatoa Nature Reserve. Besides the Javan rhino, the park is crucial for the survival of other species in serious danger, many of which are endemic to the island. Perhaps this is why the park can only be reached by sea from Labuhan and why access is strictly controlled.

202 top The undergrowth in Ujung Kulon National Park abounds with floral species, whose growth is encouraged by the annual average of 118 inches of rain. At least 50 species in the protected area are endemic or extremely rare.

202 center left This magnificent atlas moth (Attacus atlas) – the largest moth in the world – was photographed as it was leaving its cocoon.

202 bottom left The Javan rhino (Rhinoceros sondaicus) is only known to exist in the protected areas of Ujung Kulon, where about 60 remain, and a Vietnamese national park, where there are no more than 15 left.

202-203 The Cigenter is one of the many watercourses that flow from Telanca Plateau, around which a complex drainage system has developed that nourishes the forests of Ujung Kulon.

203 top A primate found in many areas of Southeast Asia, the crab-eating macaque (Macaca fascicularis) has cheek pouches to allow it to carry food in its mouth.

203 bottom Covered by thick rainforest, the islands of Peucang and the nearby Panaitan formed the early nucleus of the park when it was created in 1937. The protected area now includes 170 square miles of sea that separates the islands from the Ujung Kulon Peninsula.

The Javan rhinoceros is having a bad time of it, but worse was suffered by the tiger (*Panthera tigris*), which has been extinct on the island for 40 years. And many of the mammals in Ujong Kulon – like the leopard (*Panthera pardus*), the dhole (*Cuon alpinus*), the silvery gibbon (*Hylobates moloch*), the crab-eating macaque (*Macaca fascicularis*) and many other species of endemic primates – are continually monitored. The bird population stands in much better stead, with more than 270 species recorded, including three types of stork, 11 types of pigeon and 16 species of cuckoo. The population of reptiles and amphibians is also flourishing, with two species each of python and crocodile and many types of frog and toad.

The coral reef around the coasts of Ujung Kulon consists 90% of acropore (*Acropora*) and cauliflower coral (*Pocillopora*), and the sea is inhabited by both reef and deep-water fish, making it the most abundant marine habitat in the Sonda Archipelago.

The vegetation in the park varies according to the area, but there is a prevalence of primary rainforest as a result of the enormous precipitation in the region (roughly 750 inches of rain a year). On the massif of Gunung Payung, 1,900 feet high, palms and grasses prosper under a forest roof characterized by *Dillenia excelsa*, *Pentace polyantha* and species of *Syzygium*. Open primary forest is found at Pulau Peucang, which is an area dominated by *Parinari*

Over the years three islands, Rakata, Payang and Sertung – the remains of an ancient andesitic volcano – had merged to form a single volcanic island, Krakatoa. On 26 August, the principal eruption of the island was heralded by a tremendous explosion followed by a column of ash that rose 17 miles into the sky. Over the following two days of eruptions, nearly 5 cubic miles of rock fragments were thrown into the sky and the *tsunami* (seismic sea waves) caused by the shock killed 36,000 people in the immediate vicinity.

That massive eruption – the largest we are aware of – gave rise to the new

Corymbosum, *Lagerstroemia speciosa* and *Rinorea Lanceolata* – all trees over 130 feet tall.

However, even this last corner of primary forest has undergone notable alteration as a result of man's presence, but above all following the great eruption of Krakatoa in 1883. Krakatoa is the outstanding geological feature of the park and the result of its massive eruption was to coat the ground with ash, thus causing a significant change in the composition of the soil.

cone of Anak Krakatoa ('child of Krakatoa') that began its own volcanic activity in 1930. Since then there have been 35 eruptions, each of which increases the size of the island, and the most recent of which is still in progress since its inception in 1997. Today Anak Krakatoa is 593 feet high and over a mile in diameter. It provides an exceptional opportunity for geologists and botanists to make field studies of the slow colonization of its slopes by vegetation.

Komodo National Park

INDONESIA

ISLANDS OF KOMODO, RINCA, PADAR, GILI
DASAM, GILI MOTONG, FLORES
REGISTRATION: 1991
CRITERIA: N (III) (IV)

Due to its size, the inhabitants of the islands called it buaja darat ('land crocodile'), as an adult can measure ten feet in length and weigh around 150 pounds; but the Komodo dragon (*Varanus komodoensis*) is not a crocodile, it belongs to the family of *Varanidae*, of which lizards are members. The *buaja darat* is in fact the largest representative of the order of scaly reptiles and offers researchers an exceptional chance to study evolution. Walter Auffenberg, a pioneer of the study of these descendants of the dinosaurs, said, 'When this animal decides to attack, nothing can stop it.'

This is perhaps the reason why innumerable legends have flourished about the capabilities of this fearsome predator, despite it only being able to move at most at 12 mph. What is certain is that it was to protect this extraordinary example of evolution that the islands of Padar and Rinca were declared a Nature Reserve as far back as 1938, to which the island of Komodo was added in 1965. In 1980 the Komodo National Park was set up over an area of 290 square miles. Four years later a part of Flores was added and some of the waters that encircle these islands in the Sonda Archipelago, so that the park now covers almost 850 square miles.

The morphology of the islands reflects their position in the middle of the Sonda volcanic platform. The land is marked by a continuous series of steep ridges that continue out to sea and enclose inaccessible inlets.

Komodo, the largest island, is dominated by a chain of hills aligned north to south that do not exceed 1,850 feet in height. This is a structure also seen on other islands.

The vegetation is typical of a tropical though not particularly rainy climate (31-39 inches during the monsoon season from November to April), and is predominated by grasslands of anthropic origin that cover roughly 70% of the land surface of the National Park. Some of the most widespread grasses are *Eulalia leschenaultiana*, *Setaria adhaerens* and *Chloris Barbata*, while the most common of the forest trees is the species of palm *Borassus flabellifer*.

The wildlife on Komodo includes many species of birds, reptiles and

204 top Situated in the southeast section of the Sonda Archipelago, between Sumbawa and Flores, Komodo has an area of 130 square miles and is dominated by a chain of hills that do not exceed 1,970 feet in height.

204 bottom left The Komodo dragon (Varanus komodoensis) measures up to 10 feet in length, weighs 300 pounds and is the largest scaly reptile on earth. In the past it was erroneously believed to be

poisonous like other reptiles, but its bite is so strong that it can cause serious infections and even be lethal to man. Eating mainly carcasses, the creature is a carrier of dangerous bacteria that breed in its jaws.

204 bottom right A group of 'dragons' drinks from a freshwater pool. Used to living alone or in small groups, this reptile's favorite habitat is deciduous tropical forest or, to a lesser extent, open grassland.

205 Measuring 7.8 square miles in area, the island of Padar is the only one on which the Komodo dragon is now extinct (since the 1970s), probably because its prey was exterminated by hunters.

JAKARTA

206 The attack sequence of a Komodo dragon is impressive. It has 60 large, closely packed curved teeth that make it impossible for prey to escape their grasp.

amphibians; there are also seven species of terrestrial mammals, including the endemic rat *Rattus rintjanus*. Others of interest are the macaque (*Macaca fascicularis*) and the Timor deer (*Cervus timorensis*). Komodo National Park can also boast a large coral reef that is home to one of the most abundant fish fauna in the world but whose ecosystem has been seriously threatened by poaching over the last few decades; it has not been unknown for dynamite to be used. The seas contain mammals such as the blue whale (*Balaenoptera musculus*), which is in danger of extinction, the sperm whale (*Physeter catodon*) and 10 species of dolphin, including the highly threatened dugong (*Dugong dugon*).

Equally vulnerable is the attraction of the National Park, the Komodo dragon. A recent count suggests that roughly 5,700 remain though the species seems to have disappeared from the island of Padar as no signs have been seen for several years. The reason for the danger is extensive hunting of the Timor deer, the dragon's favorite food. It is obvious that even the most terrible hunting machine in the world will have a hard time when it has no prey.

206-207 Estimated to be around 5,700 in number, the Komodo dragon population is divided between 2,900 on Komodo, 900 on Rinca, 100 or so on Gili Motong and the rest in the coastal areas of the island of Flores.

207 bottom left The genus Varanus to which the Komodo dragon belongs, is a latinization of the Egyptian word waran *meaning 'alarm'. It is derived from the legend in which the lizards of this family in the Nile warned the people of the presence of crocodiles.*

207 bottom right Some of the preferred prey of the dragon are goats, boar and the Timor deer but it is quite happy to eat birds, snakes, fish, crabs, water buffalo and even the young of its own species.

List of the Sites

The Americas

On 1 March 1872 the President of the United States, Ulysses Grant, approved the statute that the magnificent scenery of Yellowstone should be made a national park. That act officially marked the start of the conservation of the natural environment and led towards modern environmentalism.

Considering the vastness of its untouched areas and the early attention that was paid to the protection of nature, it is not surprising that the American continent overall represents one third of UNESCO's World Heritage sites. Extending from Alaska to Patagonia, and passing through the enormous green lung of the Amazon, it has an extraordinary richness of biodiversity.

For both flora and fauna, the Americas are unequalled in the variety of their environments and protected areas. Consider, for example, the huge expanses of Kluane, Wrangell-St. Elias, Glacier Bay and Tatshenshini-Alsek Parks, which are divided between Alaska, the Yukon and British Columbia; they cover over 42,000 square miles of land and form the second largest protected area on the planet. Parque Nacionál Manu, in Peru, is considered the region with the most extensive biodiversity in the world. Then there is Parque Nacionál Los Glaciares, in Argentina, which, if we exclude the Poles, is half occupied by the world's largest glacier, the Campo de Hielo Patagonico. Then there are the marine sanctuaries like El Vizcaíno in Baja California, the barrier reef in Belize and the Peninsula Valdés in Patagonia.

Naturally, the lion's share of protected areas is held by the United States and Canada, where the growth of the environmentalist movements of the twentieth century have exerted great pressure on their respective governments, even preventing important conservation areas from being sacrificed to economic interests. In recent years, even some Latin countries have rediscovered their nature. This is particularly the case in Costa Rica, which has launched conservation projects across all its territory to safeguard its natural heritage; after all, the increase in 'green tourism' is proving to be a significant source of income.

Despite the efforts made, the impact of human activities on the fragility of many ecosystems is also making itself felt in the Americas, beginning with the catastrophe being caused by deforestation in the Amazon. Each year, tens of thousands of square miles of the last virgin forest on the planet is cut down. And man's invasiveness is putting the survival of many species at risk. With reference just to the mammals, the bison (the symbol of the American frontier) is at risk, along with large predators like the puma and jaguar, strange-looking animals such as the sloth, tapir and armadillo are also endangered as are the blue and gray whales, the giants of the sea that, to look at, one would think were invincible.

Kluane/Wrangell-St. Elias, Glacier Bay and Tatshenshini-Alsek Parks

UNITED STATES/CANADA

UNITED STATES, ALASKA
CANADA, YUKON AND BRITISH COLUMBIA
REGISTRATION: 1979, 1992, 1994*
CRITERIA: N (II) (III) (IV)

*IN 1992 THE SITE WAS EXTENDED TO INCLUDE
GLACIER BAY NATIONAL PARK AND PRESERVE
AND, IN 1994, THE TATSHENSHINI-ALSEK
PROVINCIAL WILDERNESS PARK

OTTAWA

WASHINGTON D.C.

210 top A native of North America, the bald eagle (Haliaetus leucocephalus) used to nest from Alaska down to the Gulf of Mexico but it has now disappeared from the southern regions.

210-211 The Wrangell-St Elias, Chugach and Kluane mountain chains form the 'kingdom of the mountains' in North America. At 18,008 feet high, St. Elias is the second tallest mountain in the United States.

At the start of the twentieth century, the Gold Rush in the Klondike fed the myth of the American Dream. At that time, the Great North had for decades been a land crisscrossed by fur traders like John Dalton, who in 1890 opened the first fur-trading center in the Tatshenshini Basin. The era of the pioneers passed but Alaska continued to be a land of conquest for mining companies. And, today, the debate on the region's abundant oil reserves is alive in the heart of American society, as they could easily damage the environmental balance of a vast area.

In Canada, the Windy Cragg affair has just come to an end. This was a project to build the largest open-pit mine in the continent to extract gold and copper. At the start of the 1990s a group of 50 or so environmental groups combined under the name 'Tatshenshini International' and forced the Canadian government to protect a vast area of the Yukon and British Columbia, and in consequence to reimburse handsomely the mining companies involved.

This was the reason behind the creation in 1993 of the Tatshenshini-Alsek Provincial Wilderness Park, a protected area measuring 3,700 square miles. A year later, this park was subsumed in a World Heritage site that includes Kluane National Park, Wrangell-St. Elias National Park and Preserve and Glacier Bay National Park and Preserve in Canada and the United States. This complex covers an overall area of 42,500 square miles and is the second largest protected area in the world after the Great Barrier Reef.

Lying across the Alaskan and Canadian border, the region includes large mountain ranges – with Mount Logan (19,521 feet), the second highest mountain in North America – and one of the world's largest glacier systems outside of the North and South Poles. This extraordinary continental landscape features alpine scenes, arctic tundra, fiords, glacial valleys, moraines and an intricate hydrological basin that drains into the Alsek River Delta. The vegetation grows in different biogeoclimatic zones, with forests of fir (*Picea glauca* and *Picea sitchensis*), poplars

and aspens (*Populus tremuloides* and *Populus balsamifera*), birch woods at over 3,300 feet (*Betula glandulosa* and *Betula papyrifera*), and then grasses, shrubs, sedges and berries at higher levels.

The parks provide a habitat to many North American species, in particular the grizzly bear (*Ursus arctos horribilis*), American black bear (*Ursus americanus*) and the blue or glacial bear (*Ursus americanus emmonsi*), which is thought

211 top The mountains in Kluane National Park in Canada form the backdrop to Slims River Valley.

211 center The red fox (Vulpes vulpes) lives right across Alaska and Canada, with the exception of the extreme north.

211 bottom A rare case: Dall's sheep (Ovis dalli) has prospered despite being useless to man.

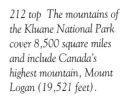

to be a chromatic variant of the black bear. Endemic species include Dall's sheep (*Ovis dalli dalli*), the insectivorous plant *Sorex alaskanus* and the ground squirrel (*Spermophilus parryi*); then there are elk, wolverine, the gray wolf, deer and lynx. The fish population numbers five species of Pacific salmon, which are a favorite catch for fishermen.

A land of fur-skinned creatures, this complex of parks is also home to many animals that, in the past, were the exploits of a successful trading business: the fox (*Vulpes vulpes*), otter (*Lutra*

canadensis), mink (*Mustela vison*), beaver (*Castor canadensis*) and muskrat (*Ondatra zibethicus*). Though the fur trade was brought to a halt following an enormous international campaign, and plans for a copper mine were thwarted, the threats to the environment have not ended. A recent proposal has been aired in the American Senate to open the parks to hunting. The International Union for the Conservation of Nature is considering this hypothesis to evaluate its impact on the fauna of the region.

212 top The mountains of the Kluane National Park cover 8,500 square miles and include Canada's highest mountain, Mount Logan (19,521 feet).

212 center With the lynx, mink and muskrat, the beaver (Castor canadensis) is one of the unfortunate fur animals that attracted adventurers to the north at the start of the twentieth century.

212 bottom Living in the grasslands, tundra and deciduous and conifer forests, the gray wolf (Canis lupus) is one of the most adaptable mammals in existence. With 60,000, Canada has the largest population of wolves in the world.

212-213 Hoge Pass lies at a height of 6,610 feet in the Donjek Mountains in Kluane National Park. The area was set up as a wildlife reserve in 1942.

213 bottom left Owing to the reduction in habitat and its low reproduction rate, the grizzly (Ursus arctos horribilis) has been classified as a 'vulnerable species' by the Committee on the Status of Endangered Wildlife. The residual population across Alaska, British Columbia and the Yukon is between 40,000 and 60,000.

213 bottom right The Alaska-Yukon moose (Alces alces gigas) is the largest of the four subspecies of existing moose. It is not unusual for males to weigh 1,300 pounds.

212

214 *Living in many oceanic habitats, the humpback whale (Megaptera novaeangliae) form their reserves of body fat in the cold seas before migrating to subtropical waters during winter for the breeding season.*

215 top left *Classified as Delphinus orca by Linnaeus, the killer whale was later renamed Orcinus orca when a new genus was created. A symbol of the coast of British Columbia, it is one of the most intelligent and ferocious marine predators.*

215 bottom left *A killer whale swims beside its calf. Families usually comprise three to 25 individuals but may extend to 50.*

215 right *Lying 80 miles long from the base of Mount Logan to Yakutata and Disenchantment Bays, Hubbard is the longest glacier in Alaska to flow into the sea.*

Wood Buffalo National Park

CANADA

ALBERTA
REGISTRATION: 1983
CRITERIA: N (II) (III) (IV)

216 top A group of white pelicans alights on Slave River, one of the three watercourses that form the large internal delta of Lake Athabasca. Situated on the migratory routes, Wood Buffalo National Park has 227 species of birds, including the very rare American crane.

216 bottom Two black bear cubs (Ursus americanus) are at play, but not for long: the mating season and weaning period are the only periods these solitary animals spend in company.

I t is very unusual that a peaceful country, respectful of nature like Canada, should have been hit recently by an environmental argument of international proportions. At the start of the 1990s, the naturalist associations rose up against the decision by the federal government to cull a number of wood bison, also known as wood buffalo, *(Bison bison athabascae)*, a robust subspecies of the American bison, of which 2,500 survive in Wood Buffalo National Park.

As the name suggests, the park was created in 1922 with the specific aim of protecting this gigantic mammal,

which, at the time, was down to just 1,500 in number.

The herds had in part been struck by an apparently contagious form of tuberculosis and brucellosis, and cattle breeders were worried that the epidemic would infect their herds. The naturalists, however, argued against the reasoning of the breeders, saying that the bsion had suffered from this disease for 75 years and there had never been a case of a breeding animal having been infected. Temporarily, at least, the naturalists have won their case and the wood bison can continue to graze quietly in the national park. The park lies in the province of Alberta, is on the border of the Northwest Territories and, with a size of 18,500 square miles, is larger than Switzerland. Though for the most part an immense plain devoid of any dramatic natural characteristics, the area of the park includes important topographic features of importance such as saline lowlands, the most interesting karstic zone in North America, and the large inland delta formed by the Peace, Athabasca and Slave Rivers that flow into Lake Athabasca.

The climate is continental, with short hot summers and long winters so cold that the ground is frozen from September to June. The vegetation is dominated by coniferous forests of fir *(Picea glauca* and *Picea mariana)*, pines *(Pinus banksiana)*, larch *(Larix laricana)* but also poplars *(Populus balsamifera* and *Populus tremuloides)*.

The star of the national park, the wood bison, is in fact a hybrid subspecies as a few years after the

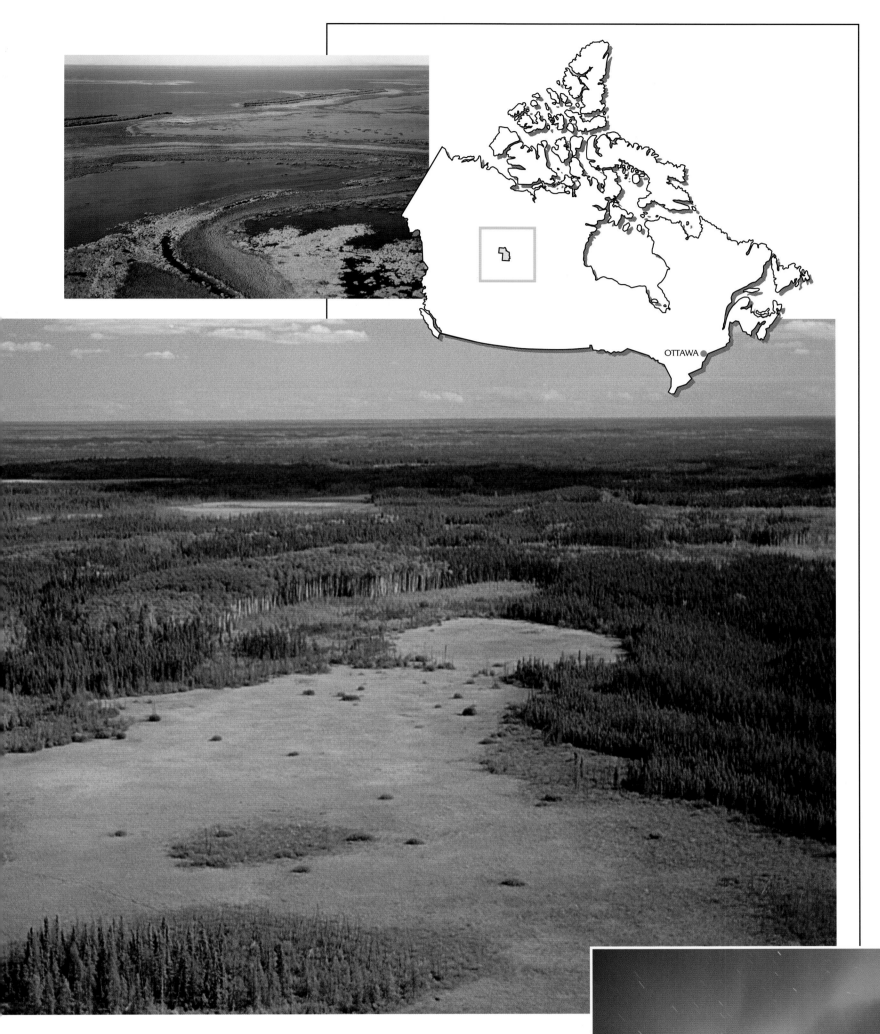

OTTAWA

216-217 There are huge clearings in the fir, pine and larch forests in Wood Buffalo National Park. The park, which covers 17,000 square miles of land, includes North America's largest grasslands.

217 top The Peace, Athabasca and Slave Rivers flow into the Peace-Athabasca Delta. A dam draws off a part of the water, which means that the lake may dry out slowly, causing incalculable environmental damage.

217 bottom One of the most spectacular natural phenomena to be seen, the Aurora Borealis gives out a bright, almost supernatural light over the forests of Wood Buffalo National Park, situated between 58 and 60 degrees north.

creation of the protected area the
Canadian government settled 6,000
head of American bison there (*Bison
bison bison*) to repopulate the area.
There is also the highly rare American
crane (*Grus americana*) (only
discovered in 1954) which lives in the
remote zones of the park and, as a
result of careful protection, has
increased in number from just 21 to
over 130. Overall, Wood Buffalo is
home to 46 species of mammal,
including the black bear (*Ursus
americanus*), grizzly (*Ursus arctos
horribilis*), gray wolf (*Canis lupus*),
Arctic fox (*Alopex lagopus*), moose
(*Alces alces*), lynx (*Lynx canadensis*),

Canadian beaver (*Castor canadensis*)
and mink (*Mustela vison*). And as the
region is a crossroads of at least four
migratory routes, the shores of Lake
Athabasca provide nesting places for
227 species of birds.

But who knows for how long,
because the Peace-Athabasca Delta is
gradually drying out. This will cause
the loss of food supplies and, at the
same time, make access easier for
predators. Once again, at least in part,
the reasons for this change are owing
to human action, in particular the
construction of Bennett Dam, which
has limited the flow of water to the
delta since 1969.

*218 top Meadows of
sedges and copses of aspen
cover the land near Gros
Beak Lake. The aspen
grows mostly in mountain
woods and favors very wet
zones.*

*218 bottom Created in
1922 to protect the wood
bison, the park's original
population of just 1,500
has now grown to 2,500.*

*218-219 The bison in
Wood Buffalo National
Park is probably a hybrid
between the rare wood
bison (Bison bison
athabascae) and the
American bison (Bison
bison bison), which was
introduced to the area to
repopulate it.*

219 bottom left A black bear scratches its back energetically against a tree. An adult usually weighs between 220 and 330 pounds, but can occasionally reach 500 pounds.

219 bottom right The wapiti, or elk, was originally given the scientific name Cervus canadensis, *which was later changed to* Cervus elaphus *as it is in fact a subspecies of the Eurasian deer.*

Canadian Rocky Mountains parks

CANADA

ALBERTA AND BRITISH COLUMBIA
REGISTRATION: 1984*
CRITERIA: N (I) (II) (III)

*THE BURGESS SHALE SITE, INSCRIBED ON THE
WORLD HERITAGE LIST IN 1980, HAS NOW BEEN
SUBSUMED INTO THIS SITE

In 1886, when the geologist R. G. McConnell of the Geological Survey of Canada discovered the Burgess Shale fossil deposits, the workers on the Canadian Pacific Railway had already made their personal collections of trilobites. Thanks to the pioneering work of the construction of the railway, the Canadian government had created a nature reserve of 10 square miles around the mineral springs of Cave and Basin, thinking, as the directors of the railway did, that one day they would become a tourist attraction.

That act marked the beginning of the string of national parks in Canada and the place formed the nucleus around which the Rocky Mountains Park was constituted two years later.

Basin National Historic Site.

Today the area includes four national parks – Banff National Park, Jasper National Park, Kootenay National Park and Yoho National Park – and three provincial parks –Hamber Provincial Park, Mount Assiniboine Provincial Park and Mount Robson Provincial Park – making a total of 8,907 square miles of protected land along the border of Alberta and British Columbia.

Geologically, the Canadian Rocky Mountains are formed by schist, dolomite, sandstone and limestone, and were created between the Precambrian era and the Cretaceous period. They range in height from 3,280 feet to Mount Robson's 12,972 feet and have several large glaciers, the biggest of

which is the Columbia Icefield that covers 125 square miles.

The continental climate has fostered the development of three ecoregions – montane, subalpine and alpine – that alternate depending on altitude and exposure to atmospheric agents. The classified species include 996 vascular plants, 243 mosses, 407 lichens and 53 bryophytes. The mountain region is covered with forests of Douglas fir (*Pseudotsuga menziesii*), white spruce (*Picea glauca*) and poplars (*Populus tremuloides* and *Populus balsamifera*). At a height between 5,905 and 6,900 feet, the subalpine region (which is the most extensive with over 445 square miles of forest) is dominated by firs (*Picea engelmannii* and *Abies lasiocarpa*) and pines (*Pinus flexilis* and *Pinus contorta*).

The name of the park was changed to the Banff National Park in 1930. As the years passed, the Rocky Mountains became the symbol of environmental conservation in Canada, and to commemorate that first protected area, the hot, emerald-green springs in Banff have been renamed the Cave and

220 top left After a drop of 75 feet, the Maligne River dives into a spectacular gorge that the violence of the river has dug out of the limestone rock.

220 bottom left The elk (Cervus elaphus) is the largest of the deer family. Unlike the others, evolution has given it an upper canine tooth, which, in the nineteenth century, became a fashionable item of jewelry.

220 bottom right At an altitude of 4,921 feet, Moraine Lake is one of the pearls of Banff National Park. This was the first park instituted in Canada and was opened in 1885 with the name Rocky Mountains Park.

221

221 left In the heart of Jasper National Park, Medicine Lake has the Maligne River as a tributary but it does not seem to have an emissary. In fact, the lake is drained by one of the largest underground water systems in North America.

221 right The redness of the antlers is given by the presence of surface blood vessels and indicates the sex and youth of this moose. Only males have antlers, which usually start to grow at around one year of age.

OTTAWA ●

222-223 Peyto Lake is one of the most spectacular in the Canadian Rocky Mountains. The local lakes are fed by glaciers, the largest of which, the Columbia Icefield, has an area of 125 square miles.

222 bottom At 11,870 feet, Mount Assiniboine is a dramatic, isolated pyramid of limestone in the heart of Assiniboine Provincial Park. It dominates Lake Magog, around which a rich wild fauna abounds. Overall, the protected area of the Canadian Rocky Mountains encloses four national parks and three provincial parks, making a total of 8,880 square miles.

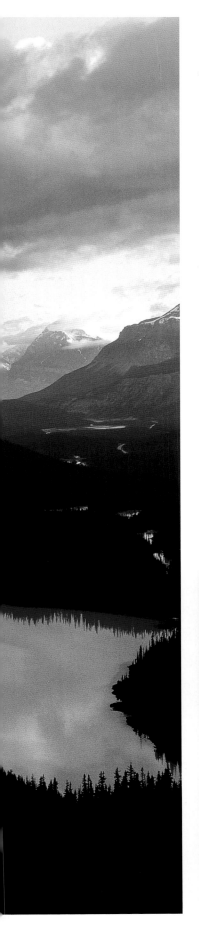

Higher up, the alpine flora includes low species such as *Salix arctica* and *Betula glandulosa*, heathers, like *Cassiope tetragona*, and rosales (*Dryas integrifolia* and *Dryas hookeriania*).

The most representative mammals are the herbivores that have their habitat in the alpine meadows. They include the mountain goat and mountain sheep (*Oreamos americanus* and *Ovis canadensis*), the pika (*Ochotona princeps*), which is a sort of hare and the hoary marmot (*Marmota caligata*); there are forest mammals like the moose (*Alces alces*), the elk (*Cervus canadensis*) and the caribou (*Rangifer tarandus*); and carnivores such as the gray wolf (*Canis lupus*), the grizzly bear (*Ursos arctos horribilis*), the American black bear (*Ursus americanus*), the lynx (*Lynx canadensis*) and the puma (*Puma concolor*).

Of the 280 species of birds, mention should be made of the northern three-toed woodpecker, the partridge (*Lagopus*

223 top *At one time distributed right across Canada, the puma (Felis concolor) now only lives in the Rocky Mountains. Male adults can reach a length of 9 feet and weigh close to 200 pounds.*

223 center *The gray wolf (Canis lupus) has only recently returned to the Rocky Mountains. A long study in Banff National Park estimates there are about 40 living there.*

223 bottom *During their migration across North America, each autumn thousands of golden eagles (Aquila chrysaetos) take refuge along the eastern slopes of the Rocky Mountains.*

leucurus), the gray jay (*Perisoreus canadensis*), Clark's nutcracker (*Nucifraga columbiana*) and, of course, the golden eagle (*Aquila chrysaetos*).

With the exception of a plan for an open-pit coal mine just outside Jasper National Park – which would seriously compromise the health of the area – the Rocky Mountains do not seem subjected to grave environmental risk, despite the fact that every year they receive almost 10 million visitors.

OTTAWA

224 top It is unknown what the function of the bony crest of the Parasaurolophus was, but perhaps the animal required a horn for communication purposes.

224-225 The rocks in the provincial park were deeply furrowed by the movement of the water during the melting of the icefields.

225 top Hoodoos are unusual sandstone mushroom-like formations a few miles from Drumheller and one of the park's attractions.

Formed by the wind and water, they dissolve very quickly when the stone that covers and protects them is eroded by the atmosphere.

225 center The progressive emersion of ancient layers of sediment has unearthed more than 300 complete dinosaur skeletons and thousands of fossil fragments.

Dinosaur Provincial Park

CANADA

SOUTHERN ALBERTA
REGISTRATION: 1979
CRITERIA: N (I) (III)

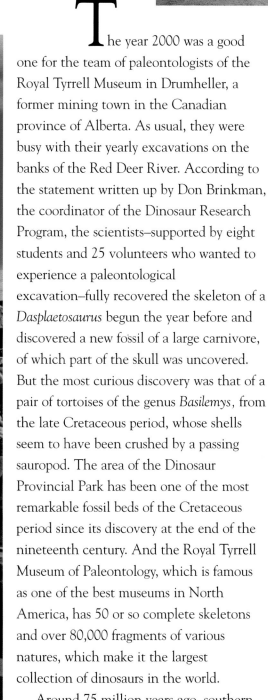

The year 2000 was a good one for the team of paleontologists of the Royal Tyrrell Museum in Drumheller, a former mining town in the Canadian province of Alberta. As usual, they were busy with their yearly excavations on the banks of the Red Deer River. According to the statement written up by Don Brinkman, the coordinator of the Dinosaur Research Program, the scientists–supported by eight students and 25 volunteers who wanted to experience a paleontological excavation–fully recovered the skeleton of a *Dasplaetosaurus* begun the year before and discovered a new fossil of a large carnivore, of which part of the skull was uncovered. But the most curious discovery was that of a pair of tortoises of the genus *Basilemys*, from the late Cretaceous period, whose shells seem to have been crushed by a passing sauropod. The area of the Dinosaur Provincial Park has been one of the most remarkable fossil beds of the Cretaceous period since its discovery at the end of the nineteenth century. And the Royal Tyrrell Museum of Paleontology, which is famous as one of the best museums in North America, has 50 or so complete skeletons and over 80,000 fragments of various natures, which make it the largest collection of dinosaurs in the world.

Around 75 million years ago, southern Alberta – where the Dinosaur Provincial Park lies – was a coastal plain on the edge of the Bearpaw Sea. The climate was then subtropical, which allowed an extensive fauna to develop, including the first mammals as well as fish, amphibians, birds and the large reptiles that dominated the world, the dinosaurs. Over the geological eras, an intricate river system built up a bed of sediments nearly 2,000 feet thick that covered the carcasses of many animals. About 15,000 years later, the erosive action of the glaciers cut gashes in the sediments, like the twisting beds of the Red Deer River and Judith River, revealing the fossil remains of these creatures.

From a botanical viewpoint, Dinosaur Provincial Park is of no particular interest, but the layers of sandstone and schist exposed by glaciation have revealed an extraordinary cross section of the world of the dinosaurs. Between 1979 and 1991, 23,347 finds were made, including 300 skeletons of dinosaurs belonging to 35 different species. These numbered creatures from the *Hadrosauridae*, *Ornithomimidae*, and *Nodosauridae families*, and even some of the most feared predators of the Cretacean period, Tyrannosaurus Rex.

The relative mildness of the modern climate permits hoofed animals to survive the winters, like pronghorn (*Antilocapra americana*) and mule and white-tailed deer (*Odocoileus hemionus* and *Odocoileus virginianus*). The local fauna includes 150 species of birds, such as the golden eagle (*Aquila chrysaetos*), the prairie falcon (*Falco mexicanus*), the ferruginous hawk (*Buteo regalis*) and the pigeon hawk or merlin (*Falco columbarius*).

The number of visitors to the Dinosaur Provincial Park is on the increase but it remains a quiet place for the species that inhabit it, as the tourists are more interested in searching for fossils. Large discoveries are fairly rare event as the excavations only last a few weeks during the summer but disappointed visitors are always able to console themselves with the treasures of the Royal Tyrrell Museum.

225 bottom Large dinosaur bones in the foreground stick up out of the sediment in Dinosaur National Park. Those found on the site (one of the richest fossil beds from the Cretaceous period) belong to 35 different species.

Gros Morne National Park

CANADA

NEWFOUNDLAND
REGISTRATION: 1987
CRITERIA: N (I) (III)

Six hundred million years, ago the landmasses that became Europe and North America began to separate. Colossal tectonic movements created deep fissures between the two continents, which were in part filled by magma that rose from the lowest layers of the earth's crust.

With the passing of geological eras, the divide increased to form a sea and, on the American continent, violent jolts formed the Appalachian Mountains. Subsequently, Europe and North America began to approach one another once again as a result of the emersion of the ocean crust. Then came the Ice Age during which everything was covered by a thick white layer. When the glaciers melted, they cut

a catalogue of evolution as they contain fossils of all species that lived during the Precambrian and early Paleozoic eras.

Facing onto the Gulf of St. Lawrence and the Belle Mare Strait that separates the island from Labrador, Gros Morne National Park encloses 700 square miles of some of the most spectacular scenery in Canada. The Long Range Mountains are studded with glacial lakes, waterfalls, steep valleys and, as it descends towards the sea, by cliffs, fjords, large sandy zones, brackish marshland and sand dunes up to 100 feet in height.

The flora is abundant owing to the high humidity brought by the ocean breezes and is divided into 36 distinct vegetal communities. Here 711 species of vascular plants and 401 bryophytes

have been catalogued which represent 60% of the flora on the island of Newfoundland. Most dominant are the woods of conifers, with black pines and red fir in the higher zones, whereas the tundra of herbaceous plants and various species of heather is prevalent in the marshy areas.

Although there are rare species in other parts of Canada, for example the lynx, there is little fauna on the island except for caribou, musk ox, the occasional brown bear and salmon in the rivers of the Long Range Mountains; whales and seals are found in the ocean waters around the island. On the other hand, Newfoundland has 235 species of avifauna comprising arctic, northern and sea birds.

through the mountains like a knife from the peaks to the sea.

The history of the geological events and continental drift can be seen most clearly in what is today Gros Morne National Park. Situated along the west coast of the island of Newfoundland, it follows the line of the Long Range Mountains, the layers of which are like

226 top right The common puffin (Fratercula arctica) is a clumsy bird with a multicolored beak that lives in the northern areas of the Atlantic Ocean. It spends winter on the open sea and moves to the coasts only in spring for the mating season.

226 bottom left and right The spectacular splash of a humpback whale (Megaptera novaeangliae) in the cold waters of the North Atlantic Ocean. The name of this giant marine mammal means 'large wings' and refers to its

powerful pectoral fins. Other whales to be seen in Gros Morne National Park are the pilot whale (Globicephala melaena), minke whale (Balaenoptera acutorostrata) and the finback whale (Balaenoptera physalus).

227 To the west the rocky cliffs of Gros Morne National Park give onto the Gulf of St. Lawrence in the area of Green Gardens, a region generally used for animal grazing. Newfoundland is thought by some to have been where the Vikings landed on American soil.

OTTAWA

The diminution of the fauna is a result of hunting, which has been practiced since time immemorial by the communities of Native Indians and Inuit, and of the fishing industry and cod salting, which occurred on both sides of the Belle Mare Strait from the early nineteenth to the mid-twentieth centuries.

In 1973, when the park was created, the Native Americans were obliged to abandon their settlements in the protected area. Today they mostly live in Rocky Harbour, the coastal village where the park's visitors' center is located. It was also where Giovanni Cabot, the first European to reach Newfoundland, landed in 1497. It seems that it was Cabot who coined the term 'redskin' for the natives, as the first men he came upon on the island had their faces smeared with a ritual unguent made from the fat and blood of seals.

228-229 The caribou (Rangifer tarandus) is the only cervid in which both sexes have branched antlers.

228 bottom left Gros Morne is a nesting place for the American bald eagle (Haliaetus leucocephalus), and many arctic, northern and deep sea birds.

228 bottom right A majestic moose (Alces alces) grazes in the grasslands of Newfoundland.

229 top The golden light of an Arctic sunset washes over Norris Bay and Bonne Bay in the heart of Gros Morne National Park.

229 center Threatened elsewhere in Canada, the Canadian lynx (Lynx canadensis) is still numerous in Newfoundland.

229 bottom Distributed from Alaska to Siberia, the musk ox (Ovibos moschatus) gets its name from the strong smell of musk its thick coat gives off.

Waterton Glacier International Peace Park

CANADA/UNITED STATES

CANADA, ALBERTA
UNITED STATES, MONTANA
REGISTRATION: 1995
CRITERIA: N (II) (III)

OTTAWA

WASHINGTON D.C.

In the document that instituted the Waterton-Glacier International Peace Park, signed in Spring 1932 by the Canadian and American governments, the goodwill and cooperation between the two countries were clearly emphasized. Prominence was also placed on the agreement with another organization, though much less powerful: the Confederation of the Blackfoot, the North American Indians that had inhabited the area from time immemorial and who consider Chief Mountain – that stands in the center of the border park – the symbol of their tribe.

The creation of the first international park on earth had the merit of opening the way to other agreements whose principal intent was conservation of the environment, regardless of border politics. However, this longsighted measure was not the creation of the functionaries of the two large countries, but of two adventurers who lived on the edge of the law: these were John George 'Kootenai' Brown

and Henry 'Death on the Trail' Reynolds who, in 1911, first dreamed up the possibility of creating a united territory – probably around a campfire in these mountains. The idea later reached the ears of the Rotary Club of Alberta and its sister club in Montana, and it was these two organizations that took upon themselves the preliminary diplomacy that was to lead to the historic signatures.

The natural border between the 203 square miles of the Waterton Lakes National Park in Canada and the 1,564 square miles of the Glacier National Park in the United States runs through a narrow lake on the 49th parallel. The two areas have the same geomorphological features. The landscape is constituted by grasslands and mountains up to 8,200 feet high. The stratigraphy of the territory shows major geological events that took place over the span of 1 million years, the most important of which is the Lewis Fracture, during which Precambrian

230-231 Situated on the eastern edge of the Rocky Mountains, Waterton Glacier International Peace Park has its highest point on Mount Cleveland at 10,469 feet. Despite its name, the park has no glaciers, simply permanent snowfields.

231 top right Famous as the symbol of the United States, with a wingspan of over 8 feet, the magnificent bald eagle (Haliaetus leucocephalus) is one of the largest birds of prey in the world.

231 center Believed to be extinct in the region, the gray wolf (Canis lupus) was sighted in the mid-1980s, first in Glacier National Park and later in Waterton Lakes National Park. Today there are about 40 in at least three different groups.

231 bottom During the long Arctic winter, an elk scavenges beneath the snow on the edge of a coniferous forest. Once common across the whole continent, these large ungulates prefer grasslands and open woods to forests.

rocks were pushed up to cover the younger and softer Cretaceous formations, thereby revealing deposits of stromatolites. The Waterton-Glacier Park region is also affected by the confluence of three of the continent's large drainage systems: from here waters run west towards the Columbia River, east to the Missouri and north to the Saskatchewan Plain.

From a climatic point of view, the area is the meeting point between the continental Arctic and Pacific Ocean systems, and this phenomenon has resulted in a peculiar flora. This is divided into five ecoregions, the most important of which are the alpine tundra – containing plants like the alpine poppy (*Papaver pygmaeum*) – and the subalpine forest dominated by birch trees.

The park is known for it's profuse fauna with 241 species of birds and 61 species of mammals, including gray wolves, coyotes, black bears and 200 grizzly bears. It also acts as a corridor for the migrations of elk, bison and deer, which are of fundamental importance to the health of their gene banks. Perhaps more than anything else, it is these ungulates that symbolize that nature does not have and can never be subjected to borders.

232

232 top left Waterton Glacier International Peace Park has a population of over 200 grizzlies (Ursus arctos horribilis) and a large community of American black bears (Ursus americanus).

232 bottom left The moose (Alces alces) is easily recognizable by the spread of its antlers and its long nose. It is a solitary animal that winters in the mountain and subalpine zones of the Rockies.

232 right The elk, or wapiti, is the more robust subspecies of Cervus elaphus. The adult male stands 4.5 feet high and weighs 650-1000 pounds.

232-233 The gully into which the turbulent waters of Avalanche Creek flow is one of the most interesting natural environments in Glacier National Park in Montana.

233 top Seen here beyond the expanse of bear grass, the sparkling turquoise waters of Lake Grinnell are fed by the snows of Mount Gould.

Yellowstone National Park

UNITED STATES

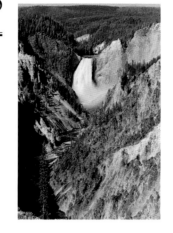

WYOMING, MONTANA AND IDAHO
REGISTRATION: 1978
CRITERIA: N (I) (II) (III) (IV)
INSCRIBED ON THE WORLD HERITAGE
IN DANGER LIST IN 1995

234 *Unique in the world, the incredible plays of color in the Giant Prismatic Spring (Yellowstone's largest thermal spring) are created by algae and microorganisms in the water and by mineral deposits on the banks.*

235 *top left An area rich in geothermal phenomena, the Porcelain Basin is named after the whiteness of its limestone deposits. It has several geysers; this is Africa Geyser, which gives off continuous puffs of steam.*

When William Hanna and Joseph Barbera created the willful bears Yogi and Boo boo, and the patient red-jacketed ranger whose duty it was to protect the picnic baskets of the visitors to Jellystone Park, it was clear they had based their ideas on the astounding Yellowstone Park in North America. The creation of this, the first national park in the world, by President Ulysses Grant on 1 March 1872, opened the era of environmental conservation.

In 1870, when the United States was still suffering the wounds of the Civil War, the son of the senator for Montana, Walter Trumball, organized an expedition to Yellowstone led by General Henry D. Washburn to check tales brought back by the region's earliest explorers. In 1807, John Colter had returned from a mission to the frontier territories, telling of valleys that ended in lakes of boiling mud, fumaroles, jets of steam and hot springs, which together formed a Dantesque vision of hell. The stories circulated enough for the phrase 'Colter's Hell' to be coined.

Armed only with these tales, Washburn and his companions soon discovered a steam vent that rose 100 feet into the air in a fountain of boiling water. This was what was later to become Yellowstone's most famous geyser, Old Faithful, which was so named for the regularity of its eruption (every 74 minutes).

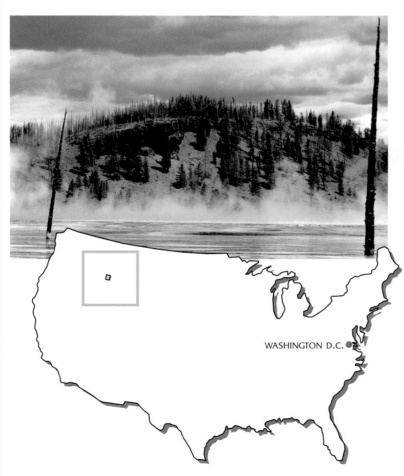

235 *bottom left In the pale winter atmosphere, the steam from the Giant Prismatic Spring creates an interesting color effect against the background of conifers.*

235 *bottom right Mammoth Hot Springs form spectacular travertine terraces created by the resurfacing of water rich in carbonic acid. They are the clearest surface indication of the volcanic forces at work in Yellowstone's subsoil.*

235 *top right Lower Yellowstone Falls run into a bright yellow gully, though the color here is nothing to do with the name of the river or Park. 'Yellowstone' refers to the color of the rock where the Yellowstone river meets the Missouri 620 miles to the east.*

WASHINGTON D.C.

This was only the first of the many surprising natural phenomena the expedition discovered during that glorious expedition. In the park's 3,468 square miles, there are more than 10,000 geothermal phenomena and more than 300 geysers – two thirds of the world's total. Formed by an accumulation of rhyolites dating to 65,000 years ago, Yellowstone Plateau has the peculiarity of lying above the crater of an ancient volcano in a zone where – following vulcanist phenomena – the earth's crust is often just a few miles thick.

Consequently, the heat from the

dramatic and colorful effect. There are also fumaroles, craters and lunar landscapes like Firehole River, where the water flows over a bed of boiling springs, creating a ribbon of steam for a long stretch of its course. The comparatively ordinary Yellowstone River flows into a spectacular canyon with striking waterfalls that drop into Yellowstone Lake. The lake has a drainage area of 137 square miles, a perimeter of 110 miles and is one of the largest alpine lakes in the world.

Almost 80% of the park is covered by forest, most of which is pine (*Pinus contorta*). The large range over which

236 top A young elk, or wapiti, rests near one of Yellowstone's many watercourses. Despite the huge influx of tourists, the wildlife in the park has been successfully conserved.

236 center left According to historical sources, moose (Alces alces) were rare in Wyoming around 1872, the year in which Yellowstone was declared a national park. However, the protection measures taken have led to a large increase in its numbers.

earth's interior warms the water that circulates through the intricate underground drainage system and sends it violently up through the subsoil in the form of vapor when the pressure becomes excessive.

However, Yellowstone contains much more than geysers. There are phenomena like the Grand Prismatic Spring, whose sulfurous crystalline water deposits salts on the banks, creating a

236 center right Bison (Bison bison) are the largest mammals in Yellowstone and the only ones completely free in the United States.

236 bottom Eradicated in the area in the 1930s, the gray wolf (Canis lupus) was reintroduced in 1995 to help control the burgeoning number of ungulates. In 2002, 10 groups were counted.

236-237 Although it is becoming rather rare in other areas of the country, the elk (Cervus elaphus), or wapiti, has its last stronghold in Yellowstone. The population in 1998 was estimated to be 25,000.

237 top A Yellowstone wapiti snorts in the cold autumn air. Cool in summer, the local winter temperature dives to an average 10°F.

238 top Bison often fall
victim to the cold Wyoming
winters. In 1996 more than
1,000 died, but fortunately
in 1998 there were still
roughly 2,200 left.

238 bottom The almost
3,500 square miles of
Yellowstone Park contains
the largest number of
geysers (around 300, 66%
of the world total) and
geothermal phenomena in
the world.

the forests stretch, from 5,600-11,360 feet, has encouraged the establishment of various botanical communities (including 1,100 species of vascular plants), semi-arid steppe and alpine tundra.

Apart from the roughly 200 grizzlies (*Ursus arctos horribilis*) and many black bears (*Ursus americanus*) on which Yogi and Boo boo were based, Yellowstone has eight indigenous species of ungulates such as elk (*Cervus elaphus*), mule deer (*Odocoileus hemionus*), American bison (*Bison bison*), moose (*Alces alces*), bighorn sheep (*Ovis canadensis*), pronghorn (*Antilocapra americana*), Rocky Mountain goat (*Oreamnos*

reintroduce the animal, and the project has been successful.

1995 was the unhappy year that UNESCO placed Yellowstone National Park on the World Heritage in Danger list. The reason was the plan by a Canadian company to construct a mine to extract gold, silver and copper just a few miles from the park's north-east boundary.

As the mine would have lain

upstream of three torrents that flowed into Yellowstone, it would have threatened to pollute the water and cause damage to the ecosystem. The Clinton Administration placed a moratorium on the project before reaching an agreement with the company involved. The park was saved by a payment of 65 million dollars; nonetheless, the Administration was accused by certain pressure groups of having ceded jurisdiction of American territory to the United Nations. Yet Yellowstone was and remains the worldwide symbol of the history of conservation.

americanus) and white-tailed deer (*Odocoileus virginianus*).

Species under threat include the bald eagle (*Haliaeetus leucocephalus*), peregrine falcon (*Falco peregrinus*) and the largest example of its genus, the trumpeter swan (*Cygnus buccinator*).

Some years ago wolves (*Canis lupus*) were reintroduced to the Canyon and Lamar Valley, having been exterminated in the 1930s with the approval of the local authorities as they threatened local herds.

It was only some decades later it was realized that, being the largest predator of the ungulates in the area, wolves were irreplaceable in maintaining the dynamic balances of the Yellowstone ecosystem intact.

In 1995, therefore, it was decided to

239 top Yellowstone Park is 80% covered by coniferous forest. Most of these are tall pines from the species Pinus contorta.

239 center left Formidable predators, the bald eagles (Haliaetus leucocephalus) in Yellowstone share the position at the top of the food chain with peregrine falcons, wolves and coyotes.

239 center right With the return of the wolves, the coyotes (Canis latrans) have had to modify their hunting territories and, to deal with the new threat, cohesion within the packs has notably increased.

239 bottom The Rocky Mountain bighorn sheep (Ovis canadensis) is easily recognized by the long curved horns of the male. The resident population in Yellowstone is considered to be little more than 200 individuals.

Redwood National Park

UNITED STATES

CALIFORNIA

REGISTRATION: 1980

CRITERIA: N (II) (III)

240 top Mountain lions (Felis concolor) avoid flat, open land, preferring higher terrain and forests, which are better suited to their tactic of ambushing prey and for protecting their young.

240-241 The giant sequoia (Sequoia sempervirens) in Redwood National Park are often associated with the indigenous species Douglas fir (Pseudotsuga menziesii).

WASHINGTON D.C.

The English and Spanish ignored northern California until the mid-nineteenth century, when the discovery of gold in the region led to the Gold Rush. This, in turn, led to the exploitation of the immense forest resources of the state, beginning with the sequoia (*Sequoia sempervirens*) that grew along the whole of the coastline to the north of San Francisco. In the past, local natives used these trees to build canoes and houses.

The sequoia is an extraordinary legacy of the gigantic evergreen conifer forests that used to dominate the temperate areas of the planet during the Jurassic period, but today it is limited to California and Oregon. It takes a sequoia 400 years to reach maturity and it lives to an age of 2,000 years. Its dry, thick bark is rich in tannin, which protects it from fire and parasites. The tallest tree in the world grows in the Redwood National Park and has reached a height of 367 feet; in 1933 in the same area, an older sequoia was cut

down whose rings showed it to be over 2200 years old.

The National Register of Historic Places estimates that 96% of the original sequoia forests have been irredeemably lost and that 42% of what remains lies within the Redwood National Park. Created in 1968 with the aim of preserving the last sequoia forests, the park covers 172 square miles, to which can be added the 10 square miles of Del Norte Redwoods State Park, the 15 square miles of Jedediah Smith Redwoods State Park and the 22 square miles of the Prairie Creek Redwoods State Park.

Redwood stretches along 34 miles of rocky coast and overlooks dizzying drops into the Pacific Ocean and the occasional sandy beach. The vegetation is very rich, with 856 species of which 699 are

indigenous. These latter include the Douglas fir (*Pseudotsuga menziesii*), the western hemlock (*Tsuga heterophylla*), the tanbark oak (*Lithocarpus densiflorus*), the grand fir (*Abies grandis*), the Sitka spruce (*Picea sitchensis*) and the Oregon maple (*Acer macrophyllum*). The fauna boasts large communities of 75 types of mammal (with lynx, elk, silver fox, black bear, otter and puma), 400 species of birds, many fish, and invertebrates, which generally inhabit the tidal area. However, the unquestioned attraction of the Redwood National Park is the sequoia, partly because its safeguarding marked a crucial step in the history of conservation. At the end of the nineteenth century, when exploitation of the sequoias reached its peak, almost all the forest area was owned privately, so logging continued without obstacle until 1918 when the paleontologists Henry Fairfield Osborn, Madison Grant and John C. Merriam instituted the Save-the-Redwoods League, an *ante litteram* environmental association

through which it was proposed that large tracts of forest should be purchased for conservation reasons. Between 1920 and 1960, the organization placed 170 square miles of forest under protection – then entrusted this land to the California Department of Parks and Recreation before it was turned into the Redwoods National Park – a part of which, already exploited by logging companies, was reforested.

Logging of sequoias continues in unprotected areas, despite the protests of environmental groups, but these trees have shown that they are strong survivors, thanks to a very unusual capability: besides their normal sexual means of reproduction, a sequoia can regenerate by rooting from a large branch or from the roots of a fallen tree, thereby creating a clone of itself.

241 top The sequoia is the tallest and largest organism in the vegetal world and is also very special: it is said, for example, that no human has ever seen one caused to topple by natural causes.

241 bottom left Sequoia are very long living owing to the large quantity of tannin in their trunks. Tannin inhibits attack by insects and makes these trees very resistant in the event of fire.

241 bottom right A young mule deer (Odocoileus hemionus) watches carefully from the edge of a clearing. Areas of transition between woodland and grassland are the preferred grazing land of this defenseless animal; and they are hunted ruthlessly outside of the protected areas.

240 bottom Situated in the counties of Humboldt and Del Norte in northeast California, the park is about 50 miles long and varies in width between 300 yards and 9 miles.

Yosemite National Park

UNITED STATES

CALIFORNIA
REGISTRATION: 1984
CRITERIA: N (I) (II) (III)

242 top left Covering an area of more than 1,160 square miles, Yosemite obtained the status of national park on 1 October 1890. Currently the protected area is visited by over 4 million visitors a year.

242 bottom left The 'incomparable valley', as Yosemite Valley is nicknamed, is a perfect example of glacial erosion. The perfectly vertical sides of the mountains on either side were created by the advance of the glaciers in the gorge formed by the Merced River.

One of the most famous photographs taken by the master Ansel Adams was titled 'Monolith, the face of Half Dome' and showed the granite wall that looks down on Yosemite Valley. In order to get the receding view of this immense block, Adams was obliged to carry his heavy equipment up onto a shoulder of the Half Dome. It was that day in Winter 1927 that Adams decided to dedicate his life to photography, with the result that he spent the next 30 years of his life in Yosemite Valley. Probably discovered by the first colonists in 1833, this astounding canyon was dug out by the Merced River in the granite of the Sierra Nevada, and it rivals the equally famous Yellowstone for being the first protected area in history. Though Yellowstone became the first national park in 1872, Yosemite Valley and the Mariposa sequoia forest were recognized as an inalienable part of the public heritage by a document of 30 June 1864, which was signed by President Lincoln. Later, worried by the exploitation of the Sierra Nevada by gold hunters, the insistence of naturalist, poet and mountain climber John Muir convinced President Theodore 'Teddy' Roosevelt to accord Yosemite the status of a national park too. On 1 October 1890, the first tourists arrived to admire the region that was to inspire generations of artists and writers. Today Yosemite National Park, whose boundaries were repeatedly enlarged up to 1984, has an area of 1,190 square miles and receives over 4 million visitors a year. All the protected area (from a height of 2,200 to 13,116 feet), is dominated by the mountains

242 right This view of the valley is taken from Glacier Point, one of the most spectacular in Yosemite. Sited on the edge of a sheer drop, it offers an extraordinary view over the most fascinating rock formations in the park.

243 Partially hidden by the winter mist, the granite block known as El Capitan rises over 3,000 feet from the valley floor. A delight for rock climbers, it was first scaled in 1958.

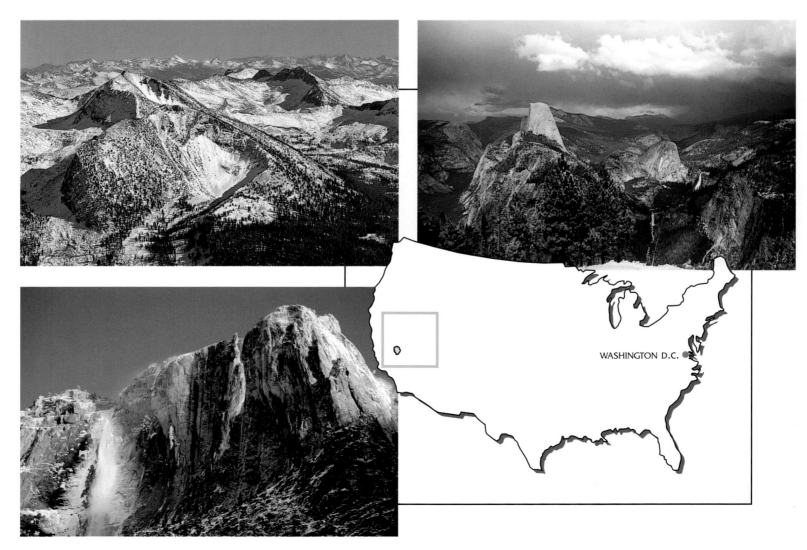

WASHINGTON D.C.

244 top Also called cougar and mountain lion, the puma (Felis concolor) is not uncommon in Yosemite despite being included on the list of endangered animals by the U.S. Wildlife Service.

244-245 Sunset over El Capitan (left) and Half Dome, another of the geological marvels in the park. Half Dome gets its name from the dome-shaped cut in the rock by the passage of the glaciers.

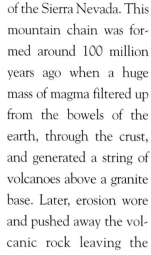

245 top With a leap of nearly 1,000 feet from a saddle on El Capitan, Horsetail Falls is the most famous of the many waterfalls in the park.

245 bottom left Three woods of sequoia (Sequoiadendron giganteum), covering 417 acres, survive in the park. The most famous individual tree is the Grizzly Giant, which stands 213 feet tall.

245 bottom right Fed by five streams that run down from the Sierra Nevada, Mono Lake's huge basin of volcanic tufa provides a habitat for a large variety and number of birds.

of the Sierra Nevada. This mountain chain was formed around 100 million years ago when a huge mass of magma filtered up from the bowels of the earth, through the crust, and generated a string of volcanoes above a granite base. Later, erosion wore and pushed away the volcanic rock leaving the granite below exposed. Yosemite Valley is a narrow canyon tens of miles long with rock walls up to 3,100 feet high and is the result of fluvial and glacial erosion over the last tens of thousands of years. This action has created not only Half Dome but also the El Capitan monolith – a block of granite that rises over 3,000 feet from the valley floor and from which the 1,000-foot Horsetail Falls cascades from the top. The glaciation has also left

damaged by logging and fires resulting from a mistaken understanding of how best to conserve the environment. It was only at the end of the 1970s that it was understood that the use of controlled fires prevents excessive thickening of the undergrowth and avoids the risk of much more serious damage if uncontrolled fires get started. The park provides a habitat to more than 230 species of birds, including the American bald eagle (Haliaeetus leucocephalus), the peregrine falcon (Falco peregrinus) and the great gray owl (Strix nebulosa). Of the 74 recorded mammals, there are the yellow-bellied marmot (Marmota flaviventris), the coyote (Canis latrans) and the mule deer (Odocoileus

U- and V-shaped valleys, moraines and glacial circles. This is the setting for 27 botanical communities and 16 types of forest. The forests are composed of silver fir (Abies alba), pine (Pinus contorta) and Norway spruce (Picea abies), but also noteworthy are species like the Californian black oak (Quercus kelloggi), Douglas fir (Abies douglasii), various other pines (Pinus sabiniana, Pinus lambertiana and Pinus monticola) and juniper (Juniperus occidentalis). In Mariposa, Merced and Tuolumne there are three sequoia woods (Sequoiadendron gigantum) that together cover 420 acres; they have been repeatedly

hemionus). Even more rare are the martens (Martes americana and Martes pennati), the wolverine (Gulo luscus) and the puma (Puma concolor).

Yosemite is also home to a community of 300-500 black bears (Ursus americanus). Over recent decades, the pressure created by tourism has introduced human food to them, which has affected their behavior. Some bears, which have become too aggressive, have had to be shot by rangers. Thus there is also the risk that they too will end up being restricted to certain areas or even disappear from Yosemite.

WASHINGTON D.C.

246 Considered one of
the wonders of the world,
the Grand Canyon is 278
miles long and nearly
5,000 feet deep, and has a
width that varies between
600 yards and 19 miles.

247 top Also known as
the bobcat, the American
red lynx (Lynx rufus) is
an elegant creature of
medium size that is
frequently seen on the
South Rim.

Grand Canyon National Park

UNITED STATES

ARIZONA
REGISTRATION: 1979
CRITERIA: N (I) (II) (III) (IV)

Looking down for the first time on the chasm of the Grand Canyon, the naturalist Donald Culross Peattie said he was aware of the 'will of God', and the writer J. B. Priestley described the spectacle of the Colorado River winding through the immense rock walls as 'the Last Judgment of nature'. Both these remarks – which make recourse to the ultramundane to explain the magnificence of the Grand Canyon – date to the end of the nineteenth century, when America was discovering the aesthetics of nature. Until then, the huge landscapes of the Wild West were seen rather as lands to be conquered and exploited.

The Grand Canyon has been known to the white man for centuries, since 1540, when it was discovered by the Spanish army captain, García Lopez de Cardenas, who was sent north by the viceroy of Mexico in search of the seven legendary golden cities of Cibola; but with such an ambitious commission, his arrival at the Grand Canyon only caused him disappointment. In consequence, the only subsequent visitors to the area were missionaries whose goal was more to save the souls of the Navajo and Hopi natives than to record geological phenomena or botanical oddities. Even Major John Wesley Powell, the veteran of the Civil War, who, leading an expedition of nine, was the first to descend the rapids of the Colorado, was less interested in geographic or naturalistic wonders than ethnological aspects. The expedition lasted three months, during which three members of the team lost their lives, but at the end of the study on the languages spoken by the natives, the Bureau for American Ethnology was set up in the Smithsonian Institution. However, the extraordinary beauty of the Grand Canyon affected Major Powell and his descriptions stirred the curiosity of his geological colleagues in the prestigious scientific institute.

The magnificence of the Grand Canyon's scenery defies any definition. This spectacular gorge is 4,900 feet deep, 277 miles long and between 1,800 feet and 20 miles wide. The Colorado River has an average flow of 850 cubic yards per second and at least 100 rapids. The horizontal rock layers in the Grand Canyon were formed over a period of 2 billion years and provide samples from the four main geological eras: the Precambrian, Paleozoic, Mesozoic and Cenozoic. It is therefore a field site of scientific interest only matched in degree by its physical beauty; no one can

247 bottom left In the area of the Grand Canyon the prairie hawk (Falco mexicanus) shares the territory with the rarer peregrine falcon (Falco peregrinus anatum).

247 bottom right The number of coyotes (Canis latrans) in the park is on the increase to the extent that measures have been taken to control its population.

248 top left The conifers on the edge of the South Rim – like the Utah juniper and Pinon pine – are species able to hold water in their roots for long periods.

248 top right Snow is not unusual at higher levels. The North Rim has a damper climate than the South Rim, therefore its vegetation is more varied and abundant.

248-249 The colorful stratification of the Grand Canyon is caused by ferrous minerals that take on red, orange, yellow and green hues when oxidized.

249 top Formed over a period of 2 billion years, the horizontal layers of the Grand Canyon bear witness to the four main geological eras: Precambrian, Paleozoic, Mesozoic and Cenozoic.

remain untouched by the splendor of the rocks smoothed by the ceaseless action of the water and by the incredible colors created by the different compositions and age of the rocks. And up on the Kaibab Plateau at the top of the canyon, it is easy to find the remains of fossilized coral, shells, seaweed and even fish.

There are innumerable lookout points along the canyon carved by the Colorado, and 'natural sculptures' the names of which once more refer to deities; for example, the Diana Temple and the Shiva Temple, though the presence of this latter god is highly improbable in this part of the world. These 'sculptures' have always been sacred to the Hopi natives who believe them to enclose the spirits of their ancestors.

The two sides of the Grand Canyon – the South and North Rims – are different worlds. The former is mostly a desert with various species of cactus, agave and yucca as well as species of conifer, like the Utah juniper and the Pinon pine, able to retain water for a long time in their roots.

The North Rim has a damper, cooler climate, and therefore more abundant vegetation, with conifer forests of Douglas and Ponderosa pines, and, in the more protected valleys, communities of aspen and birch. The result of this diversity is a difference in the fauna of the two sides of the canyon, though some species, like the coyote, puma and American goat are present on both. An example of a species living on one side only is, on the South Rim, a rare indigenous subspecies of rattlesnake (*Crotalus viridis abyssus*). Another interesting case is the Kaibab squirrel that inhabits the North Rim, and the Albert squirrel that is on the South Rim. Despite being descended from a single ancestor, the different conditions on either side of the river have led to two distinct species evolving.

Those able to travel freely between the two sides are the more than 300 species of birds recorded in the area, of which there are at least 60 pairs of peregrine falcons, making this the largest population of this species in the southern United States.

The discovery of the natural beauties of the Grand Canyon at the end of the nineteenth century coincided with the dawn of mass tourism. In 1901 a railway was built to the South Rim and, a year later, the luxurious El Tovar Hotel was opened, with Theodore Roosevelt being one of its first guests. Like many of the early visitors, the President came for 'sport' as hunting was allowed even though a forest reserve was instituted in the Grand Canyon way back in 1893. It is estimated that between 1900 and 1905 alone at least 600 pumas were shot. The institution in 1919 of the Grand Canyon National Park under Woodrow Wilson finally put an end to that disaster for the wildlife of the area. Now, the animals and birds have only to deal with the 5 million visitors to the canyon, all armed with cameras.

249

249 bottom The first white man to see the Grand Canyon was the Spanish army captain García Lopezde Cardenas in 1540.

250-251 Yaki Point Lookout (where this photograph was taken) offers one of the most remarkable views of the enormous Grand Canyon.

Great Smoky Mountains National Park

UNITED STATES

TENNESSEE AND NORTH CAROLINA
REGISTRATION: 1983
CRITERIA: N (I) (II) (III) (IV)

There are now very few places where the natural environment has remained intact, identical to how it was before the appearance of the human race. It may seem paradoxical but one such place is the Great Smoky Mountains, which are enclosed within a national park visited by 8 million people a year, more than any other protected area in the United States.

Lying at the southern tip of the long chain of the Appalachian Mountains and covering 807 square miles of land, the Great Smoky Mountains National

252 top right Glaucomys volans *is the smallest tree squirrel. It is a nocturnal rodent that shares the local habitat with many other small and medium sized mammals, from foxes to marmots.*

252 bottom The Newfound Gap Road (the only road through the park) allows the visitor to appreciate the variety of the botanical species in the Smoky Mountains. Here the lower levels are dominated by maple and birch.

Park, established in 1926, contains steep mountains up to 6,560 feet high separated by wide valleys.

The central section is a continuous rocky crest with a complex drainage system that contains 1,900 miles of impetuous mountain torrents.

The park also encloses 45 hydrographic basins and everywhere water lies close to the surface.

With these characteristics, and a climate that alternates hot, sticky summers with relatively mild winters, it is not surprising that 95% of the landscape is covered by vegetation. What makes the Smoky Mountains National Park unique is that it is the last refuge of species from temperate or northern latitudes that proliferated during the Pleistocene epoch.

Its vegetal mosaic comprises approximately 1,500 flowering plants, of which 130 are arboreal, and a total of 2,200 cryptogams.

Around 20% of the forest is virgin, whereas the areas at low altitudes that were cleared over the centuries to make agriculture possible are now like laboratories for botanists as they reveal the successive stages that flora grows back.

The area has been shown to contain 14 types of forest. At the highest levels, there is the world's largest area of red fir, which shows relationships with the forest communities in Maine at the extreme northeast of the United States, and with Ontario and Quebec in Canada. Lower down, the evergreen conifers are joined by maples and birch and, in some valleys,

there are up to 20 species of broadleaf deciduous trees in an area of just 600 square yards.

The wealth of flora is matched by the variety of the fauna, including 50 or so indigenous mammals.

Easily found are the numerous black bears (*Ursus americanus*) and deer (*Odocoileus virginianus*), even if the park is best known for medium-sized mammals such as the red fox, gray fox, lynx, raccoon, badger, skunk, marmot

252-253 About 2,200 cryptogams have been identified in the Great Smoky Mountains National Park, including several northern temperate species that have survived to the modern day from the Pleistocene epoch.

253 top Of the myriad waterfalls in the park, Grotto Falls is the only one that has a path that passes behind the sheet of water.

253 bottom The color of the leaves begins to change at the end of August at the top of the mountains, and spreads into the valleys during October when the beauty of the park reaches its maximum splendor.

and a number of different types of squirrels and bats. There are more than 200 birds and the watercourses provide a habitat for 30 species of salamander, the largest variety in the world.

At the start of the nineteenth century, the bison and *wapiti* or elk (*Cervus elaphus*) became extinct in the region, but the elk was reintroduced successfully in 2000.

That same year, puma and coyote were seen, having migrated there from other areas, which attests the health of the environment.

The animals represented two more pieces in the jigsaw of the recreation of the world that was known to the Cherokee and European pioneers.

In addition, the park contains the largest collection of nineteenth-century wooden huts in the United States, and this fact has also meant that the Smoky Mountains have been inscribed on the National Register of Historic Places.

Everglades National Park
UNITED STATES

FLORIDA
REGISTRATION: 1979
INSCRIPTION ON THE WORLD HERITAGE
SITES IN DANGER LIST: 1993
CRITERIA: N (I) (II) (IV)

254

Americans rightly claim a founding role in the conservation policies of the world's natural heritage but still the national conscience is not completely clear. Whereas America created the myth of the wilderness with the creation of the Grand Canyon and Yellowstone National Parks, an area that was of equal interest in southern Florida did not arouse the slightest interest.

The Everglades is an inhospitable area, it is true. The hot, damp climate of what seems no more than a swamp infested by mosquitoes and alligators is not particularly inviting, but the Pa-Hay-Okee ('Grass River' as the Seminole Indians call it), which flows at an imperceptible rate for 130 miles from Lake Okeechobee to the Bay of Florida and reaches a width of 50 miles, is the only tropical ecosystem in North America. And, paradoxically, recognition of its value coincided with its inexorable decline.

When President Harry Truman instituted the Everglades National Park in 1947, there were only 500,000 inhabitants in southern Florida. In 1985, the year the state authorities raised the alarm, the population had reached 6 million and industrialization had produced a catastrophic environmental disaster. The Everglades habitat had been reduced by 20%, 14 species of animal were in serious danger of extinction and

254 top Communities of mangroves of the species Rizophora mangle, Avicennia germinans and Laguncularia racemosa grow alongside the canals and river estuaries, offering a perfect habitat to many birds, fish and crustaceans.

254 center The undisputed master of the park is the American alligator (Alligator mississippiensis). This ferocious predator feeds on birds, fish, turtles, crabs, otters, frogs and, occasionally, members of its own species.

254 bottom There are 16 species of waders in the park, including Egretta caerulea (illustrated here) whose numbers are diminishing worryingly. It is estimated that its numbers have declined by 93% over the last 50 years.

WASHINGTON D.C.

all the aquatic fauna were contaminated by mercury. Furthermore, the flora was threatened by 221 species of exotic infestant plants. In 1993, inscription of the site on the list of World Heritage sites in danger caused tens of millions of dollars to be set aside for what is one of the largest environmental cleaning programs in the world. Nonetheless, today, the situation seems even more serious.

Spread over 2,300 square miles, the

254-255 Covering 2,317 square miles, the Everglades National Park is the only tropical ecosystem in North America. Botanists are drawn by the huge quantity of vegetal species – 60-70% – found in the Caribbean area and the high proportion of endemic species.

255 top The 'River of Grass' flows at an imperceptible speed for 125 miles between Lake Okeechobee and Florida Bay.

255 right Although less rare in the Everglades than the white pelican, the brown pelican (Pelecanus occidentalis) is suffering from mercury poisoning of the fish that form the basis of its diet.

park contains many different habitats,
from the marine environment of the Bay
of Florida to the drier environment near
Lake Okeechobee, where 200 tropical
plant species live close to pines
characteristic of temperate climes.
Between these two extremes there are
several communities of mangroves,
which live where the salt and fresh
waters meet. Further inland there are
mudflats covered by herbaceous plants,
water meadows and communities of
cypress that have developed the ability
to survive in stagnant water. Above all,
there is the 'Grass River' that advances
just 100 feet a day and has a depth of 10
feet in the center and less than 3 feet at
the sides; the river is punctuated by
islands on which oaks and red maples
grow.

Though the population is falling,
there are 800 aquatic and terrestrial
animal species in the Everglades. The
one that causes most worry is the
manatee (Trichecus manatus), of which
only 1,000 or so remain. The manatee is
closely followed by the Florida panther
(Felis concolor coryi); of the 30 remaining,
more than half now wear a radio-collar
so that their movements can be
monitored. With regard to the bird
population, the many species of waders
are of concern as their numbers have
fallen 93% in the past 50 years.

Enjoying good health, however, are
most of the 60 species of reptiles and
amphibians. The undisputed king of the
Everglades is the American alligator
(Alligator mississippiensis), which is the
most ferocious predator in the park.
Visitors, nevertheless, are more afraid of
the 43 different species of mosquito that
proliferate exponentially in the swamps:
between them they lay 10,000 eggs for
every square foot of land. They too are
protected, as they are a fundamental link
in the food chain, though that does not
bring peace of mind to the tourists.

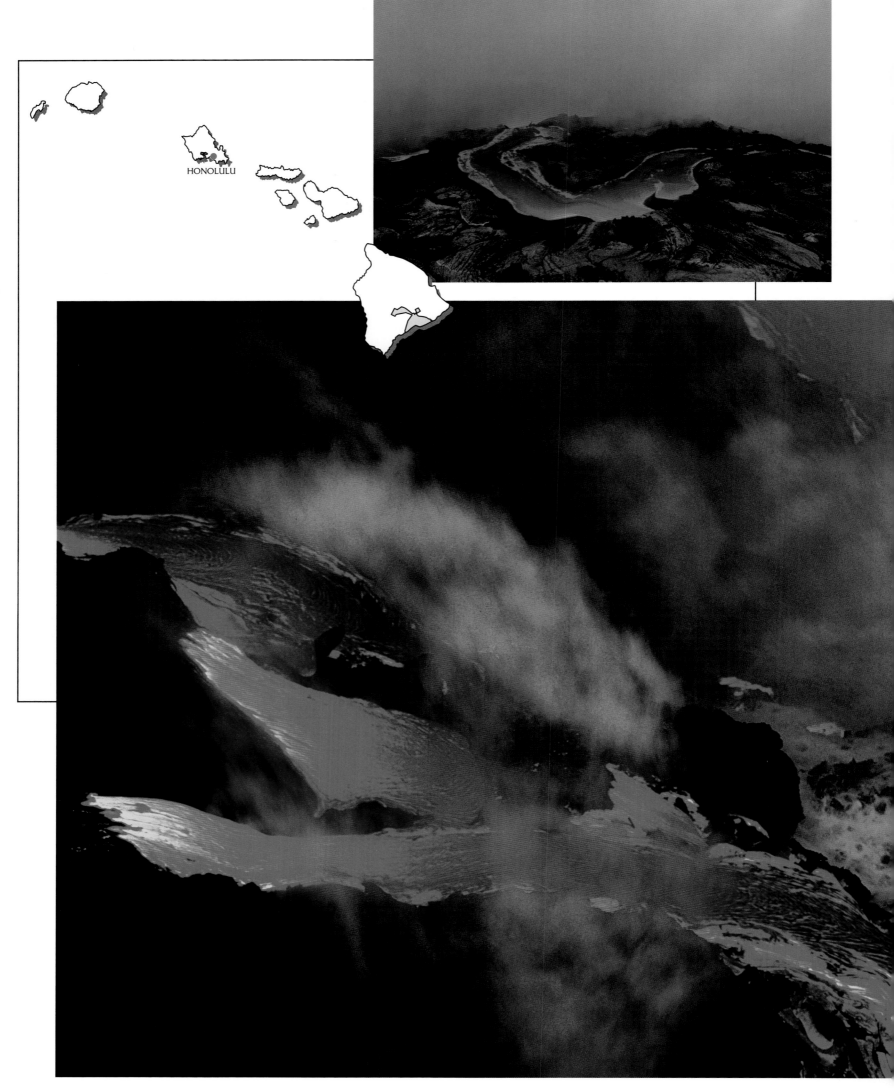

HONOLULU

258 top A river of
incandescent lava flows
over a pahoehoe field. This
Hawaiian word has
entered the international

geological vocabulary
to define a very smooth
basalt lava surface with
a fibrous crust like
bread.

258-259 The lava that
has been exuded for
20 years uninterruptedly
from Kilauea – 4,100
feet high and considered

the most active volcano on
the planet – flows into
the Pacific Ocean
producing large clouds
of vapor.

259 The ceaseless
eruption of Kilauea has
been a tourist attraction
since 1840. In 1866
the volcano was visited

by Mark Twain who
praised its beauty.
In 1912 the U.S.
Geological Survey
observatory was built.

Hawaii Volcanoes National Park
UNITED STATES

HAWAII
REGISTRATION: 1987
CRITERIA: N (II)

Lieutenant James King, on board James Cook's 1779 expedition, estimated the height of Mauna Loa to be 16,020 feet. A few years later, the barometric measurements taken by botanist Archibald Menzies (the first to reach its peak) were the first to record it fairly accurately, with a reading of 13,563 feet. In fact, according to the U.S. Geological Survey Hawaiian Volcano Observatory, founded in 1912, Mauna Loa in the southwest of Hawaii is 13,678 feet high.

When, however, the roughly 16,400 feet from the bottom of the ocean are added, and the 26,250 feet of the depression that has been formed by the upward thrust of the volcano, at a total height of over 55,000 feet (10.5 miles), Mauna Loa is the tallest mountain in the world, almost double the height of Everest. It is certainly the most voluminous as it contains approximately 20,000 cubic miles of volcanic rock and covers an area above sea level of 2,035 square miles.

It is one of the most active volcanoes on earth, with 33 eruptions recorded in the historical period, but even this figure is easily beaten by its neighbor Kilauea, which was in continuous eruption for over 20 years up until 1907 and then began again in fits and starts in 1952 before another continuous eruption started in 1983 and which has so far shown no signs of abating. This type of eruption is referred to as 'Hawaiian'; it is rarely explosive and features a continuous flow of lava that often spills from the side of the volcano.

Over millennia, these flows of fluid magma have deposited layer over layer of lava that have produced the spectacular volcanic panorama of the island of Hawaii.

Both volcanoes are part of the Hawaiian National Park created in 1916 and later extended to cover its current area of 359 square miles.

Instituted to preserve the landscape modeled by 70 million years of geological evolution, the park has

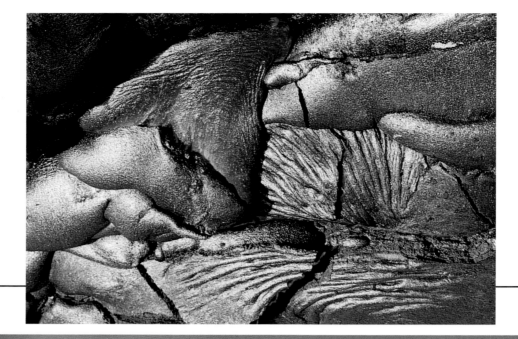

260 top A small triangular
tongue of lava creeps into
the already cooled deposits
of magma, cracking them
with its pressure and
creating the typical woven
appearance of the
pahoehoe.

260-261 The lava from
Kilauea slides into the sea
from the top of a cliff.
The uninterrupted
accumulation of large
quantities of magma has
given the island of Hawaii
a lunar landscape.

become the refuge of autochthonous
plant and animal species.

The isolation of the Hawaiian
Archipelago and the peculiar nature
of the soil have encouraged the growth
of botanical communities with a high
percentage of endemic species even
though, as is typical of islands in general,
the biodiversity is relatively
less than that of continental areas.

The ferns are of particular importance,
as they represent a substantial
percentage of the indigenous flora that
still prevails at altitudes above 4,900
feet, whereas imported plants have
contaminated the environment below
2,000 feet.

The only original mammal to inhabit
Hawaii is the *Lasiurus cinereus*, the most
common bat in the Americas.

The birds are of great interest with
several exemplifying adaptive radiation.

261 top Kilauea is the
most active volcano in the
world and Mauna Loa is
the largest, formed by
20,000 cubic miles of
volcanic rock. The
mountain's overall height
from its base on the bottom
of the ocean 5 miles down
exceeds 55,000 feet.

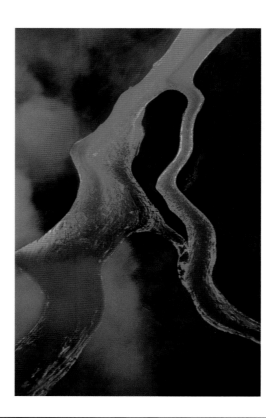

261 bottom Kilauea
originated between
600,000 and 300,000
years ago. The incessant
eruptions of the last two
centuries are probably a
reliable indicator of the
behavior of this volcano
over the last 100,000
years.

262 and 263 The eruptions of Mauna Loa and Kilauea were studied in detail during the twentieth century. They are spectacular sights but the degree of fluidity of the magma expelled means that the eruptions are rarely explosive in character. In general the incandescent lava seeps out from cracks in the side of the cones. This type of eruption is referred to scientifically as 'Hawaiian'.

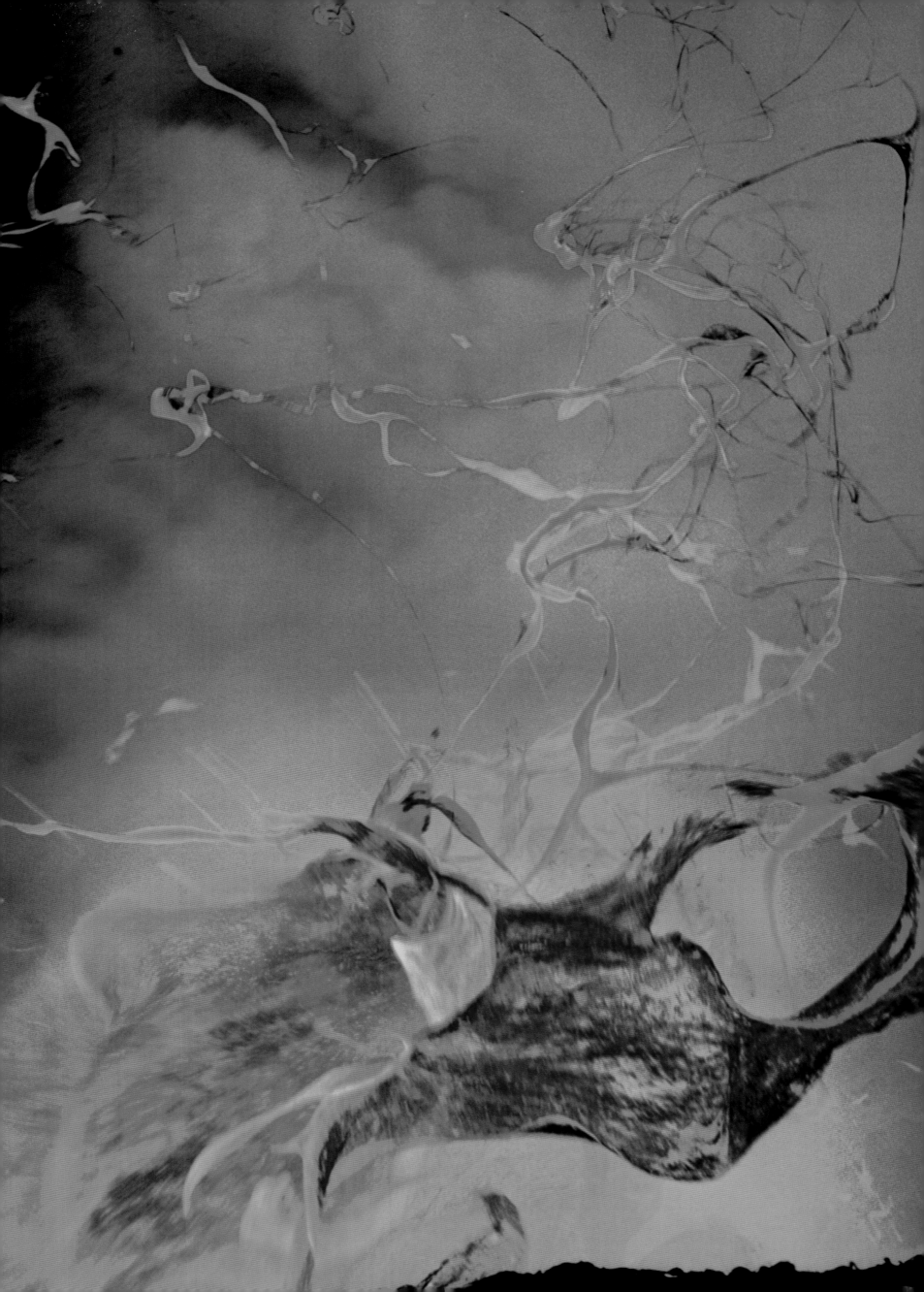

264 Akaka Falls is one of the loveliest waterfalls in Hawaii. It falls 440 feet down a face covered completely in mosses. The surrounding forest, in which giant ferns dominate, was declared a territorial park in 1923.

265 top Kilauea's crater seems quiet in this picture but the volcano only appears to be sleeping. The eruptions from the cone exit from the cracks low down on the sides of the mountain.

Many endemic species are rare or endangered; these include the *akepa* (*Loxops coccineus*), the *akiapola'au* (*Hemignathus wilsoni*), the Hawaiian petrel (*Pterodroma sandwichensis*), the omao (*Phaeornis obscurus*), the *apapane* (*Himatione sanguinea*), the *elepaio* (*Chasiempis sandwichensis*), the *amakihi* (*Hemignathus virens*) and the *iiwi* (*Vestiaria coccinea*).

The entire park, unfortunately, is seriously compromised by the invasiveness of the species introduced by man. Wild goats and pigs have destroyed entire areas of indigenous plants and the mongoose has decimated the reptile population.

The *nene* (*Branta sandvicensis*), the last survivor of nine species of endemic wild goose, recently elevated to being the symbol of Hawaiian conservation, has suffered from hunting and from alteration of its natural habitat. Estimates say there were around 25,000 when James Cook arrived but no more than 50 were left in the mid 1940s.

A program of reintroduction begun in the 1970s has had some success but the survival of the *nene* is still dependent on man's care.

265 bottom left The ohelo (Vaccinium reticulatum) is an endemic berry that only grows on the islands of Hawaii and Maui. Its rare fruits are one of the favorite foods of the nene (Branta sanvicensis), the last species of wild goose on Hawaii.

265 bottom right The unusual haleakala (Argyroxiphium sandwicense) is perhaps the plant that best typifies Hawaii. Thanks to the island's isolation, 90% of the flowering plants on Hawaii are endemic but this heritage is greatly threatened by imported species.

Whale sanctuary of
El Vizcaíno

MEXICO

BAJA CALIFORNIA
REGISTRATION: 1993
CRITERIA: N (IV)

266 top With a maximum length of 28 inches, olive ridley sea turtle (Lepidochelys olivacea) is the smallest sea turtle. It lives both in the pelagic or open sea water as well as along the coast but prefers the calm waters of lagoons such as those of El Vizcaíno.

MEXICO CITY

266-267 The dramatic white cliffs of Baja California are perennially battered by the ocean waves. Migration routes bring thousands of Pacific whales to this area to breed.

267 top left and center left The coast of El Vizcaíno has countless beautiful bays with crystalline water.

267 right The growing pressure exerted by tourism is becoming a serious threat to marine mammals in the area of El Vizcaíno, for example, these Californian sea lions (Zalophus californianus). Recently, the colony at Morro Santo Domingo decided to move away because of the intrusive human presence.

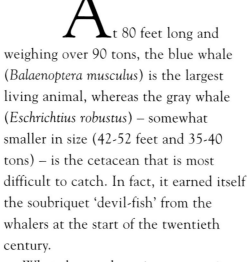

At 80 feet long and weighing over 90 tons, the blue whale (*Balaenoptera musculus*) is the largest living animal, whereas the gray whale (*Eschrichtius robustus*) – somewhat smaller in size (42-52 feet and 35-40 tons) – is the cetacean that is most difficult to catch. In fact, it earned itself the soubriquet 'devil-fish' from the whalers at the start of the twentieth century.

What the two have in common is the long migration that they make from the winter season in the Arctic Ocean and the Gulf of Alaska to the milder temperatures of the coastal lagoons Ojo de Liebre and San Ignacio in Baja California. Here they spend about three months for the mating and calving season. The return trip is over 12,500 miles long, which they make by following the western coastline of North America.

The whales have found protection in the calm lagoons of El Vizcaíno since 1933 when Mexico banned whale hunting, becoming a member of the International Whaling Commission soon after the Second World War.

The El Vizcaíno Biosphere Reserve extends over 9,600 square miles (it includes the El Vizcaíno desert, the Bahia Sebastian Vizcaíno and numerous coastal lakes) and although it was only instituted in 1988, the two lagoons, Ojo de Liebre and San Ignacio (that together measure 1,430 square miles) have been under protection since 1972.

In the 30 years since the decision was taken, the population of gray whales has increased from 1,000 (when it was thought to be on the road to extinction) to 27,000, with 900 young born each year in the waters of El Vizcaíno.

The situation of the blue whale is much more precarious despite the northern Pacific population increasing from 1,200 to 1,700 and having a world total of 12,000.

Situated in a region with a particularly dry climate (annual precipitation averages 4 inches), the two lagoons are surrounded by coastal dunes dominated by low shrubs and, in stretches, by the northern tips of a mangrove forest.

267 bottom A flock of white pelicans (Pelecanus erythrorhynchos) in flight near the coast. Thanks to the favorable climate, El Vizcaíno is home to 192 species of birds.

Guanacaste Conservation Area

COSTA RICA

PROVINCES OF GUANACASTE AND ALAJUELA
REGISTRATION: 1999
CRITERIA: N (II) (IV)

The people in the area call it *arribada* but it is more like a full-scale invasion by the 250,000 turtles that arrive on the beaches of Naranjo and Nancite between August and December to lay their eggs. There is no better place in Central America to witness this spectacle. The first to arrive are the green turtles (Chelonia mydas), followed shortly after by the many olive ridley turtles (*Lepidochelys olivacea*) and giant leatherback turtles (*Dermochelys coriacea*). To prevent the creatures being disturbed, the Pacific Ocean Protection Zone here stretches 12 miles out to sea, but the Guanacaste Conservation Area, which was established in 1989 by the Costa Rican government, also includes beaches and huge coastal plains and reaches right over to the Atlantic Ocean across the Cordillera Guanacaste.

The turtles' nesting site is only one of the many attractions in the Area. Covering 463 square miles of land and 193 square miles of sea, it is an exceptional set of different ecosystems, as well as being a laboratory of crucial importance to the study of tropical faunal and botanical species. The forest that covers a vast portion of the Area has been divided into seven vegetation zones and, to give an example, in the dry tropical forest alone, 20 different associations of plants have been recorded that correspond to as many types of land and different exposures to the wind. And in the wet tropical forest, there is the world's highest concentration of guaria morada

280 top right A howler monkey (Alouatta palliata) looks out from a safe position in Parque Nacionál Santa Rosa. This primate shares the area with the capuchin monkey (Cebus capucinus).

280 top left Rincón de la Vieha is the largest volcano in the area (6,286 ft.). From here 32 rivers and 16 torrents flow into the Tempisque, the river that is of vital importance to the population of the province of Guanacaste.

280 bottom left The Guanacaste Area de Conservación covers 37 freshwater and brackish lagoons that need to be protected. Some of them are homes to remarkably intact mangrove forests.

280 bottom right The Orosí Volcano lies in the western zone of the protected area. This volcanic area has a high calcium carbonate content and many pailas (small boiling mud craters).

SAN JOSÉ

281 top Just over a mile long, Nancite Beach lies in Parque Naciónal Santa Rosa. Overall the protected area covers 463 square miles on land and 270 at sea. Its fauna and flora represent 65% of Costa Rica's total.

281 bottom About 12 miles of beach in the protected area are where the arribada – the arrival of 250,000 sea turtles to lay their eggs – takes place between August and December.

282 top With a noisy beating of wings, a splendid scarlet macaw (Ara macao) takes to the air. Sought after by illegal bird traders, this is the largest parrot in the world.

282-283 A tree frog (Hyla crepitans) clutches a palm fruit securely. Palms prosper in forests near the coast where trees from the Clusia species dominate.

283 top Surprised by the photographer, a palm viper (Bothrops lateralis) coils itself. In the province of Guanacaste 500 species of reptiles have been recorded, half of which are snakes.

283 bottom A small blue butterfly sucking nectar creates a garish contrast with a red Heliconia flower. Guanacaste's protected area provides a habitat to roughly 5,000 species of butterfly.

(Cattleya skinneri), the beautiful orchid that is the national flower of Costa Rica.

In the 37 brackish coastal lagoons – of which Puerto Soley, Cuajiniquil, Santa Elena and Potrero Grande are the largest in Central America – mangroves grow in abundance, including rare species like Rhizophora mangle, Avicenna

province of Guanacaste.

The terrestrial fauna numbers 2 million species of insect (of which there are 5,000 butterflies alone), 500 birds and many mammals requiring conservation: the white-lipped peccary (Tayassu pecary), margay (Felis wiedii), capuchin monkey (Cebus capucinus) and the howler monkey (Alouatta palliata).

nitida and Conocarpus erectus.

In the middle of the Cordillera, there is also a freshwater lake that lies in the Rincon de la Vieja – a volcano with three craters, the largest of which lies at an altitude of 6,290 feet.

The last large eruption occurred in the 1980s but the fumarole and the pailas (boiling mud baths) at the base of the volcano are evidence of its continuing activity.

Rincon de la Vieja gives rise to 32 rivers and 16 torrents that all flow into the Tempisque, a river of vital importance to the farmers in the

Surprisingly, this natural paradise has also been of importance to the history of Costa Rica: the Guanacaste Conservation Area encloses the Parque Nacional de Santa Rosa, which was named after the hacienda founded in 1580. In 1856 the main building was the setting for the 'Battle of Santa Rosa', the first and fundamental step on the way to the country's independence from Spain.

The colonial-style building was declared a National Monument in 1966 and today is the head office for administration of the protected area.

Parque Nacionál Darién

PANAMA

PROVINCE OF DARIEN
REGISTRATION: 1981
CRITERIA: N (II) (III) (IV)

PANAMA

For the Emberà, Wounaan and Kuna peoples, the arrival of Columbus on the coast of Panama in 1502 and, a few years later, the foundation of the city of Santa María Antigua del Darién were not exactly good news. Colonization brought profound disruption to their customs. The survival of these peoples was aided by the unusual resemblance of the fruit of the tagua tree (*Phytelephas macrocarpa*), a species of palm, to the ivory of elephant tusks.

Until the invention of plastic, expert carving of the tagua fruit by the indigenous people of Darién supplied them with a source of income and the Spaniards with a good commercial profit. The tree provided such things as buttons, jewelry, dice and chess pieces; during the Victorian era, even very costly objects were passed off as being carved from ivory when they were really tagua. Despite the development of the area that the Panama Canal has brought, the indigenous communities have continued to maintain a hunting and slash-and-burn existence and still make carvings of idols from the fruits of the tagua tree, partially as a result of the unspoilt environment of the Parque Nacionál Darién where their villages lie.

Established in 1980, the park lies on the Colombian border where North and South America meet geographically, botanically and zoologically. Covering 2,300 square miles, it stretches from the Pacific coast to the 6,150 feet of Cerro Tacarcuna, the highest peak in the Serranía del Darién. Formed by volcanic rock covered by sedimentation, this strip of land between the two continents has repeatedly submerged and re-emerged over the geological eras.

It most recently reappeared at the start of the Pleistocene epoch.

Within its boundaries lie beaches, cliffs, mangrove forests, freshwater meadows, marshes, palm groves and the largest tropical forest in Central America. The rainforest features an ecosystem with the greatest biodiversity in the region and a vault 130-160 feet high whose most common species is the *cuipo* (*Cavanillesia platanifolia*), with reddish orange leaves.

A widespread species in the mountain forests is the *cativo* (*Prioria copaifera*), along with epiphytes, bromeliads and orchids, of which there are at least 40 endemic species.

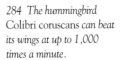

284 The hummingbird Colibri coruscans *can beat its wings at up to 1,000 times a minute.*

285 top and center *The vault of the tropical forest of Darién is between 130-160 feet high.*

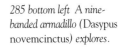

285 bottom left A nine-banded armadillo (Dasypus novemcinctus) *explores.*

285 bottom right A common potoo (Nyctibius griseus) *is perfectly camouflaged on the top of a branch.*

The Pacific mangrove swamps provide a habitat for the red mangrove (*Rhizophora mangle*) and *Avicennia nitida, Laguncularia racemosa, Mora oleifera* (V) and *Pterocarpus officinalis*.

Studies on the fauna have not been very extensive but, even so, many endemic species have been noted, including the rodent *Orthogeomys dariénsis*, and the small marsupial *Marmosops invictus* from the didelphid order.

All five American cats are present: the jaguar (*Pantera onca*), puma (*Felis concolor*), ocelot (*Felis pardalis*), margay (*Felis wiedii*) and jaguarundi (*Felis yagouaroundi*).

There is also the capybara (*Hydrochoerus hydrochaeris*) and endangered species such as the bush dog (*Speothos venaticus*), the giant anteater (*Myrmecophaga tridactyla*), the spider monkey (*Ateles fusciceps*) and Baird's tapir (*Tapirus bairdii*).

The park is also home to the world's largest community of harpy eagles (*Harpia harpyja*).

The latest threat to this tropical paradise is the construction of the Panamerican highway that runs from Alaska to Argentina.

This large artery had already harmed indigenous populations elsewhere, but an agreement between the Panamanian government and the Interamerican Development Bank has warded off, for the moment, the danger that its construction and use would represent to the delicate ecosystem of the Darién.

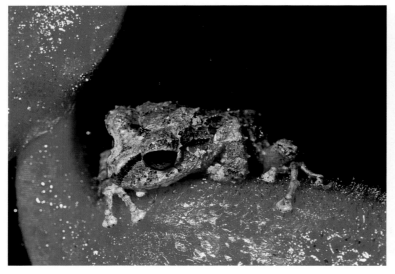

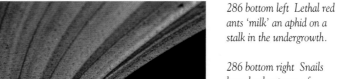

286 top A dangerous boa constrictor (Boa constrictor imperator). In this subspecies, the females are larger than the males and can reach a length of 7 feet.

286 center left and right The fauna in Darién includes strange creatures like the frog Eleutherodactilus spp. and grasshopper (Markia histrix) whose body is covered with quills.

286 bottom left Lethal red ants 'milk' an aphid on a stalk in the undergrowth.

286 bottom right Snails love the dampness of Darién where rainfall varies between 100-140 inches a year.

287 A frog of the genus Leutherodactylus on top of a ginger plant.

Parque Nacionál Canaima
VENEZUELA

STATE OF BOLIVÁR
REGISTRATION: 1994
CRITERIA: N (I) (II) (III) (IV)

One of the first books written on the subject of the conservation of the natural environment was a novel: *The Lost World* by Sir Arthur Conan Doyle. Better known as the creator of Sherlock Holmes, the author drew his inspiration for the lost world of his novel from the *tepuy*, the flat-topped, polychrome sandstone mountains in the state of Bolivár in Venezuela.

In fact, Conan Doyle never saw a *tepuy*. He was probably struck by the enthusiastic reports by the naturalists at the Royal Society, who were the first to explore that immense and remote area of Latin America. It is so vast that its principal feature was not discovered until 1937 when Jimmy Angel, an American adventurer searching for the mythical El Dorado, left Panama in a small plane and landed on the Auyán-*tepuy*. He set off

Falls is one of the largest tourist attractions in Venezuela and, since 1964, has been part of Parque Nacionál Canaima, which, covering 11,580 square miles, is the sixth largest park on the planet. It lies to the south of the Orinoco on the Brazil-Guyana borders and is composed of three physiogeographic areas: the gently undulating lowlands at a height of between 1,100 and 2,100 feet, the Gran Sabana plateau between 2,600 and 4,900 feet and the tops of the *tepuy*, which range from 3,250 and 9,220 feet, the highest of which is Roraima. The park is also the source of the Río Caroní, which, with its many tributaries, supplies water to Guri Dam where 60% of Venezuela's electricity is produced.

Geologically, the territory is formed by Precambrian rocks modeled by 600 million years of erosive processes. The vegetation of the lowlands and the Gran Sabana is

than 500 species of orchids grow in the park.

Although not particularly abundant, the fauna includes 118 species of mammals, 550 birds, 72 reptiles and 55 amphibians. Those on the International Union for the Conservation of Nature's Red List are the giant armadillo (*Priodontes maximus*), giant anteater (*Myrmeophaga tridactyla*) and margay (*Leopardus wiedii*). Birds like toucans, parrots and hummingbirds are easier to sight, if only for their bright-colored plumage. In contrast, it is highly unusual to encounter the shy and silent king of the forest, the jaguar.

In 1993 an anonymous character entered the Guinness Book of Records for having ceded to the Venezuelan state 278 square miles of forest adjacent to the park, the largest area of land ever donated for reasons of conservation.

288 top Less majestic than Angel Falls, the Jasper Waterfall is one of the marvels of the Gran Sabana, a region modeled by 600 million years of erosion.

again a few hours later, this time on foot, as he was unable to restart his plane, and 11 days later he reached civilization. When he arrived, he was able to show a bagful of gold nuggets and, above all, tell of his discovery of the world's largest waterfall.

In his honor, the waterfall was named Angel Falls. It is 3,287 feet high (15 times the size of Niagara) and the water takes 14 seconds to fall from top to bottom. Angel

characterized by herbaceous plants and shrubs of the genus Mauritia (known as *morichales* by the local population), while wet tropical forest grows with great biodiversity with many endemic species near the watercourses, on the slopes and in the canyons of the *tepuy*. Numerous carnivorous plants grow in the *tepuy* system (called Pantepuy by botanists). It is estimated that between 3,000 and 5,000 species of phanerogamous plants and ferns, and more

288 bottom left A shy and suspicious cat, the jaguar (Panthera onca) is almost impossible to spot in the park. Although fairly diverse, the fauna in Canaima is not abundant.

288 bottom right The 11,600 square miles of the Parque Nacionál Canaima is the sixth largest protected area on Earth.

289 With a total height of
3,287 feet and a free fall of
2,647 feet, Angel Falls is
the world's tallest waterfall;
fifteen times higher than
Niagara. The water takes
14 seconds to complete the
drop.

CARACAS

The Galápagos Islands
ECUADOR

REGISTRATION: 1978, 2001
CRITERIA: N (I) (II) (III) (IV)

290 top The incandescent magma flowing from the sides of the volcano near Punta Espinosa on the island of Fernandina is a magnificent sight. Fernandina is the westernmost island in the archipelago and lies a few miles south of the equator.

290 bottom A group of Brachycereus nesioticus cactus prospers near Punta Espinosa on Fernandina. The island has had no plants or wildlife introduced by man and is one of the very rare natural environments left on the planet.

It was in 1835 that the young naturalist Charles Darwin reached the Galápagos Islands on H.M.S. Beagle and recognised: 'a highly unusual group of finches, similar to one another in the structure of their beak, their short tail and the form of their body and plumage […]. Observing this gradation and diversity of structure in a small and very homogeneous group of birds, one can truly imagine […] that a species has been altered so as to perform different purposes.' A further 24 years were to pass before his theory took shape in his book *On the Origin of Species*.

In this book Darwin proposed different postulates, amongst which was a gradual and continual evolution of living species, the descent of all organisms from a common ancestor and the selection of the next generation through the 'survival of the fittest' in the struggle for existence. And those brownish birds that belonged to 13 species, together known as Darwin's finches, played a decisive role in the development of the theory of evolution.

In truth the Galápagos Islands, discovered exactly 300 years earlier by the Bishop of Panama, Tomás de Berlanga, have experienced every sort of vicissitude. Originally uninhabited, in the seventeenth and eighteenth centuries they became the refuge of pirates and buccaneers who stopped off there to fill up with fresh water and the famous giant tortoises, which they loaded on board live so they could eat fresh meat. Fascinated by these exceptional creatures – after which the islands are named, *galápago* is Spanish for tortoise – Darwin too found the taste delicious, underlining in his notes how good the meat tasted when roasted in its shell as well as the soup made with younger tortoises.

Owing to the almost complete isolation of the islands, like Darwin's finches, the giant tortoise (*Geochelone elephantopus*) are an extraordinary example of evolution, growing to weigh 550 pounds and able to live for more than 100 years. Although they have been classified as a single species descended from a few individual tortoises that reached the Galápagos in remote history, there are in fact 14 subspecies, three of which are now extinct, while of another there is only one remaining. It is unknown whether the adaptations that have occurred over the millennia would allow a cross

QUITO

290-291 With a dark, bare landscape often marked by eruptive phenomena, and home to many marine iguanas, Fernandina is an inhospitable island yet contemporaneously the most interesting on the archipelago.

291 top The landscape of Bartolomé, the youngest and most spectacular island in the archipelago, is decidedly lunar. It is formed by a series of half-moon beaches and picturesque lava formations, the best known of which is Pinnacle Rock.

291 bottom left Punta Suarez on Hood Island is famous for this blowhole that spurts water between 50 and 100 feet into the air depending on the force of the waves.

291 bottom right A small crater lies in Santiago, the east coast of which has a huge pahoehoe lava field resulting from a violent eruption in 1897.

292-293 The majestic great frigate (Fregata minor) reproduces only once every two years because it takes more than one year to wean the chicks. This photo shows a female with her young

292 bottom The waved albatross (Diomedea irrorata) is able to spend a full year without touching land. At Gardener Bay on Hood Island there are 10,000 pairs, almost the entire world population.

293 top A falcon attacks a giant tortoise (Geochelone elephantopus), of which there are roughly 150,000 on the archipelago.

between different populations. With the arrival of whale hunters – including Hermann Melville who found inspiration for his novel *Moby Dick* here – the fate of the tortoises seemed at hand. It is estimated that over 100,000 have been hunted, leaving a population of roughly 15,000.

Lying just south of the equator and 500 miles from the coast of South America, the archipelago is composed of 13 major islands, seven smaller ones and 100 or so tiny islets and reefs over a total of 3,100 square miles. It is formed by volcanic lava and magma and still has several active volcanoes.

When the islands were annexed by Ecuador in 1832, the Quito government began a project of colonization that led

islands. Both were registered as World Heritage sites in 1978 and 2001 respectively.

Finches and tortoises apart, the Galápagos Islands are an extraordinary open-air laboratory to study the fauna and flora, which has evolved independently, resulting in the highest percentage of endemism in the world. In total the endemic species include over 300 fish, 1,600 insects, 80 spiders, 300 coleopteras and 650 mollusks. There are also endemic species of sea birds like the flightless cormorant, an albatross, three gannets and two gulls. In addition the archipelago is home to the only penguin to live in tropical waters, sea lions and the Galápagos seal, which was highly prized by

293 bottom left The blue-footed booby (Sula nebouxii) is not endemic to the Galápagos but is also found in the Gulf of California and other areas of the Pacific.

293 bottom right The only non-flying cormorant, the Phalacrocorax harrisi is one of the species most at risk on the archipelago.

to the settling of various communities. The current population of roughly 18,000 is concentrated in the capital, Puerto Baquerizo Moreno, and the two towns of Puerto Ayora and Santa Cruz. In 1959, 97% of the archipelago's surface area was designated a national park and in 1986 a marine reserve was instituted to protect the waters that surround the

nineteenth-century fur hunters.

The reptiles merit a separate description as they have evolved freely in an environment void of predators. There are geckos, snakes, lava lizards and land iguanas, but special mention must be made of a marine iguana, the only species of aquatic lizard in the world. Practically every rock in the

Galápagos is inhabited by these reptiles, which live on the land but feed in the water on algae. Their population, estimated to be 200,000-300,000, is under serious threat from the oil that leaked in 2001 from the tanker *Jessica*. The June 2002 edition of *Nature* magazine reported that the mortality rate of the marine iguanas on the island of Santa Fe had increased exceptionally since the accident.

The Galápagos have an extremely fragile ecosystem that human presence has already profoundly altered. In 1976 a group of wild dogs attacked a colony of 500 land iguanas, killing them all, and in the 1990s poachers killed at least 120 giant tortoises. If this were not enough, the work of the Charles Darwin Foundation, which looks after the archipelago, is hard pushed by the Ecuadorian government, which, since the 1980s, has established incentives for the islands to be populated and the number of inhabitants is growing at around 8% a year.

294 top left A prevalently terrestrial animal, the marine iguana (Amblyrhynchus cristatus) is also able to swim and feeds exclusively on seaweed. Other iguanas do not share this custom and so the marine iguana has an almost unlimited source of food but is vulnerable to marine predators.

294 top right Almost every rock in the Galápagos is a home to marine iguanas. The total population of this species is estimated at 200,000-300,000. The concentration along the coast reaches roughly 3,000 every 1,000 yards.

294 center An endemic subspecies of the Californian sea lion, the Galápagos sea lion (Zalophus californianus wollebaeki) probably swam to the island, settled and began to differentiate from its nearest relatives.

294 bottom Genetically close to Magellan penguins, the Galápagos penguins (Spheniscus mendiculus) can survive in the archipelago's equatorial waters thanks to the cold Humboldt Current that reaches Fernandina and Isabela Islands.

294-295 A group of sea lions lazes on the beach of Mosquera Island. Like the penguins and cormorants, the numerous population of this marine mammal has suffered from el Niño. During the event of 1997-98, the population of the main colonies was reduced by 48 percent.

295 top A green turtle (Chelonia mydas) takes pains to lay her eggs safely on a beach of Bartolomé but, just a few yards away, a Galápagos buteo (Buteo galapagoensis) awaits its moment.

296 top Dominated by the
bulk of Huascarán, the
Lagunas Llanganuco form
the most famous series of
lakes in the park. The
protected area covers 296
sparklingly clear lakes of
glacial origin.

LIMA

296-297 At 22,205 feet
high, Nevado Huascarán,
called 'Corazón del Parque',
is the highest mountain in
the Cordillera Blanca in the
province of Ancash north of
Lima. It is the second
highest peak in all of the
Andes after Cerro
Acongagua (22,834 feet).

297 top The Cordillera
Blanca has the highest
tropical mountain chain
in the world with
27 peaks over 19,685
feet, 663 glaciers and
41 rivers that flow
into the Rio Santa,
Marañon and Pativilca
basins.

Parque Nacionál Huascarán

PERU

DEPARTMENT OF ANCASH
REGISTRATION: 1985
CRITERIA: N (II) (III)

The world's largest bromeliad only grows at a height of between 12,140 and 13,800 feet on the sunniest and most sheltered side of Quebrada Pachacoto in the Cordillera Blanca. The 28,000 examples that live there can reach a height of 33 feet and, during its single spectacular blooming in its 100-year lifespan, it produces thousands of flowers and millions of seeds. The *Puya raimondii* owes its name to Antonio Raimondi, a nineteenth-century Italian traveler and scientist, who dedicated his life to exploring Peru on behalf of the University of Lima.

The *Puya raimondii* is, however, only one of the many attractions in the Parque Nacionál Huascarán, established in 1975 to protect the area of the Cordillera Blanca, the highest range in the Peruvian Andes and its tropical zone. The park runs for 110 miles north to south between the Callejón de Huaylas and Callejón de Conchucos and has a maximum width of 13 miles. Covering 1,312 square miles, it encloses 27 peaks over 19,680 feet high, 663 glaciers, 296 lakes and 41 torrents, which run into the three rivers, the Santa, Pativilca and Marañon.

Spread over a territory that ranges from an altitude of 8,200 to the 22,205 feet of Mount Huascarán (the second highest mountain in the Andes), the park has seven different habitats with a wide array of microclimates, from wet mountain forest to fluvial tundra. This wide variation enables roughly 800 species of high Andean flora to grow that belong to 340 genera and 140 families. Particularly interesting are the remains of forests of *queñual* (a tree of the genus *Polyepis* similar to cork oak) and the many orchids of the genera *Orchis* and *Masdevallia*.

Although hunting has drastically reduced the animal population, the Cordillera Blanca is home to a dozen of species of mammals, including the puma (*Felis concolor incarum*), spectacled bear (*Tremarctos ornatus*), pampas cat (*Oncifelis colocolò*) and vicuna (*Vicugna vicugna*).

The birdlife is more composite with 112 species, some of which are rare, like the Andean condor (*Vultur grypnus*),

297 center A paradise for hikers from all over the world, the Parque Nacionál Huascarán has the best equipped and laid-out paths in Peru.

297 bottom The huge mass of the Nevado Huandoy (20,981 feet) stands in the northern area of the Cordillera Blanca. The mountain chain is of volcanic origin and still has a certain degree of seismic activity. The last dramatic tremor was in 1970.

giant coot (*Fulica gigantea*) and puna hawk (*Buteo poecilochrus*).

Yet the true value of the Parque Nacionál Huascarán is its morphology, which has few rivals on earth. Its snowcapped mountains – the tallest of which are Huascarán and Huandoy – are favorite destinations of climbing expeditions. The thousands of hikers that visit the park each year limit their treks to the shores of the beautiful glacial lakes such as the Lagunas Llanganuco, Laguna de Siete Colores

and the Gran Laguna de Conococha, from which the Rio Santa flows.

The Cordillera Blanca can also make an unusual boast. In one of its most inaccessible areas, where only a few expert climbers have ventured, there stands a mountain of almost 20,000 feet that has the precise outline of a pyramid. It is called the Nevado Alpamayo and, in 1966, a poll in the German magazine *Alpinismus* voted it the 'most beautiful mountain in the world'.

LIMA

300 top left Considered to be the area of the globe with the greatest biodiversity, Parque Nacionál Manu is home to 15% of the world's species of birds and at least 13 endangered animals.

300 top right The lianas are one of Manu's marvels. During a recent sample census, 79 belonging to 43 species were found in an area of just 2.5 acres.

300-301 Parque Nacionál Manu covers an area of 5,920 square miles ranging in altitude from the 1,200 feet at Rio Manu and the 13,120 feet of Cerro Huascár.

301 top The orchids of the genus Epidendrum can be recognized by their pendulous petals and were believed sacred by pre-Inca and Inca cultures. Orchids are common in the forests of Peru: in Manu alone roughly 3,000 species have been catalogued.

Parque Nacionál Manu

PERU

Departments of Madre de Diós and Cuzco,
Provinces of Manu and Paucartambo
Registration: 1987
Criteria: N (ii) (iv)

301 center It has still not been possible to classify the vast population of invertebrates inside the park but it is estimated that there are roughly 500,000 arthropods. This group of butterflies includes the species Urania leilus *and* Panacea prola.

Hunted to the edge of extinction for its skin, the black caiman (*Melanosuchus niger*) is a distant relative of the dinosaurs of the Mesozoic era; it can reach 20 feet in length and is one of the most ferocious predators in the Amazon watershed. Famous for their multicolored plumage, the parrots in the *Ara* genus are the largest in the world and can reach a length of over 3 feet from head to tail. The jaguar (*Panthera onca*) is the largest and most powerful feline in the Americas; it hunts by night and its preferred prey are tapirs, deer, caimans and turtles, and it is the only natural predator of the anaconda.

The giant anteater (*Myrmecophagidae tridactyla*) is a toothless mammal with a tongue up to 24 inches long that it inserts into ants' nests.

And the giant otter (*Pteronura brasiliensis*) is, despite the family it belongs to, a predator that can reach up to 6.5 feet long and is known by the name 'river sea lion' in the Amazon Basin.

All these unusual creatures have two things in common: the first is that they are included on the International Union for the Conservation of Nature's Red List of endangered species, and the second is that they all live in the Peruvian Amazon, in the vast Parque Nacionál Manu, which botanists and zoologists consider the protected area with the greatest biodiversity on earth.

It covers an area of 5,800 square miles and is named after the Rio Manu, a tributary of the Amazon.

The park covers the entire watershed of the Manu as well as that of the tributaries of the Rio Alto Madre de Diós. It lies to the east of the Peruvian Andes and ranges from a height of 1,200 to 13,100 feet. Its morphology i s prevalently alluvial plateaus and hilly lowlands composed of sedimentary rocks from the late Tertiary period (from 110-1 million years ago).

The mountainous area above a height of 4,900 feet is characterized by earlier sedimentary and metamorphic rock (more than 440 million years old).

The extension and the variety of altitudes over which the park lies mean that there is a contemporary presence of diverse atmospheric conditions, ranging from dry Andean to the wet

301 bottom The forest of Parque Nacionál Manu is so intricate and its biodiversity so rich that a census is impossible. A recent study recorded 1,147 species of vascular plants in an area measuring 2 square miles.

tropical climate of the Amazon. Consequently, the degree of biodiversity of the fauna and flora that inhabit the park is so high that only estimates can be made. From a botanical standpoint, no overall survey has bee in restricted areas generally lying on the plateaus. A recent study on just 20 square miles near the research station of Cocha Cashu identified 1,147 species of vascular plants of which 200 were found in an area of just 2.5 acres.

In particular, there were 18 species of *Ficus* as opposed to the 15 found in

the rest of Peru.

Then there were 79 species of liana, of which 43 were discovered in an area of only 1,120 square yards.

With regard to fauna, Manu National Park is even more exceptional. Given that the areas studied are flat lands, it can be

estimated that the total number of species is far greater than the 800 so far recorded, even though this number already represents 25% of the birds in Latin America and almost 15% of those in the world. Passing to the mammal population, there are 13 species of monkey and at least 100 bats and to the long list of animals in danger there must be added the giant armadillo (*Priodontes maximus*), the ocelot (*Felis pardalis*), the Andean mountain cat (*Oreailurus jacobita*), the north Andean huemul (*Hippocamelus antisensis*) and the

302 top The nearest relation to the cuckoo, the hoatzin (Opisthocomus hoazin), with a large reddish-brown crest, could be described as being prehistoric in appearance.

302 center left If they were not 'frozen' by the camera, the wings of this hummingbird (Phaetornis hispidus) would be invisible owing to the speed of their movement.

302 center right Recognizable for its bright plumage, the scarlet macaw (Ara macao) is the largest and most threatened parrot in the world. Extremely sociable, it lives in noisy groups on clay walls.

302 bottom The garish colors of a Heliconia rostrata are irresistible to hummingbirds, who are the usual pollinators of this plant. Common in the Amazonian area, there are eight families of Heliconiae.

303 Just 1.5 inches long, the cricket frog (Hyla crepitans) is able to jump 50 inches, i.e., 36 times its body length.

304 top The tamarin (Saguinus fuscicollis) is a small, agile daytime primate that lives in the primary forests of Peru, Bolivia, Brazil, Ecuador and Colombia. The weight of an adult only just exceeds 11 ounces.

spectacled bear (*Tremarctos ornatus*).

In addition, Manu is home to 12 species of reptiles belonging to seven different families and 77 species of amphibians.

But the incredible inventory of the animal kingdom in this park is dominated by the invertebrates: though there is no list available of the species present, it has been estimated that Manu contains roughly 500,000 species of arthropods.

This may have been the reason that the region began to be studied from the end of the 1950s, when the zoologist Celestino Kalinowski started making endless collections of birds, mammals and reptiles to sell to the world's most important museums.

In the years that followed, studies were undertaken on the primates, birds and plants until, in 1981, the World Wildlife Fund succeeded in finding the funds to contribute to the construction of the Cocha Cashu biological station that can accommodate 20 or so researchers.

The only other human inhabitants of the Parque Nacionál Manu are a few hundred indiginous peoples belonging to three ethnic groups: the Machiguenga, Amahuaca and Yaminahua. Little is known of them

other than the fact that their small communities exist on a subsistence economy based on hunting and slash-and-burn agriculture.

Conservation of Manu also means protection for these peoples besieged by the attractions of a world they could not understand.

304 center A margay (Felis wiedii) is similar to an ocelot. Here it makes an agile leap during a nocturnal hunt.

304 bottom The brilliant colors of the rainbow boa (Epicrates cenchria cenchria) appear after the second year of life.

304-305 *Proverbially slow, the sloth (Bradypus tridactylus) is a curious, tailless creature with visible ears. Practically defenseless, it lives on the highest branches and is solitary in its habits.*

305 *top Durukuli from the genus Aotus (these are two Aotus trivirgatus) are the only primates in the Americas to have nocturnal habits. With large eyes and strongly developed rear legs, they do not weigh much more than a couple of pounds.*

306 top left and right Rio Manu, from which the park takes its name, is a tributary of the Amazon. Like the tributaries of the Rio Alto Madre de Dios, its entire basin lies within the park.

306 center The size of a large dog, the capybara (Hydrachaeris hydrachaeris) is the biggest rodent in the world. A semi-aquatic animal, it lives in groups of five or six individuals.

306 bottom A group of Terecay side-necked turtles (Podocnemis unifilis) is busy sunbathing in calm, shallow water in Manu park. An indigenous species to the Amazon Basin, the Terecay feeds on plants and fruits that fall into the water.

306-307 The jaguar (Panthera onca) is the largest and most powerful feline in the Americas. Nocturnal, it feeds on tapirs, deer, caimans and turtles and is the only natural predator of the anaconda.

307 top left A distant relative of the dinosaurs of the Mesozoic epoch, the black caiman (Melanosuchus niger) now only lives in remote areas of the Amazon Basin. It is estimated that during the nineteenth century indiscriminate hunting reduced the number of this reptile by 99% for its highly prized skin.

307 top right The giant otter (Pteronura brasiliensis) is also known as the 'river sea lion'. It can reach 6'6" in length and weigh 70 pounds.

Parque Nacionál Noel Kempff Mercado

BOLIVIA

DEPARTMENT OF SANTA CRUZ
REGISTRATION: 2000
CRITERIA: N (II) (IV)

No one knew the Parque Nacionál Huanchaca better than Professor Noel Kempff Mercado.

He was a naturalist who had dedicated his professional life to the exploration and systematic study of the wild 5,600 square miles constituted by the plateau, after which the park was named, and by a vast plain furrowed by many rivers that all

flowed into the Amazon.

For the professor and his three pupils, 6 September 1986 should have been a day like any other.

They left at dawn with the aim of reaching Huanchaca cliff in the early afternoon but perhaps it was simply their presence that disturbed a bunch of smugglers carrying drugs into Brazil, who killed them barbarously.

In memory of the scientist, two years after his death, the Bolivian government decided to dedicate this park to him.

At the same time, it began to take drastic measures to protect the

extraordinary natural environment that – owing to poaching, indiscriminate deforestation and sinister activities – was in serious danger.

About 10 years ago, the Fundación Amigos de la Naturaleza was set up with state backing which, thanks to the 'Adopt an Acre' project, succeeded in finding funds to double the size of the protected land.

In addition, in partnership with the Bolivian government and three giant American energy companies, it promoted the world's largest forest project for the capturing of greenhouse gases. According to estimates, with the investment of 10 million dollars to promote sustainable development of the area, in 30 years the emission of 25-36 million tons of carbon dioxide, caused by deforestation, will have been avoided.

The Parque Nacionál Noel Kempff Mercado is one of the largest wild areas in the Neotropics and has a very high level of biodiversity.

Situated in the zone where the Amazonian forest meets the biogeographic province of Cerrado (which has a dry climate), it is divided into at least five vegetation zones, that range from the evergreen forest on Huanchaca Plateau, with trees up to 150 feet tall, to the fluvial zone along the Iténez and Paraguá Rivers.

In total there are 4,000 classified species of vascular plants, of which there are many species of liana and a 100 or so types of orchid.

The variety of the habitat provides the substrate for an extremely profuse

308 left Though it may live in dry habitats, the giant anteater (Myrmecophaga tridactyla), as large as a badger, lives prevalently on alluvial plains where termites form the basis of its diet.

308-309 Covering a little under 2,000 square miles, Parque Nacionál Noel Kempff Mercado has at least five vegetative zones. One of these, the evergreen forest, dominates the Huanchaca Plateau with trees up to 150 feet tall.

fauna of 139 mammals, 620 birds, 74 reptiles, 62 amphibians and 254 fish. Zoologists, however, continue to make discoveries, especially with regard to amphibians, small mammals such as bats, reptiles – like a rare species of black caiman (*Melanosuchus niger*) – and insects, for instance, several endemic beetles.

The vast grassy areas in the southern part of the plateau are one of the last habitats of the pampas deer (*Ozotoceros bezoarticus*), while the equally rare swamp deer (*Blastocerus dichotomus*) lives on the plains affected by seasonal floods. Endangered mammals include marsupials like the Glironia venusta and Monodelphis kunsi, the giant otter (*Pteronura brasiliensis*) and the plate otter (*Lutra longicaudis*).

Thanks to its flora and fauna and the international efforts made to protect the ecosystem, the park is a place of primordial fascination.

Exactly what struck, more than a century ago, Sir Arthur Conan Doyle, who took inspiration from the forests of Latin America for his novel *The Lost World*.

309 top right The jaguar (Panthera onca) is also a skilful hunter in the water and even feeds on crocodiles. It usually attacks its prey at the temporal bone on the skull, unlike other cats that generally go for the neck.

309 center right In need of protection, the giant otter (Pteronura brasiliensis) is a highly sociable water-dwelling mustelid. It usually lives in communities of five to eight individuals.

309 bottom left The freshwater dolphin (Inia geoffrensis) has a pinkish translucent skin owing to its high level of surface vascularization that is particularly evident on the belly.

LA PAZ

Pantanal Conservation Area

BRAZIL

STATES OF MATO GROSSO AND
MATO GROSSO DO SUL
REGISTRATION: 2000
CRITERIA: N (II) (III) (IV)

The hyacinthine macaw (*Anodorhynchus hyacinthinus*) has a wingspan of 3 feet and cobalt blue plumage. It can live to an age of 80 and, in the wild, eats prevalently the fruit of the *acurí*, a palm endemic to Brazil. Besides its beauty and longevity, the largest parrot in the world has other gifts; it is a perfect companion, becomes fond of its owner and is able to repeat phrases in human language and do exercises of ability. The result of these qualities means that on the illegal animal market (which is estimated to be worth 5 billion dollars a year), a single macaw costs between 8,000 and 10,000 dollars.

310 Pantanal lies in an area of ecological tension between the Cerrado (i.e., the dry savannah in central Brazil) and the semideciduous forests of the southeast. The interaction between the vegetative habitats has created an extraordinary biodiversity.

310-311 Covering 89,000 square miles, the Pantanal is the largest freshwater marsh ecosystem in the world. UNESCO has placed a representative section that lies entirely in Brazil under protection.

Roughly 2,500 hyacinthine macaws live in captivity but there are only about 3,000 still living free in the Pantanal, an area of 920,000 square miles (almost as big as Great Britain), of which 560,000 square miles lie in Brazil and the rest is distributed between Bolivia and Paraguay. Poachers who capture the birds live for resale, or who kill caimans for the equally profitable skin market, consider the Pantanal a 'nature supermarket'. For scientists, on the other hand, it is one of the largest and most interesting ecosystems in the world. For this reason UNESCO registered a representative section of the Pantanal in its list of World Heritage sites in 2000. This section is the 725 square mile Pantanal Matogrossense National Park, which lies entirely in Brazil, is also considered of international importance by the Ramsar Convention.

The territory has a variety of ecological subregions: river channels, intricate gallery forests, permanent marshes and islands, floating islands of fluvial vegetation, called *camalotes*, and grassy plains subject to seasonal flooding. The principal source of water in the Pantanal is the Cuiaba, a river 560 miles long that flows into the Río Paraguay. During the rainy season between October and March, roughly two thirds of the Pantanal is submerged to create a huge sheet of water about 10 times the size of the

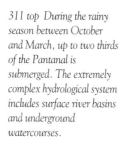

311 top During the rainy season between October and March, up to two thirds of the Pantanal is submerged. The extremely complex hydrological system includes surface river basins and underground watercourses.

311 bottom left The main water source in the Pantanal is the Rio Cuiaba, which flows roughly 620 miles southwest inside the protected area before joining the Rio Paraguay.

BRASILIA ●

Everglades in Florida.

The diversity and interaction of the different habitats is reflected in an immense variety of plant species, though to date they have not been widely studied. They grow in an area of ecological tension between the dry savannah of central Brazil and the semi-deciduous forests of the south. Besides its dense fluvial vegetation and many herbaceous plants in the alluvial plains, the Pantanal is famous for its immense expanses of palms and lilies and for a curious, softwood fig-tree called *figueira mata-pau* ('tree-killer fig') as, in order to

311 bottom right A giant anteater (Myrmecophaga tridactyla) explores a baía, a plain subject to seasonal flooding. It features semideciduous vegetation of small trees and shrubs.

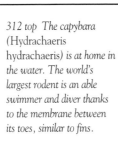

312 top The capybara (Hydrachaeris hydrachaeris) is at home in the water. The world's largest rodent is an able swimmer and diver thanks to the membrane between its toes, similar to fins.

312 bottom left A green anaconda (Eunectes murinus) waits for a meal in the aquatic vegetation. These reptiles are very prolific: at least 40 are born in a single clutch. At birth they are already 18 inches long.

312 center Despite their harmless appearance, the giant otter (Pteronura brasiliensis) is one of the region's greatest predators. They feed on fish, crabs, snakes and even caimans and eat 10 pounds of food a day.

312 bottom right A magnificent example of a banded tiger heron (Tigrisoma lineatum) has successfully made a catch.

survive, it has to wrap itself around the palms in a spiral.

Zoologists deem the Pantanal to be one of the wet zones with the largest variety of species, which, including the cursorily studied category of invertebrates, roughly totals the amazing figure of 150,000. There are 80 or so mammals, including the jaguar, ocelot, giant anteater, armadillo, tapir and capuchin monkey. The largest mammals are the elegant swamp deer (*Blastocerus dichotomus*) and the capybara

312-313 With a population of caimans (Crocodylus jacare) estimated at around 10 millions, the Pantanal is the area with the highest concentration of crocodiles in the world. It is said that there are 22 'visible' in every square mile.

313 bottom Although just in the 1980s around 130,000 yellow anaconda (Eunectes notaeus) skins were put on the black market, having been hunted in the Pantanal, this reptile is still very common in the area.

(*Hydrochoerus hydrochaeris*), which, at a weight of 66 pounds, is the largest rodent in the world. The birdlife numbers 656 species belonging to 66 families; in addition to the hyacinthine macaw and 26 other sorts of parrot, there is a large number of herons, egrets and other aquatic birds. The symbol of the Brazilian park is the jabiru (*Jabiru mycteria*), a crane, whose white plumage has a red ring on the lower part of its neck. With a wingspan of 9 feet, it is one of the most majestic fliers in the world. The 400 or more species of fish make the Pantanal the largest freshwater fish reserve in the continent, and the roughly 10 million caimans (*Crocodilus*

yacare) give the area the largest concentration of crocodiles on the planet. Their reputation as being dangerous to man is unmerited, given that caimans are not very aggressive, but the same is not true of the anaconda (*Eunectes murinus*), the most common reptile in the Pantanal.

Aside from poaching, the Pantanal's ecosystem is threatened by two massive engineering projects that would affect a vast part of its territory. The first is the construction of a 2 billion dollar gas pipe between Río Grande in Bolivia and Rio de Janeiro. The second, which according to scientists would literally change the characteristics of the

314 top The Pantanal is an excellent habitat for the jaguar judging by the size of those that live there. However, it is estimated that only one adult remains for every 25 square miles of territory.

314 bottom The roseate spoonbill (Ajaja ajaja) gets its coloring from the level of carotene in the crustaceans it feeds on.

environment, is the creation of the Idrovia, a network of navigable canals 2,140 miles in length, as part of a joint project between Argentina, Bolivia, Brazil, Uruguay and Paraguay. Put on paper at the end of the 1980s, this network would halve the cost of goods' transport, which are currently all carried by road. So far the work has not been begun owing to the massive costs involved, which would be difficult to support by the countries suffering serious

314-315 The fish commonly known in Brazil as the peraputangaha *has a very particular diet: its favorite food is the water*

lily. The presence in the Pantanal of 400 species of fish makes this area the largest freshwater fish reserve in the continent.

economic difficulty – or perhaps because of the campaign being waged across all of Brazil to save the Pantanal. Although most Brazilians did not even know of its existence until 1990, they suddenly became impassioned about its fate that year. Thanks to a television soap opera called 'Pantanal', which narrated the lives and loves of a family of animal breeders who lived in a *fazenda* on the edges of the protected area, the country was glued to the set for months.

315 bottom During the mating season, two male egrets (Casmerodius albus) fight bitterly while in flight.

Atlantic Forest South-east Reserves

BRAZIL

States of Paraná and São Paulo
Registration: 1999
Criteria: N (ii) (iii) (iv)

At one time the Brazilian Atlantic rainforest stretched from Rio Grande do Norte to the coastal area of Rio Grande do Sul to form a thin stretch of dense vegetation between the Atlantic Ocean and the arid Planalto Plateau. In 1984, the World Wildlife Fund launched a dramatic appeal in which the Mata Atlantica was referred to as the second most threatened habitat in the world after the forest of Madagascar. The appeal claimed that only 9% of the original surface area of the extraordinary forested area remained.

Following the appeal, in 1991 the Mata Atlantica Biosphere Reserve was set up, and in 1999 UNESCO included Discovery Coast Atlantic Forest Reserves in the World Heritage list. The reserves include the Atlantic Forest Southeast Reserve and a set of eight protected areas in the states of Bahia and Espírito Santo that together cover 432 square miles. The Atlantic Forest Southeast Reserve lies in the states of Paraná and São Paulo and comprises 25 protected areas that cover 1,807 square miles.

Geologically, the Atlantic Forest Southeast Reserve is one of the oldest regions in the world, having been generated by faults during the Tertiary period and intrusions of volcanic origin. The Serra do Mar mountain chain, which separates the coastal plains from Planalto, is formed by Cambrian granite and magmatic gneiss in which limestone massifs have given rise to karst in the zones of Apiapí, Iporanga and Eldorado Paulista.

Owing to its isolation from other types of forest, the Mata Atlantica is typified by one of the highest percentages of endemic species in the world. Over 50% of its 10,000 types of tree and 92% of its amphibians are unique to the region. In some parts, the vegetation is so thick that 450 species have been counted in a single hectare. The composition of the vegetation varies with the altitude (which rises from sea level to 4,600 feet) and with the soil type that alters with distance from the coast. The low level forests are dominated by large trees belonging to the Fabaceae, Lauraceae, Myrtaceae and Euphorbiaceae families, which can reach 100 feet in height. At greater altitude, palms of the type *Euterpe edulis* grow, which is a species in danger. Between 2,950-4,250 feet the rather lower forest of Podocarpus and Clusia grows, which is extremely rich in epiphytes, orchids and bromeliads.

The fauna includes 120 species of mammals, including the jaguar (*Panthera onca*), ocelot (*Leopardus pardialis*), bush dog (*Speothos venaticus*), the La Plata otter (*Lutra longicaudis*) and 20 or so bats. There are also various species of primates in danger, such as the woolly spider monkey (*Brachyteles arachnoides*). Of the 350 species of birds recorded, two that stand out are the great harpy eagle (*Harpia harpyja*) and the red-tailed Amazon parrot (*Amazona brasilensis*).

In spite of the efforts made to conserve the area, the Mata Atlantica has shrunk further to 7% of its original size, losing an estimated 1,930 square miles between 1985 and 1990. Even after the institution of the protected area, illegal activities such as mining, the felling of palms and the construction of new settlements has taken place. In 1997 the Instituto Brasileiro do Meio Ambiente e dos Recursos Naturais Renováveis estimated that within 50 years the Atlantic forest might be completely destroyed.

316 top The Atlantic Forest Southeast Reserve is one of the oldest regions in the world. It was created by faults during the Tertiary period with intrusions of volcanic origin.

316 bottom left Known in Brazil as the 'iguaniñha', the lizard Enyalius inheringii is spread right across the Mata Atlantica area.

316 bottom right The forest of Serra da Graciosa, that lies at altitudes between 2,950 and 4,250 feet, has many bromeliads, epiphytes and orchids.

317 top A superb bromeliad grows in the dense Serra da Bocaina forest in the state of São Paulo. The Mata Atlantica has one of the highest percentages of endemic speicies on the planet but

BRASILIA ●

has been reduced by 7% from its original size.

317 bottom The endemic species of sloth, Bradipus torquatus, is considered in danger of extinction. The forests of the Mata Atlantica are home to 120 species of mammals.

A map that the Duke of Ferrara, Ercole d'Este, received in November 1502 shows for the first time an island named Ilha de Quaresma off the Brazilian coast. The map allows us to suppose that the island was discovered around Easter time during a year immediately preceding this date by one of the expeditions sent to these regions. Some attribute the discovery to Gaspar de Lemos, a captain in the Cabral fleet who was sent back to Portugal to announce the discovery of Santa Cruz. Others believe that the news was given

by an expedition of which little is known, while others again give the credit directly to Fernao de Loronha.

What is certain is that the island was first described by Amerigo Vespucci, who embarked in 1503 on the ships of Gonçalo Coelho, and that, one year later, it was given by Dom Manuel I to Fernao de Loronha as payment for the precious cargo of wood that he had brought from Brazil. Since then, the mysterious island and the entire archipelago to which it belongs have been called – incorrectly – Fernando de Noronha.

Instituted in 1988, the national marine park that comprises the Fernando de Noronha Archipelago covers an area of 44 square miles, 85% of which is made up of the waters that surround the islands. The Biological Reserve of Atol das Rocas, on the other hand, was created in 1978 and covers 163 square miles. The former comprises 21 islands, islets and emerged rocks that are the peaks of a vast volcanic underwater mountain chain that rises 13,100 feet from the bottom of the Atlantic. The chain was created between 12 and 2 million years ago, as is shown by its morphology of pyroclastic deposits, lava, cones and volcanic apertures.

The latter, the Atol das Rocas, is a formation of reefs that lies on a substrate of underwater rock over an area measuring just under 3 square miles. During high tide, only two sandy islets can be seen, which rise no more than 10 feet above the water level, whilst at low tide the entire reef ring with its border of sand banks becomes visible. This ring surrounds a vast lagoon that is no more than 16 feet in depth.

Despite a reduced biodiversity owing to the isolation of the habitat, the vegetation on the archipelago has strong affinities with the forests on the Brazilian coast, with the exception of a small area of mangroves (*Laguncularia racemosa*), which is the only community of this genus existent in the southern Atlantic. Of the 400 species classified, three are endemic: gameleira (*Ficus noronhae*), mulungo (*Erythina velutina*) and burra leiteira (*Apium escleratium*). Atol das Rocas, in contrast, has an island vegetation of salt-resistant grasses and a few palms and cassowaries that were introduced by fishermen.

A refuge for marine and terrestrial birdlife, the archipelago has three endemic species of birds: the noronho vireo or sebito (*Vireo gracilirostris*), the cucurata (*Elaenia spectabilis ridleyana*) and the *arribaçã* (*Zenaida auriculata noronha*). There are also 95 species of fish, a population of 1,200 dolphins (*Stenella longirostris*) and the two turtles *Chelonia mydas* and *Eretmochelys embricata*. However, the most unusual species in Fernando de Noronha is unquestionably one of the two reptiles endemic to the island: the two-headed snake (in fact a limbless lizard) *Amphisbaena ridleyana*.

Outside of the park, the human population on the archipelago is only just over 2,000 for whom the main income has passed from fishing to tourism, even though strict rules are enforced. The maximum number of visitors each year is 15,000 and each of these is obliged to pay a high environmental tax so that non-selected people are prevented from staying on the islands for too long. The Atol das Rocas, on the contrary, has no tourists, and only scientific expeditions are allowed to visit.

318

318 top The two 'brothers' of the Ilha dois Irmãos appear off Fernoña de Noroña. The archipelago is formed by the peaks of a large underwater mountain range of volcanic origin that rise over 13,000 feet from the bottom of the ocean.

318 center The red-footed booby (Sula sula) is one of the 150,000 seabirds that nest on the Atol das Rocas.

318 bottom As with the other 95 species of fish in the area, grunts (Haemulon parrai) prosper in the waters of the Fernando de Noroña Archipelago thanks to the distance from the continent and position of the islands on the course of the equatorial currents.

318-319 Between December and June, the Praia do Leão – named after a small island shaped like a sea lion – is where green turtles (Chelonia mydas) come to nest.

Fernando de Noronha and Atol das Rocas

BRAZIL

STATE OF PERNAMBUCO
REGISTRATION: 2001
CRITERIA: N (II) (III) (IV)

319 bottom The dazzling livery of a crab on the rocks of Ponta das Caracas. In all 72 species of crustaceans have been registered in the archipelago.

BRASILIA ●

Iguazú Falls
ARGENTINA/BRAZIL

PROVINCE OF MISIONES (ARGENTINA),
STATE OF PARANÁ (BRAZIL)
REGISTRATION: 1986
INSCRIPTION IN THE WORLD HERITAGE LIST
IN DANGER IN 1999-2001
CRITERIA: N (III) (IV)

It rises in the Serra do Mar, not far from the Atlantic Ocean and runs 800 miles along the Paraná plateau receiving the waters of 30 tributaries and widening to almost a mile across. But it is only after this docile jaunt that it earns itself the name that it has been given by the indigenous peoples: Iguazú. In the Guaraní language, the name Iguazú (or *Iguaçú* in the Brazilian transliteration) means 'great water'. Even more impressive is the spectacle of the river as it launches itself from a semicircular amphitheater of basalt lava 2.5 miles wide and 260 feet high in a curtain of 275 separate falls. Accompanied by crashing thunder and the immense mass of vapor shot through by rainbows, this extraordinary place has been described as 'the most beautiful border in the world'.

Iguazú Falls are shared between Argentina and Brazil. 'Only' 2,700 feet of the falls lie on Brazilian territory but, in recompense, it is from a natural Brazilian observation point that visitors have the best view of the Garganta del Diablo (Devil's Throat), the falls' most famous cataract. After its drop, the river rushes into a canyon just 260 feet wide (over which the Puente Tancredo Neves has been built to unite the two countries) and runs for 20 or so miles before flowing into the Río Paraná.

To protect the falls and subtropical forest that, thanks to a constant humidity level of 80-90%, covers almost all the area adjacent to the falls and the many islands in the river, the Argentine and Brazilian governments long ago set up two national parks. In both territories the wet subtropical forest is rich with species of ferns, including the gigantic *Dicksonia selowiana*, bamboo, lianas and other climbing plants, bromeliaceae and epiphytes, of which there are 80 different types of orchid. The banks of the river are typified by the association of the tree *Aspidosperma polynerum* that can reach a height of 100 feet, with numerous species of palms, such as *Euterpe edulis*.

The fauna is also varied and interesting, including many mammals in danger of extinction. There is the giant otter (*Pteronura brasilensis*), jaguar (*Panthera oncha*), giant anteater (*Myrmecophaga tridactyla*) and puma (*Felis concolor*). There is also an enormous variety of birds, including five species of toucan and many parrots.

In recent years, pressure from humans has raised worries for the protection of the ecosystem. Three sizeable urban centers lie at the edge of the parks: Foz do Iguaçu in Brazil, Puerto Iguazú in Argentina and Rio de la Plata in nearby Paraguay. In Foz do Iguaçu alone (which had 30,000 inhabitants in 1960 and now has 200,000) there are 160 hotels and it is estimated that the Brazilian section of the park receives 1 million visitors a year. The guards in both parks have reported illegal fishing and indiscriminate cutting down of palms as their hearts are considered a food delicacy. But perhaps the greatest danger to the falls lies with the gigantic Itaipu dam opened in 1991 a little downstream of the falls. Though, on the one hand, the 12.5 million kilowatts produced by the hydroelectric plant provide 40% of the needs of Argentina and Brazil, on the other hand, it has caused notable morphological and climatic imbalances.

320-321 The 'great water' – this is the meaning of the word iguazú in the Guaraní language – leaps into a semi-circular basalt amphitheater 236 feet deep and nearly 3,000 yards across.

320 bottom left With constant humidity of 80-90%, the area around Iguazú Falls is covered by an intricate subtropical forest with many species of ferns, bamboos, bromeliads, lianas and orchids.

320 bottom right The Ramphastos toco, with its striking bill, is one of five species of toucan in the park. In the area next to the falls 422 species of birds have been recorded.

321 top The rainbow created by the spray that rises from the base of the waterfall makes the sight of the Garganta del Diablo even more spectacular. This is the most famous of the 274 cataracts in Iguazú.

Parque Nacionál Los Glaciares

ARGENTINA

PROVINCE OF SANTA CRUZ
REGISTRATION: 1981
CRITERIA: N (II) (III)

BUENOS AIRES

322-323 Covering an area of 96 square miles, the Perito Moreno Glacier is an arm of the immense Campo de Hielo Patagónico. In complete contrast to other glaciers in the region and most of the planet, its mass is constantly on the increase.

322 bottom An iceberg opens a passage along the Canál de los Tímpanos, which is a narrow stretch that connects the Perito Moreno Glacier with the main basin of Lake Argentino. Situated on the 50th parallel, the lake is the southernmost of the great Andean lakes in Argentina.

323 top *The menacing and overhanging blue face of Perito Moreno is 3 miles across and up to 200 feet high.*

Although he was only 25 years old, Francisco Pascasio Moreno was already on his fifth voyage to the inhospitable land of Argentinian Patagonia when, on 15 February 1877, he found himself standing before one of the most spectacular sights in that region: an immense glacial lake stretched out at the feet of the southern Andes into which large glaciers slid slowly down the mountain sides.

In fact he was not the first to discover the lake; that honor belonged to second lieutenant Valentin Feilberg, who had visited the region four years previous but thought he had arrived on the shores of Lake Viedma some tens of miles further north. It was Moreno, therefore, who named the lake, which he baptized Lake Argentino, using the rather rhetorical speech sometimes heard from great explorers.

Many years later the most fascinating natural feature of the zone was named in his honor; the glacier Perito Moreno in which the word 'perito' is the title he was given at the end of the nineteenth century when the government asked him to deal with the delicate question of the border between Argentina and Chile. Spread over an area of about 96 square miles, the Perito Moreno is a strip of the Campo de Hielo Patagónico, the largest iced area in the world outside of the polar caps. A legacy of the ice that covered the Southern Hemisphere during the last Ice Age, the Campo de Hielo covers 5,400 square miles and its many arms stretch into the wide valleys eroded by the movement of ice over the millennia.

The Perito Moreno is one of these arms, and its mass is in continuous increase as it is fed by the Campo de Hielo. The glacier

overlooks Canàl de los Tímpanos, a narrow passage that connects the Brazo Rico and the Brazo Sur to the main section of Lake Argentino. At regular intervals the front of Perito Moreno – 3 miles wide and 200 feet high – reaches the opposite bank, thereby blocking the channel and preventing the exchange of the two bodies of water. That causes a rise in the waters of Brazo Rico of up to 80 feet. With the increase in pressure the glacier begins to fracture and water enters the ice, whereupon it collapses in a thunderous crash. During the twentieth century, this spectacular phenomenon was repeated every 30 years or so, the last in 1988.

Though extraordinary, the Perito Moreno is only one of the 47 main glaciers to be found in the 1,722 square miles of the Parque Nacional Los Glaciares instituted in 1937. Nor is it even the largest, as it is exceeded in size by the Upsala (230 square

323 bottom *There are 47 glaciers in Parque Nacionál Los Glaciares, besides roughly 200 secondary glaciers (i.e., measuring just over 1 square mile). Overall, ice covers 1,000 square miles of the protected area.*

324 top Though all less than 13,000 feet high, the three peaks of Cerro Torre, Torre Egger and Cerro Stanhardt have few rivals in the history of extreme mountaineering. The major difficulties are posed by the weather – often prohibitive – and the isolation of the region.

324-325 The majestic Cerro Fitz Roy is reflected in the cold water of Desierto Lake. The lakes in the park have an overall area of 367 square miles. The largest are Lake Viedma, in the north, and Lake Argentino.

miles) and the Viedma (222 square miles). The park also contains more than 200 secondary glaciers, each less than 1 square mile in size and not connected to the Campo de Hielo Patagonico. The size of the Campo occupies 1,000 square miles inside the park, i.e., more than 50% of its overall surface.

The glacial activity is concentrated around Lake Argentino and Lake Viedma, whose waters flow into the Rio Cruz before being carried to the Atlantic Ocean. The erosion caused by glaciation during the Quaternary epoch also created many steep, pointed Andean peaks in the area, for example, the Cerro Fitz Roy (or Cerro Chalten, which, at 11,070 feet, is the highest mountain in the park) and mounts Peineta, Heim and Agassiz. The Cerro Torre, on the other hand – at 10,262 feet, the second highest mountain in the region – is rounded.

Being mostly covered by glaciers and lakes, the Parque Naciónal Los Glaciares has little fauna or flora, but there are two well defined phytogeographic formations: these are the sub-Antarctic forest and the Patagonian forest. The former is spread over the mountain slopes and characterized by the ñire and *guindo* (*Cohiue magallanico*) trees, as well as by various species of beech, one of which is the *lenga* (*Nothofagus*

pumilio). A recent observation has been the return of the Guaitecas cypress (*Pilgerodendron uviferum*).

The Patagonian steppe is composed of grasslands featuring the extremely widespread *calafate*, the notro, *saúco del diablo* and the *topa-topa*. The *calafate* is a bush that produces bittersweet berries and the *notro* is recognizable by its lovely red leaves.

A full survey has not yet been completed of the park's fauna, mostly because there is very little information on the vertebrates that inhabit the region with the exception of the birds. There are a hundred or so species of birds, including the Andean condor (*Vultur gryphus*), which nests at high altitude in colonies called condoreras. The most notable mammals are the puma (*Felis concolor*), the gray fox (*Duscicyon griseus*), the piche, which is a small armadillo, the guanaco (*Lama guanacoe*) and the huemul (*Hippocamelus bisulcus*).

During recent years, Patagonia has experienced growing tourism but no danger has been registered to the local flora and fauna. Experts are instead worried by the contraction of the glaciers caused by global warming. Recent satellite photography has shown that all the glaciers in the Campo de Hielo are shrinking – except for one, the Perito Moreno.

325 top left In the clear air of a Patagonian autumn, the terrain at the foot of Fitz Roy is tinted with the bright hues of a sub-Antarctic beech forest of Nothofagus pumilio.

325 center left Cerro Torre is the sharp peak on the left, and Fitz Roy the tall one on the right. They flank a wide glacial valley in one of the loveliest mountain scenes in the world. Generally, the Andes are almost completely isolated from human activity.

325 top right The north face of Cerro Torre is swept by a storm. This formidable granite tower – considered one of the most difficult to climb in the world – was first conquered in 1959 by climbers Cesare Maestri and Toni Egger.

325 bottom From the top of Loma del Peque Umbado, dawn reveals the glorious scenery of Fitz Roy (also known as Cerro Chaltén at 11,073 feet) and Cerro Torre (at 10,262 feet).

Península Valdés

ARGENTINA

Province of Chubut, Patagonia
Registration: 1999
Criteria: N (IV)

BUENOS AIRES

It has a curved body with no dorsal fin and, on its head, incrusted with splotches of keratin, there are two blowholes from which it expels its characteristic spout of vapor. An adult can reach 43 feet in length and weigh over 40 tons.

The black right whale belongs to the suborder Mysticeti and its scientific name is *Eubalaena australis*, the 'whale of the south'. It is one of the most fascinating and threatened mammals in the world and, for this reason, was declared a national monument in 1985 by the Argentine Congress. Although it has been protected since 1936, like many other large cetaceans it has suffered ruthless hunting and only in recent years has there been a significant increase in its numbers. Today there are roughly 3,000, of which 500 travel to the tranquil waters of the Golfo Nuevo and Golfo de San José in the Península Valdés to mate. They arrive at the start of winter and, between June and September after 12 months gestation, the females give birth to a single calf 16 feet long.

Discovered in 1779 by Juan de la Piedra, the Península Valdés was given its name by the Italian explorer Antonio Malaspina, who visited the region between 1789-94, and named it after Antonio Valdés, the Spanish Minister of Naval Affairs, who had sponsored the expedition. Joined to the mainland by an isthmus 22 miles long, the vast peninsula occupies an area of over 1,500 square miles. It sticks out into the Atlantic and its coastline is a string of gulfs, bays and cliffs formed by marine sediments during the Miocene epoch where it is not difficult to find fossils of marine fauna.

Although it knew a fleeting moment of glory at the end of the nineteenth century when its salt deposits in Salina

Grande were exploited, today the peninsula has only 220 inhabitants who make their living from sheep-breeding. Yet since 1983 when the entire peninsula was designated a nature reserve, the increasing number of visitors has encouraged development of an economy based on tourism that has not yet seemed to disturb the environmental balances.

Exposed to the cold Atlantic winds,

the vegetation on Península Valdés is short and shrublike, typical of the Patagonian steppes where 18 different communities of shrubs and herbaceous plants have been recorded. One of the most interesting areas of the peninsula from a conservation standpoint is the Reserva naturál Isla de los Pájaros created in 1967 to protect the nesting places of seabirds. The absence of

326-327 A humpback whale makes a spectacular splash.

326 bottom left Completely arid, the shoreline of the Golfo Nuevo is formed by marine sediments containing many fossils.

326 bottom right The almost closed, shallow waters of the Golfo San José offer an important refuge to marine fauna.

327 top left Of the 181 species of birds in the peninsula, the magellanic penguin (Spheniscus magellanicus) is the most numerous. Each year, during the breeding season, the five colonies here number almost 40,000 nests.

327 top right A southern elephant seal (Mirounga leonina) calls to the females in the colony.

327 center In the nineteenth century, the southern right whale (Eubalaena australis) constituted 78% of all whales caught.

327 bottom A humpback whale swims with her calf. The whales arrive between April and June at the end of the southern winter and head southwards again at the end of the summer, between December and February.

328-329 and 328 bottom Appearing suddenly in a whoosh of spray, a killer whale (Orcinus orca) seems to throw itself at the shore. This is the start of a dramatic attack on a sea lion (Otaria flavescens). The predator follows its prey under the watchful eyes of the impotent members of the colony, who give off cries of alarm.

humans on the island (access has been prohibited to tourists since 1975) provides 181 species of birds with an ideal habitat. The community includes gulls, cormorants, egrets, terns and a colony of Magellanic penguins (*Spheniscus magellanicus*) that numbers over 40,000 active nests.

The shallow waters of the inlets and the beaches of the peninsula offer shelter to other sea mammals: the Southern elephant seal (*Mirounga leonina*) and the Southern sea lion or 'lobo marino de un pelo' (*Otaria flavescens*). The sea lions arrive to reproduce between December and February, establishing themselves at the foot of the promontories protected by high cliffs that prevent access to land predators. The most serious threat to these creatures continues to be man: not attributed to the ruthless hunting practiced from the sixteenth century up to a few years ago, but to the progressive occupation of their habitats by new settlements.

329 *The diet of the killer whale is based on fish and squid, but every so often they attack large, even adult, mammals such as sea lions and elephant seals. Their hunting technique is honed to perfection: they hurl themselves up the shallow seabed with the incoming waves, grab their prey and slide back into deeper water aided by the backwash.*

330-331 *A herbivorous mammal and ruminant of the camelid family, the guanaco (Lama guanacoe) is the most characteristic inhabitant of Argentinian Patagonia. Their population on the Península Valdés numbers about 2,200.*

330 bottom *Fairly widespread in South America below the equator, the fox can be found even in desolate regions like Patagonia. The abundance of its prey means it prospers in Península Valdés.*

*331 center right Only 8
inches long and weighing
11 ounces, the
Microcavia australis lives
in arid environments and
has adapted to survival on
few alimentary resources.*

*331 bottom right
Introduced into Argentina
at the end of the nineteenth
century, the common hare
immediately colonized the
country and entered into
competition with the marà,
or Patagonian hare
(Dolichotis patagonum),
whose existence is
increasingly threatened.*

*331 top left The only
nocturnal bird of prey
in the Americas, the
horned owl (Bubo
virginianus) covers
a vast area from the
Arctic to Patagonia.*

*331 top right A small
nocturnal armadillo, the
pichi (Zaedyus pichi) is
found in the southern
regions of Chile and
Argentina down to the
Straits of Magellan.*

List of the Sites

Oceania

To Europeans at least, the history of Oceania – and in particular of Australia, which makes up most of the continent – is a recent one. The first to set foot there, in 1606, was the Dutchman Willem Janszoon, who was convinced that he had reached New Guinea. Ten years later his compatriot Dirk Hartogszoon recognized the west coast of Ptolemy's *Terra Australis Incognita,* the southern continent that the ancients believed had to exist to balance the weight of Europe and Asia. Between 1642 and 1644 another Dutchman, Abel Tasman, discovered New Zealand and Tasmania, yet Australia was not colonized until 1770 when James Cook annexed it to the British Empire.

With roughly 17 million inhabitants concentrated in the coastal areas of an island measuring 29,000 square miles, Australia still remains an incredibly wild continent. Most of its surface is desert but in its interior there are habitats of extraordinary richness, such as tropical rainforests, vast alluvial plains and dramatic mountain ranges. Apparently the oldest continent on Earth, Australia has rock formations that were created 3.5 billion years ago, and the completely independent evolution of its living species has led to a flora and fauna that are not found elsewhere. The marsupials are a perfect example: the most famous and the symbol of the country, the kangaroo, is one of the primitive ancestors of the more evolved placental mammals.

Oceania's natural heritage is not of course only to be found in Australia, and above all not only on the mainland. Of the 12 World Heritage sites, two are found in New Zealand and several others are islands or archipelagos, for example, Fraser Island, the largest sand island in the world and a paradise for megatheres, or the faraway Macquarie Island, 950 miles to the south of the continent. Then, too, Tasmania and the sub-Antarctic islands of New Zealand have many endemic species both faunal and botanical.

The most vast protected area in the world, with a surface area of more than 127,000 square miles, deserves a separate mention: the Great Barrier Reef is formed by 3,400 coral reefs and stretches for 12,500 miles off the Australian coast as far north as the waters of Papua New Guinea.

Overall, Oceania can boast a natural wealth of extraordinary diversity, and the restricted impact of human activities on its habitats means that nature in this continent reigns supreme, thanks to the strict laws that put Oceania at the top of the class for conservation policies.

Kakadu National Park
AUSTRALIA

NORTHERN TERRITORY
REGISTRATION: 1981; EXTENSIONS 1987, 1992
CRITERIA: C (I) (VI); N (II) (III) (IV)

With his feet planted solidly on the ground, and body covered with ritual paintings, the evil spirit with the unpronounceable name of Nabulwinjubulwinj triumphs on Nourlangie Rock, which towers over the alluvial plains to the west of the Australian continental scarp. The cosmogony of the Gagudju aboriginals is not limited to evil spirits: there is also Warramurrungundji, 'the mother of the earth', who, having arrived from the islands to the northeast, created child spirits and taught them how to speak and hunt. She also created the rivers, plants and animals of the world before turning herself into a rock.

The spirits of the ancestors are one

few sites registered in the UNESCO World Heritage sites both for its cultural and natural values.

Created originally in 1964 as the Woolwonga Aboriginal Reserve to protect the 300 or so people who lived there, Kakadu National Park has gradually been expanded from its initial 195 square miles to cover 7,700. It lies in a zone that is tectonically relatively stable, having been formed 2.5 billion years ago, but has been remodeled over time to display geomorphological features that illustrate much of this planet's history.

Although six geological formations can be recognized, the main element is the system created by the plateau in

334 left The saltwater crocodile (Crocodylus porosus) inhabits the Alligator Rivers area. Of the 128 species of reptiles in Kakadu, the crocodiles represent three and the snakes 39.

334 right The jabiru or black-necked stork (Xenorhynchus asiaticus) is also known as the 'policeman bird' for the color of its plumage. Unlike other species of waders, it is a solitary bird.

334-335 The alluvial plain of Magela Creek was once a sea bed. It stretches out of sight, dotted with the occasional tree.

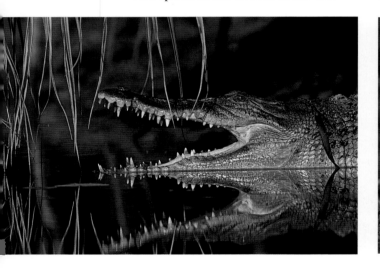

of the favorite subjects in the rock paintings of the aboriginals that have inhabited north Australia for at least the last 25,000 years, but their art also illustrates hunting, the nature that surrounded them and even their first contact with white men. The 1,000 archeological sites and 7,000 examples of aboriginal rock art are the reason why the Kakadu National Park is one of the

Arnhem Land and the continental scarp, which rises rapidly to 1,000 feet and runs 320 miles down the eastern edge. It is thought that 140 million years ago much of Kakadu was covered by a shallow sea. Once the water level dropped, the rock formation that at the time were cliffs, formed the continental scarp, and the vast plain known as Koolpniyah Surface originated at its

foot. In antiquity, crags like Nourlangie Rock used to be islands near the coast of this shallow sea.

Other features are drainage basins, alluvial plains formed by torrents that dragged sediments downstream during the rainy season, the southern hills of volcanic origin, and the estuarine flatlands that were affected by tides that used to arrive 60 miles inland.

335 top A large community of common egrets (Egretta alba) populates a coastal lagoon. These ecosystems stretch up to 60 miles inland and are inhabited by animal and vegetable species that have adapted to living on saline mud.

335 right This very young nankeen (Nycticorax caledonicus) or nocturnal heron belongs to one of the 274 species of birds classified in Kakadu National Park; these represent 33% of all those in Australia.

335 bottom Some magpie geese (Anseranas semipalmata) wander in search of food in a lagoon in flower. This aquatic bird is hunted by aboriginals for its meat.

CANBERRA

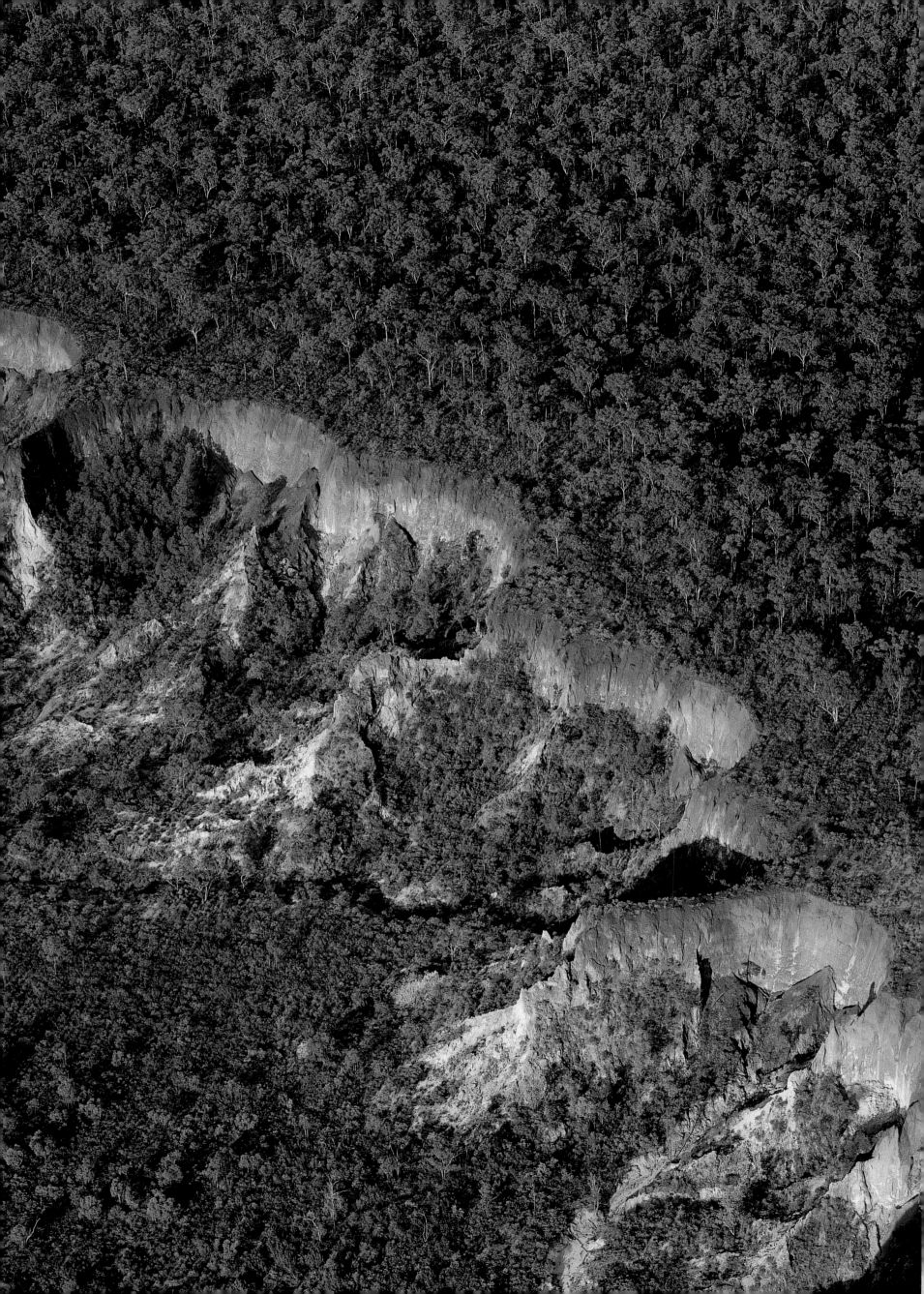

The biodiversity of the park has no equal anywhere in Australia. More than 1,600 plants have been recorded, 58 of which are considered of maximum importance for reasons of conservation, and a further 97 are rare or threatened. The flora of Arnhem Land is important, with many endemic species. The area features 13 floral communities, three of which are rainforests, seven are dominated by different species of eucalyptus and the others by salicornias, marshes of *melaleuca* and mangroves swamps along the coast.

Most of the 64 mammals in Kakadu inhabit the forests; 26 are bats, 15 rodents, eight kangaroos and possums, bandicoots and quolls. Endangered at a global level are the dugong (*Dugong dugon*) and the bat *Macroderma gigas*. Of the 128 reptiles, those declared vulnerable or threatened with extinction are the saltwater crocodile (*Crocodylus porosus*) and three species of turtle (*Caretta caretta, Chelonia mydas* and *Eretmochelys imbricata*).

The monsoon climate brings rain from November to April, and this, with the huge variety of ecosystems, has created ideal conditions for a wide assortment of birdlife. The area is home to 274 species, which is one third of all the species that inhabit Australia. Important birds are the red goshawk (*Accipiter radiatus*), Gouldian finch (*Chloebia gouldiae*) and the hooded parrot (*Psephotus dissimilis*).

Being unaffected by the presence of man, the primary threats to the environmental balance in Kakadu have historically been created by the buffalo (*Bubalus bubalis*), which damages the indigenous vegetation, thereby accelerating erosion. Once the population of the buffalo had been cut down, the worst threat to the biodiversity passed to two infestant grasses: *Mimosa pigra and Salvinia molesta*. Since 1984, significant efforts have been made to eradicate the mimosa from river estuaries, but the threat remains. As for Salvinia molesta, the infestation has reached such a point that plans have been made to control it biologically with an insect (*Cryptobagus salviniae*), which is its natural enemy. The entire area of the Magela Torrent in the northeast of the park has been put in quarantine. For the moment, the battle against *Salvinia molesta* seems to have been won, and therefore a dangerous situation of eutrophication of the waters has been avoided, and Kakadu has returned to being one of the parks with the lowest percentage of infestant grasses in the world.

336 These red rock walls near Blomfield springs in Arnhem Land stand in a section of the park that is both aesthetically and geologically spectacular.

337 top left Similar to a cathedral, this gigantic termite mound is the work of Nasutitermus triodia.

*337 top right The blue-winged kookaburra (*Dachelo leachii*) has a very distinctive sound like a human laugh.*

337 bottom There are about 1,000 archeological sites and 7,000 examples of rock art in the park, all dating to a period ranging from 25,000 years ago to the first meetings with European colonists in the seventeenth century.

338 left Twin Falls is one of the most panoramic spots in Arnhem Land and the continental scarp, which rises almost vertically 1,000 feet along the 310 miles that mark the eastern boundary of the park.

338 top right The largest section of the continental scarp – the Kombolgie Formation – was left high and dry when the seas retreated during the Mesozoic epoch. Its geomorphology has remained almost unaltered for millions of years as it is not subject to processes of sedimentation or erosion.

338 bottom right The frilled lizard (Chlamydosaurus kingii) takes its name from the layer of skin around its neck – the clamys –can measure 12 inches in diameter. Usually the frill remains closed on the animal's shoulders but opens when danger arises, the purpose being to frighten off potential predators.

338-339 *At the start of January, the piling up of black clouds heralds the first storm of the rainy season on the Arnhem Land plateau and surrounding forests.*

339 top *Arnhem Land is furrowed by ravines and torrents. The climate is mostly dry and the soil is poor. The flora is predominantly constituted by Allosyncarpia ternata, which is a broadleaf tree that only grows in Kakadu.*

340-341 *The intricate mangrove forest that cloaks the maze of canals in Hinchinbrook Island National Park numbers 30 species of mangrove. The only comparable biodiversity in the world is to be found in the same habitat in New Guinea.*

CANBERRA

The wet tropics in Queensland

AUSTRALIA

QUEENSLAND
REGISTRATION: 1988
CRITERIA: N (I) (II) (III) (IV)

Commonly known as the ribbonwood tree, but also as idiot fruit or green dinosaur, the Australian calycanthus (*Idiospermum australiense*) is a botanical species that evolved around 120 million years ago and spread only in the tropical forests of northern Queensland. It was discovered in 1902 near Cairns by the German botanist Ludwig Diels, who called it *Calycanthus australiensis*. Its peculiarity lies in the shape of its seed. Whereas the seeds of modern plants are formed of either a single (*monocotiledons*) or two (*dicotyledons*) parts, the seeds gathered by Diels had from three to five parts. Even the spiraled petals of the flower were an indication of its primitive evolution.

When Diels returned to the spot of his discovery, he found the zone had been cut down to make way for a sugarcane plantation. All trace of the Australian calycanthus was lost until 1971 when its seeds were found in the digestive tracts of dead animals. Stan Blake, a botanist in the Queensland Herbarium, gave the plant its modern name, which means 'fruit characteristic of Australia'. It is unique and therefore is the only member of the Calycanthaceae Family in the Southern Hemisphere.

This is only one of the many unusual plant species found in the tropical rainforests of Australia, which cover an area of over 3,420 square miles of which 714 are protected by 41 different national parks. Situated on the northeast coast of Queensland, the area has three geomorphological regions: a low coastal plain, an intermediate strip of continental scarp and the tableland of the Great Divide, which has an average height of 2,620

feet above sea level.

Following the separation of Australia from the supercontinent Gondwana, isolation of the continent lasting tens of millions of years has transformed the tropics of Queensland into an amazing evolutionary environment and made it one of the most important regional ecosystems in the world in terms of the number of its species and the peculiarities of many of them. The 13 types of rainforest here

are dominated by eucalyptus and acacia trees or by thick vaults of climbing ferns, fan palms (*Licuala ramsayi*) or mangroves. There are 1,161 registered species of plants representing 523 genera and 119 families, 500 of which are endemic. There are 90 species of orchid and 40 Proteaceae belonging to 13 genera. They are home to both the largest and smallest Cycadeae in the world: *Lepidozamia hopei* can reach 66 feet in height while the tiny *Bowenia spectabilis* finds shelter beneath the forest vault. A common

340 bottom left A female pademelon (Thylogale thetis) is seen here with her young. She is a small nocturnal marsupial common to all wetlands in Queensland.

340 bottom right With a drop of 1,000 feet, Wallaman Falls is Australia's highest waterfall. It is situated in the heart of Lumhotiz National Park, one of the 41 national parks in Queensland together registered as a UNESCO World Heritage site.

341 top right The Australian red cedar (Cedrela toona) is one of the most majestic trees in Queensland's forests. It can reach a height of 200 feet and has a base diameter of 10 feet. Its wood has a strong smell and the leaves an unmistakable pinkish color.

341 bottom A group of black flying foxes (Pteropus alecto) resting in the branches of a tree. Common to all of Queensland, this species feeds exclusively on fruit and nectar.

342 top The cassowary (Casuarius casuarius) is a flightless bird somewhat prehistoric in appearance. Its neck is featherless, the upper part of its head has a rigid skin like a helmet, and its feet are covered with skin similar to scales.

characteristic of the rainforests is the presence of many species in restricted areas thousands of miles from their nearest relations in Papua New Guinea, Sonda or even Latin America.

Queensland's forests provide a habitat to a large percentage of Australian species. These include two monotremes, 37 marsupials, 16 rodents, 34 bats, 370 birds, 47 amphibians and 160 reptiles. Special mention should be made of the *Coscinocera hercules*, which, with a wingspan of 10 inches, is one of the largest moths in the world. Then there is the quoll (*Dasyurus maculatus*), a strong and fierce carnivorous marsupial, and *Dendrolagus lumholtzi* and *Dendrolagus bennettianus*, two of the world's five existing tree-living marsupials.

There are at least 54 endemic species of vertebrates in the area, and perhaps the prize for the most unusual should go to the long-nosed insectivorous bat *Murina florium*, considered the most rare mammal in Australia.

342 bottom left A close relative of the quoll, Pseudocheirus peregrinus is a small tree-dwelling marsupial. The wet forests of Queensland provide a home to 37 species of marsupial.

342 bottom right Very difficult to sight thanks to its marvelous camouflage, the gecko of the species Phyllurus cornutus has a leaf-shaped tail and a coat like a common lichen.

343 The common name of the double-eyed fig parrot (Opopsitta diophthalma) is provided by their diet. Common to Australia and New Guinea, these birds eat only different species of fig.

The Great Barrier Reef
AUSTRALIA

REGISTRATION: 1981
CRITERIA: N (I) (II) (III) (IV)

The Great Barrier Reef Marine Park Act is the name of the official document with which, in 1975, the Australian government instituted what is the largest protected area in the world. With an area of 127,900 square miles, (though the zone that forms the UNESCO World Heritage site is even lager), it is 48 times the size than Texas, but the UNESCO World Heritage site is even larger, extending into the Pacific Ocean for more than 1,240 miles from Australia's east coast and from the Tropic of Capricorn to the coastal waters of Papua New Guinea.

This sweep of the Pacific contains the largest expanse of coral reef in the world. Overall there are 3,400 single reefs measuring between 2 acres and 380 square miles, roughly 300 coral islands of which 213 lack any vegetation and 618 islands that were once part of the Australian continent. The form and structure of each reef vary extremely but fall within two main types: platform reefs that are the result of radial growth and wall reefs that are usually found in areas where there are strong underwater currents.

The surface flora is poor, and prevalently *Pisonia grandis* on Heron and Musgrave Islands, whilst on Hoskin Island there is an unusual forest of pandans, *Pisonia* and *Ficus apposita*. Elsewhere there are casuarinas, which are sturdy trees named after the cassowary owing to the similarity of the branches to the plumage of the large flightless bird, and grasses of various genera. The underwater flora, however, is spectacular, with many small but very

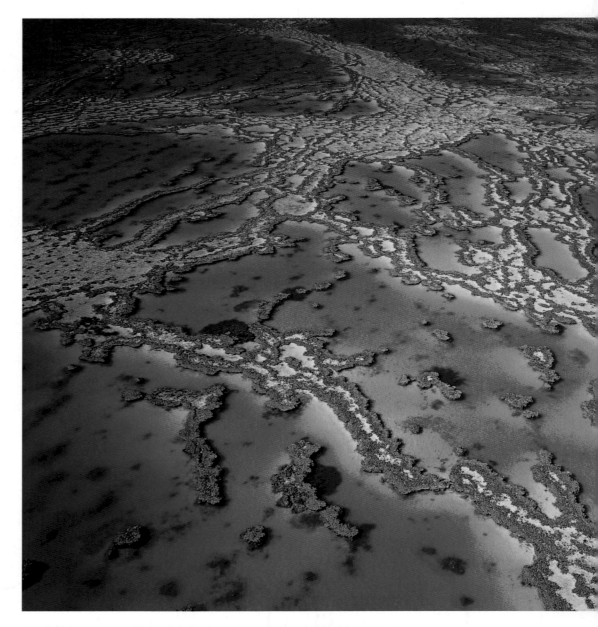

344-345 Hardy Reef is a typical platform formation of roughly 11 square miles. It is an underwater mountain of organic origin and rises 250 feet from the bottom of the ocean.

344 bottom Hardy Reef and Hook Reef together form one of the most spectacular complexes in the Great Barrier Reef. The thin dark band that separates them is a narrow passage called 'the River'.

productive algae that provide an important source of nutrition for turtles, fish, echinoderms and mollusks, besides being an important component in the formation of the reefs.

The incredible fauna of the Great Barrier Reef is indicated by statistics: there are more than 1,500 species of fish, 400 corals, 4,000 mollusks, 242 birds and an extraordinary variety of sponges, anemones, sea worms and crustaceans. There are many cetaceans, including humpback whales (*Megaptera novaengliae*), blue whales (*Balaenoptera acutorostrata*) and the killer whale (*Orcinus orca*); other mammals are the bottle-nosed dolphin (*Tursiops truncatus*), the Irrawaddy dolphin (*Orcaella brevirostris*), spinner dolphin (*Stenella longirostris*) and the Indo-Pacific humpback dolphin (*Sousa chinensis*). The islands are nesting places of worldwide importance to the green turtle (*Chelonia mydas*) and the common sea turtle (*Caretta caretta*).

Finally, the Great Barrier Reef is also the most important refuge for the dugong (Dugong dugon), which is a marine mammal (whose closest relative above sea level is the elephant) in the same family as the manatees, which Christopher Columbus believed were mermaids on his trip towards the Americas. A placid herbivore that grazes on underwater meadows and

345 top Stretching from southern Australia to Papua New Guinea and with a surface area as large as Italy, the Great Barrier Reef is easily the largest protected area in UNESCO's World Heritage sites.

345 center Heaven for divers, Heron Island lies across the Tropic of Capricorn 331 miles north of Brisbane in the Capricorn-Bunker Group. This is a section of the Great Barrier Reef measuring 4,720 square miles in area.

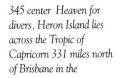

CANBERRA

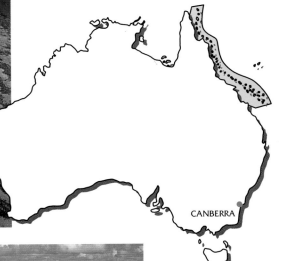

345 bottom With the coral reef lying a short distance from the beach, Heron Island is one of the unspoilt paradises of the Great Barrier Reef. Approximately 850 species of fish have been recorded in its lagoon.

346 top During their winter migration, humpback whales pass by Heron Island; sea turtles use the island to lay their eggs.

346-347 A view of the clear waters of Tongue Bay on Whitsunday Island. This is the largest of the 74 islets and islands in the Whitsunday Group.

The archipelago represents the remains of a coastal mountain range that was submerged by the rise in sea level following the end of the last Ice Age.

346 bottom left Completely uninhabited, Whitsunday Island is covered by mangrove forests, as is shown by the photograph taken from Hill Inlet.

346 bottom right Most of
the 300 cays (coral islets
that poke several feet above
sea level) were recently
formed and are still devoid
of vegetation.

347 top Whitehaven
Beach is on Whitsunday
Island. James Cook
discovered the island on
Pentecost Sunday
(Whitsunday) in 1779.

The 4 miles of this narrow
white sandy beach are one
of the favorite destinations
of the 3 million tourists that
visit the Great Barrier Reef
every year.

347

lives in coastal waters, the dugong can reach 10 feet in length and 450 pounds in weight. Recently the James Cook University in Townsville raised the alarm over the survival of this rare mammal, which has already disappeared from the seas around the Philippines, Japan, Cambodia and Vietnam. A very limited number survives, perhaps 80, in the seagrass meadows in the Andaman Sea near the southwest coast of Thailand. Even the colonies that live near Dunk Island in the Barrier Reef have been reduced in number by half recently.

During the last couple of decades, the astounding scenery of the coral reefs has become an important source of income for the aboriginal peoples that live on the islands of the Great Barrier Reef. Three million visitors a year contribute to the transition from a subsistence economy based on fishing to a more prosperous one based on tourism.

347 bottom Five hours
by steamer from
Brisbane, Lady
Musgrave Island is a
typical coral atoll. Its 35
acres of land are covered
by a forest of Pisonia
grandis that provides a
home to many birds, and
the 4.6 square miles of
lagoons were declared a
national park in 1938.

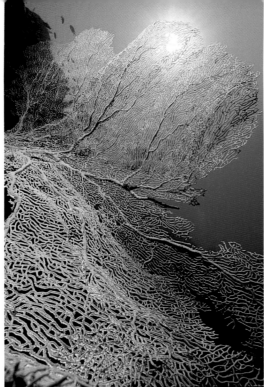

348 top left and right Pale sunlight illuminates the delicate ramifications of the colonies of gorgonias, which can take the shape of a fan (left) or bunch together to form conglomerates resembling a bush (right).

348-349 Made up of 3,400 individual reefs, the Great Barrier Reef comprises roughly 400 species of coral, which provide an extraordinary habitat for thousands of types of marine animals.

349 top Around 130 feet down the currents favor the growth of many types of gorgonias, including the flexible colonies like the one illustrated. Their ramifications spread out from a short central stem.

349 bottom There is an enormous variety in the form and structure of the reefs, though they are generally divided into two classes: platform reefs, the result of radial growth, and reefs produced by vertical growth.

350 top left A perfect example of marine symbiosis is the sea anemone and the anemone fish; the fish finds refuge among the poisonous tentacles of its host owing to its immunity.

350 top right The giant grouper (Epinephelus tukula), shown here off Lizard Island, can reach 6.5 feet in length and 220 pounds in weight.

350-351 Harmless to man, the ray's enormous size (up to 23 feet in width) and disturbing appearance has earned it the nickname 'devil's ray'.

351 left An eel peeps out of its shelter in the coral. Once thought to be dangerous to divers, this creature is curious and relatively friendly.

351 top right A school of silver jacks darts through the reef waters. With more than 1,500 species of fish and 4,000 mollusks, the Great Barrier Reef has provided the principal source of nourishment to the aboriginal peoples who have inhabited the islands for thousands of years.

351 bottom right The gray reef shark (Carcharhinus amblyrhychoides) is one of the most aggressive reef animals. It usually moves around the atolls and lagoons but some have been seen at a depth of 3,300 feet.

Fraser Island

AUSTRALIA

Queensland
Registration: 1992
Criteria: N (II) (III)

O n 13 May 1836, while sailing from Sydney to Singapore, the brigantine *Stirling Castle* ran onto the Great Barrier Reef south of Torres Strait. The captain, James Fraser, and the 18 survivors (including his wife Eliza) tried to reach shelter in Moreton Bay in the lifeboats, keeping away from the coast for fear of the aboriginals, but they were obliged to land on Great Sandy Island, which had been discovered by James Cook in 1770. Here they were captured by the Kabi people who tortured them and subjected them to forced labor until an expedition from Moreton Bay led by John Graham (one of the shipwrecked crew, who had managed to escape) succeeded in saving the only survivor, Eliza Fraser.

On her return to England, Eliza published an account of her imprisonment that became a best seller in England, but then she returned to the antipodes where she spent the rest of her days in Melbourne. This story has struck the popular imagination in Australia, inspiring writers and artists and even giving rise to a recent television serial. And of course the island where the events occurred has been named after her.

With an area of over 640 square miles, 76 miles long and between 3-15 miles wide, Fraser Island is the largest and oldest sand island in the world. Its sand mass descends to between 100 and 200 feet below sea level and is derived from granite, sandstone and metamorphic rocks. Its gigantic dunes were formed between the last interglacial period of the Pleistocene epoch (120,000-140,000 years ago) and the Holocene period (less than 10,000 years ago) when winds transported enormous quantities of sand from New South Wales and deposited them along the coast of Queensland, thus creating the island. The sands are dotted by 40 or so lakes of different nature, some of which are produced by the sinking of the sand below sea level, others by the blocking of zones invaded by water, and others still of alluvial origin.

The exceptional richness of the island water and the tropical climate have encouraged the development of a very varied vegetation. It includes eucalyptus

352 bottom left Photographed near Platypus Bay on Fraser Island, around 95 miles south of the Tropic of Capricorn, a school of humpback whales migrates southwards.

352 bottom right The dingo (Canis lupus dingo) migrated to Australia from Asia around 4,000 years ago. The 160 or so dingoes that live on Fraser Island are some of the purest in eastern Australia.

(*Eucalyptus pilularis* and *Eucalyptus signata*), palms (*Archontophoenix cunninghamiana*), kauri pines (*Agathis robusta*), species from the genus *Melaleuca* belonging to the myrtle family and populations of arboreal ferns of the genus *Angiopteris*, which are among the largest in the world.

There are few endemic species of wildlife but mention should be made of a rodent (*Xeromys myoides*), included in the Red List of species in danger, and a particularly pure population of dingoes (*Canis lupus dingo*). Of the 300 species of birds, those of interest from a conservation standpoint are the red goshawk (*Erythrotriochis radiatus*), the black-breasted quail (*Turnix melanogaster*) and the ground parrot (*Pezoporus wallicus*). Fraser Island also has a large population of reptiles, amphibians and colonies of green and loggerhead turtles.

Recent archeological research has shown that the region has been inhabited for at least 40,000 years but human settlement on Fraser Island dates to only 1,500-2,000 years ago.

Today there are various towns on the island, which depend above all on tourism. Only a few traces remain of the villages inhabited by the fearsome aboriginals that captured the crew of the *Stirling Castle*.

353 top Situated in the heart of a thick forest of Eucalyptus pilularis, Lake Mackenzie, on the west side of the island, has particularly clear water as the trees do not give off tannin.

353 center Wathumba estuary is the most important of Fraser Island's outlets. Long sandy expanses and mangroves line its banks.

353

353 bottom Great Sandy Strait is the thin arm of sea that separates Fraser Island from the mainland; it takes its name from the huge sand banks that emerge from the shallow water where turtles, fish and the occasional, rare dugong live.

352-353 Owing to its position on the migration routes of the humpback whale (Megaptera novaeangliae) from the Antarctic to the warmer waters of Hervey Bay, the ˙rge bay between Fraser ˙nd and the mainland is ˙ of 'world capital' of ˙s.

Shark Bay
AUSTRALIA

WESTERN AUSTRALIA
REGISTRATION: 1991
CRITERIA: N (I) (II) (III) (IV)

Despite its slightly worrying name, Shark Bay is also famous outside of Australia for a place where thousands of tourists are able to enjoy the wonderful experience of swimming with the friendliest of sea animals.

At Monkey Mia, dolphins have quickly developed a surprising degree of interaction with man.

In addition, Shark Bay, which covers an area of 8,500 square miles, half of which is protected by 12 parks and nature reserves, is an exceptional region of marine and terrestrial ecosystems. Shark Bay lies on the westernmost tip of Australia, has an average depth of 30 odd feet and stretches over 900 miles along the coast, covering deep sea, sandy beaches, dunes, sandstone peninsulas from the end of the Cretaceous period and cliffs 650 feet high. Lying off the coast are islands whose rocky formations are formed by fossil dunes generated during the Pleistocene on chalk and sandstone bases.

The sea has noticeable differences in salinity, from 35-40 parts per thousand (ppt), which is typical of the ocean, to the hypersalinity of Hamelin Pool at 456-470 ppt. The various salinity levels, combined with high evaporation and the dynamism of the geological and biological processes inside the marine habitat, have produced genetic adaptations in many species that inhabit the bay.

Shark Bay has the world's largest algae bed, which is spread over 1,540 square miles. It is constituted 90% by Amphibolis antartica, an alga that provides a substrate to 66 species of epiphyte. Another largest bed is the 400 square miles of stromatolites.

354 top Recognizable by its enormous pink, spoon-shaped bill and blue feet, the Australian pelican (Pelecanus conspicillatus) is a very friendly bird and does not hesitate to accept food from man.

354 bottom left Of the eight species of pelican in the world, the Australian pelican is the largest. Its wingspan varies from 8-11 feet and it weighs 15-18 pounds.

354 bottom right Hamelin Pool has the largest bed of stromatolites in the world. Considered the oldest form of life on the planet, these algae have developed a crust of carbonatic sediments.

355 top With a coastline 950 miles long, Shark Bay has low, sandy areas, dunes and even rocky cliffs. These all lie on a sandstone and chalk base created during the Cretaceous period.

355 bottom Two young osprey chicks (Pandion haliaetus) make their first clumsy attempts to fly. This is one of the 11 species of marine birds that nest in Shark Bay, but overall the local birdlife numbers 230 species.

CANBERRA

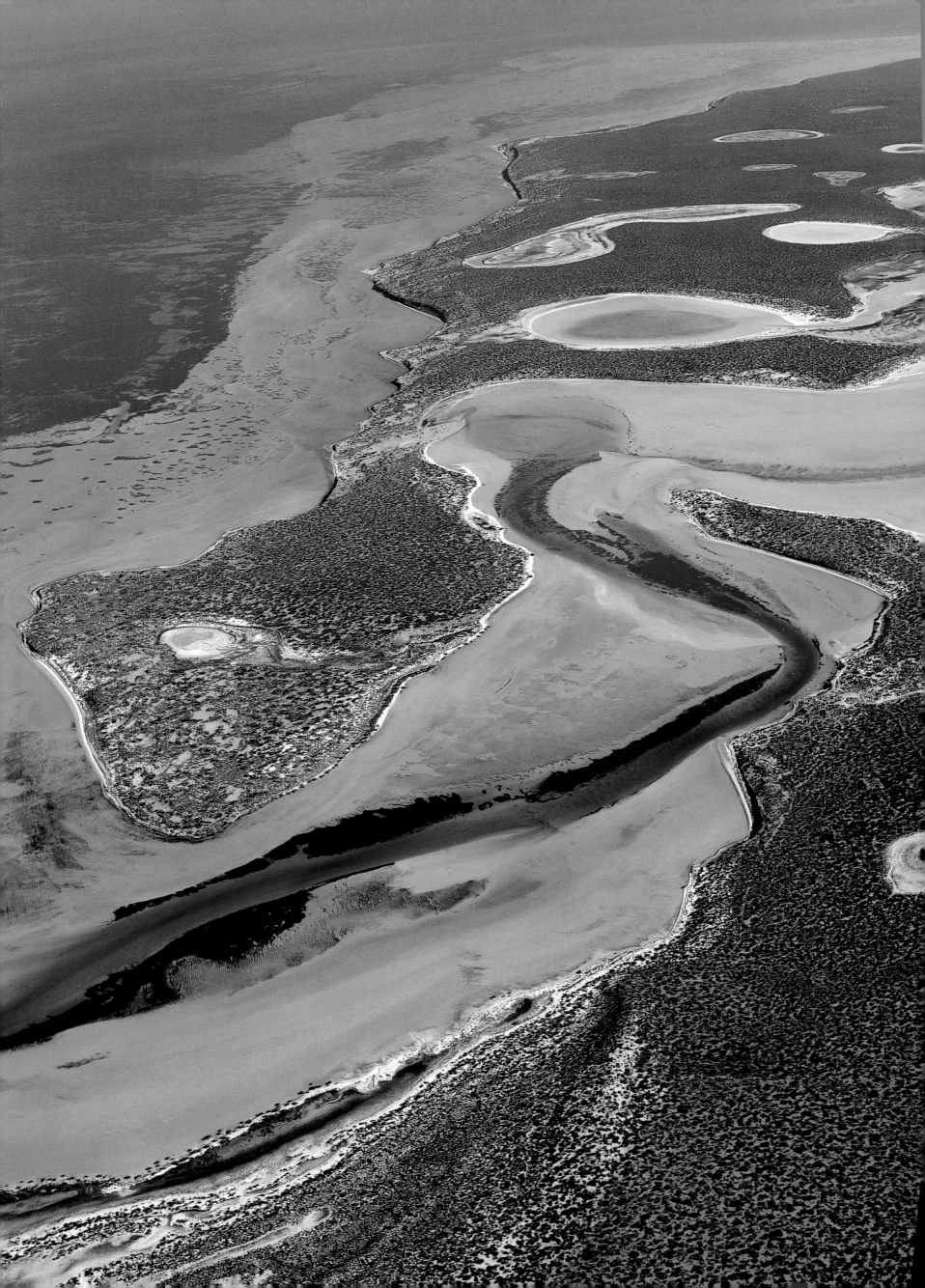

356 François Peron National Park is one of the 12 protected areas in Shark Bay. It covers 203 square miles and is named after the French zoologist who took part in Nicolas Baudin's scientific expedition in Western Australia in 1801-03.

357 top Peron Peninsula is formed by a series of bays inhabited by dugong. They find here immense beds of algae (mostly of the species Amphibolis antarctica) that overall cover 1,544 square miles of sea bed.

357 center left and right A distant relative of the ostrich, the emu (Dromaius novaehollandiae) is so numerous in Australia that it is considered harmful to the ecosystem and is kept under control with dingoes.

These algae, which have formed a cap of carbonate sediments, are thought to be one of the oldest forms of life on the planet.

The marine creatures in the bay, besides the dolphins and whales, include 10,000 dugongs, (Dugong dugon), the green turtle (Chelonia mydas) and the loggerhead turtle (Caretta caretta), which lay their eggs on the beaches of Dirk Hatog Island and the Peron Peninsula.

Of the 323 species of fish (both tropical and warm- and cold-water fish), the ones that attract attention are the tiger sharks, rays and jellyfish. The algae bed supports an incredible variety of zoophytes, crustaceans, coelenterates, lubinas and sea snakes. The coral reef is modest in size but numbers 80 species of coral and is very dynamic, owing to the Leeuvin Current, which is believed to be responsible for the good health of all Australian corals.

Finally, the population of bivalves is abundant, with 216 species, 15% of which are endemic. The land flora numbers 620 species and is dominated by eucalyptus and acacia, but, on land, it is the zoological patrimony that is of greater interest.

Of the 26 protected species in Australia, three marsupials and two rodents live on Dorre and Berrier Islands.

Shark Bay was named by the British buccaneer William Dampier, who landed there in 1699. He was a bizarre character who loved both adventure and nature. In the bay he collected samples of plants that had never been seen before in London and, perhaps to discourage others from following him, he named the bay after the sharks. It might be said that he succeeded in his intent: Shark Bay is unspoilt, and the 750 people who live there are mostly involved with the protection of the area.

357 bottom After several good years owing to heavy rains, the number of emus burgeoned so much that farm crops were seriously threatened. In some cases it was necessary to call in the Australian army.

358 top A mammal of extraordinary intelligence, the bottle-nosed dolphin (Tursiops truncatus) has developed a surprising degree of interaction with man. Thousands of tourists arrive on Monkey Mia beach to swim with these creatures.

358 center Shark Bay is home to more than 10,000 dugongs (Dugong dugon), which is an exceptionally high number for this seriously endangered mammal. The population in the bay represents 12.5% of the world total.

358 bottom The tiger shark (Galeocerdo cuvieri) is one of the most common sharks in this bay. Considered very dangerous to man, it is given this name because of the dark gray stripes on its skin.